NAPOLEON: MAN AND MYTH

Napoleon:
Man and Myth

R. BEN JONES

HODDER AND STOUGHTON
LONDON SYDNEY AUCKLAND TORONTO

ISBN 0 340 17554 0 Boards
ISBN 0 340 17555 9 Paperback

First published 1977

Printed in Great Britain for
Hodder and Stoughton Educational
a division of Hodder and Stoughton Ltd,
Mill Road, Dunton Green, Sevenoaks, Kent,
by Hazell Watson & Viney Ltd, Aylesbury, Bucks

PREFACE

Napoleon never fails to catch the public eye and the books about him and his period are legion. So much occurred in his brief period of power that historians have tended to be dominated by the story of his remarkable life and achievements, so that many of the volumes available go little beyond retelling his biography. The present volume begins by placing Napoleon within the context of his times, proceeds by studying different aspects of his career, and ends with a consideration of the reasons for his fall, an appreciation of the man himself, and a glance at his impact upon the one hundred and fifty years that have followed his death. Although Napoleon occupies the stage throughout, full consideration is given to those favourable circumstances that made it possible for this minor Corsican noble to dominate his world among a galaxy of talent. Technically, he should be referred to as Bonaparte until his assumption of the life Consulship at least, but for simplicity I have called him Napoleon. If his career was made possible by a happy combination of circumstances, at least it was Napoleon who made use of, and dominated those circumstances.

Of the many biographies of Napoleon, the principal is the great work of Lefebvre, translated into English in 1969 and published as *Napoleon 1799–1807* and *Napoleon 1807–1815* (Routledge and Kegan Paul). Holland Rose's fine work is still worthy of study, and so are the contrasted versions by Tarlé, *Bonaparte*; Kircheisen, *Napoleon* (tr. 1931) and J. M. Thompson, *Napoleon Bonaparte, his Rise and Fall* (Blackwell, 1952). Geyl's *Napoleon For and Against* (Constable, 1944) is vital reading. More recently, Felix Markham has produced *Napoleon* (Weidenfeld and Nicolson, 1963) which does not add much to his much shorter, valuable book, *Napoleon and the Awakening of Europe* (English Universities Press, 1954). The bicentenary of Napoleon's birth has produced many books, among which may be indicated Godechot's very personal *Napoléon* (Paris, 1969) and V. Cronin's chatty account *Napoleon* (Collins, 1971) and the *Annals* No 199 (March 1970) and the *Révue d'Histoire Moderne et Contempéraine* (XVII), 1970. Among the many books that lie behind much contemporary work on Napoleon are such formative studies as Vandal's *L'Avancement de Bonaparte*

(2 vols., 1902) and Madelin's gargantuan *Histoire du Consulat et de l'Empire* (1937–54). Other useful books are for instance, E. J. Hobsbawn, *The Age of Revolution* (Weidenfeld and Nicolson, 1962), J. E. Howard (ed.), *Letters and Documents of Napoleon* (Barry and Jenkins, 1961) and J. Kitchin, *Un journal 'philosophique', Le Décade 1794–1807* (Paris, 1965). G. Brunn, *Europe and the French Imperium* (Harper) and F. B. Artz, *Reaction and Revolution* (Harper), both produced in the 1930s, remain extremely useful. So does the eighteenth-century volume of Mousnier, Labrousse and Bouloiseau, *Histoire générale des civilizations* (Paris, 1959).

CONTENTS

MAPS

ACKNOWLEDGMENTS

For permission to quote copyright material the author and publishers wish to thank: Basil Blackwell Ltd for an extract from *Napoleon Bonaparte, His Rise and Fall* by J. M. Thompson; Hamish Hamilton Ltd for an extract from *The Course of German History* by A. J. P. Taylor; Harper and Row for an extract from *Europe and the French Imperium* by G. Brunn; Secker and Warburg Ltd for extracts from *The Origins of Totalitarian Democracy* and *Political Messianism* by J. L. Talmon; Weidenfeld and Nicolson Ltd for extracts from *The Campaigns of Napoleon* by David A. Chandler and *Napoleon* by Felix M. H. Markham; C. A. Watts Ltd for an extract from *An Introduction to Contemporary History* by G. Barraclough; Yale University Press for an extract from *The Heavenly City of the Eighteenth-Century Philosopher* by C. L. Becker; Princeton University Press for an extract from *The Age of Democratic Revolution* by R. R. Palmer; Harvard University Press for an extract from *The Genesis of Napoleonic Imperialism* by G. Deutsch; Cambridge University Press for extracts from *The Cambridge Modern History*, volumes VIII and IX; Routledge and Kegan Paul Ltd for extracts from *French Revolution*, volumes I and II and *Napoleon*, volumes I and II by Georges Lefebvre; Oxford University Press for an extract from *The Police and the People* by Richard Cobb.

The author wishes to acknowledge also his debt to the many scholars who have been a source of inspiration, interpretation and analysis and whose books are listed in the Preface and Further Reading sections of this book.

PART I
The Background

[1] THE LEGACY OF THE REVOLUTION

Fashions change in intellectual circles, as in others. Our present age favours the anti-hero, diminishing the significance of the individual. It was not so in the era of Napoleon. Then, there was an exaggerated consciousness of the capacity of individuals to perform great deeds, and the tremendous achievement of Napoleon makes his career admirably suited to the period of the Romantic Revival. But, in considering his era, we must guard against seduction by the fascination of a great man, and beware those historians who would present the period as a portrait of a single figure. The circumstances surrounding Napoleon's rise to power were such that others could have seized similar opportunities and become leader of France. That it was he who rose, reflects as much his good fortune as his abilities: in his ideas, either as general or as administrator, he was not especially original, rather he was exceptionally capable. His genius is to be measured in the vigour and extent of his achievement in a whole range of different fields; and an assessment of his era must begin by an examination of the historical situation which gave it birth.

In the political field, the French Revolution was the great engine of change, casting its shadow over the succeeding century and a half. In a sense, the Revolution was the culmination of the changes urged by two generations of idealists and administrators and, as no other revolution, it spoke for Europe as well as for France. The political changes it brought were fundamental: in the social field, and particularly in the economic, its impact was less profound. Its progress was disturbed and at times disruptive. After the initial crisis of 1788, the Constituent Assembly had launched upon a great programme of reform. Unwittingly, by its religious policy it provoked vigorous opposition and this hastened the onset of war in 1792. In Paris, politicians struggled for power against a background of serious foreign invasion, counter-revolutionary plots and local revolts, until the Jacobins gained control.

The Jacobins achieved remarkable success by the vigorous measures that have come to be called the Terror (1793–4). By these measures they saved the Revolution and threw back the invaders, bringing to the problem of national defence many radical solutions, in some of which can be seen early vestiges of the totalitarian methods of the twentieth century. But their achievement was at a cost in bloodshed and fear that struck like iron into the very soul of Europe's political consciousness. Robespierre was popularly cast as the principal villain, and many of the stories of the Terror were the excited exaggerations of hostile propagandists. But what matters in history is often less what actually happened, than what men thought happened, and the changes in France from 1789, reaching a climax in the Terror, were charged with an emotional significance that the historian ignores at his peril.

The Napoleonic era has been credited with bringing stability and order out of the chaos of a decade of revolution: the view is as naïve as it is untenable. There was no sudden change from chaos to order, nor could Napoleon's meteoric rise to power have been foreseen even as late as 1798. Not only had the Revolution and the Terror made an indelible impact, but the years between the fall of Robespierre and Napoleon's seizure of power, the years of the Thermidorian Reaction (1794–5) and the Directory (1795–9), were years that witnessed much work of patient consolidation. Napoleonic France stood firmly upon the basic achievements of the Revolution – indeed, some historians, taking a long-term view of administrative and political change in France, have drawn attention to the strong element of continuity in the development of her institutions. (The late Professor Cobban, rather naughtily, even suggested that the French Revolution was the creation of historians.) But the experiences of the decade of revolution bore heavily upon the years that followed, and Napoleon was never free of their burden.

If the French Revolution could claim to speak for Europe as well as for France, Napoleon, personifying a deep well of unspoken human desires and ambitions, spoke for France and could claim also to speak for Europe: his dominance over Europe was not to be repeated even in the victorious hours of the Third Reich. It is easy to see why the Napoleonic era should have attracted so much attention. But the years between it and the ending of the Terror should not be neglected, nor regarded as an entr'acte before the glory of Napoleon possesses the stage. They were years that saw the cementing of the foundations of Napoleonic France. They ended with Napoleon's seizure of power at the badly handled coup of Brumaire, but in November 1799 this was no more than an episode: few would have predicted that so glorious an era was about to begin.

[2] POLITICAL AND SOCIAL CHANGE

Three fundamental changes emerged from the Revolution to present France with a wholly new situation. The first was the destruction of the principle of divine right. Throughout nineteenth-century Europe, monarchical institutions showed a remarkable resiliency; but in France it was already clear that no government could hope to survive long without a broad basis of popular support. The Crown could no longer give the leadership that the nation demanded, as the brief Bourbon Restoration after Waterloo confirmed.

The second change was the destruction of the hopes of the nobility. During the later eighteenth century, the nobility in France and other countries had aspired to a dominant position in the administration of the country by asserting their privileges and securing the significant offices in church and state. Reformers sought to curb nobles' privileges and to open administrative offices to a wider social group in the interests of efficiency. Like their counterparts in Europe, the French aristocracy had been confident that they would be victorious in any political struggle with reformers. For this reason, when faced with reforms in 1787, they had provoked the crisis that had led to the Revolution and to the loss of their privileges and stranglehold over administrative office.

If the nobility had begun the Revolution, the bourgeoisie completed it and profited greatly, giving permanence to the Revolution Settlement and securing the future for bourgeois-dominated regimes. In fact, they had provided an answer to the conundrum that had baffled the Enlightened Despots: they had provided an alternative administrative machine, a modern one capable of indefinite expansion. By breaking the aristocratic monopoly of office, the bourgeoisie was able to lead France out of the eighteenth-century world. The careers open to those with talent, opportunity and sufficient education and social standing, gave avenues of advancement to positions of great influence to able men who formerly had little hope of more than petty local office. The same was true in the army and the navy, for the emigration of officers during the first years of the Revolution provided the opportunity for young men of talent, and sometimes with no social pretensions, to aspire to the highest commands. It was by combining the career open to talent with conscription and the new centralised administrative machine, that Carnot was able to create the revolutionary armies that were not only to save France but to secure Napoleon his hegemony over Europe.

But if the nobility had suffered defeat, it had not suffered destruction. Those who had emigrated often crept back during the Consulate and Empire, some of them to fill local administrative office. Counter-revolutionaries made much of the Jacobins' forced sale of national lands, once the property of the emigrated nobles; but, in fact, there was no expropriation of a class, only of certain individuals, and that for political reasons. The balance of ownership of landed wealth (the Church apart), if shrewdly altered, was not radically disturbed. Attempts to redistribute property (as, for example, the Laws of Ventôse, Year II), conspicuously failed, and with the death of Robespierre, the bogey of social revolution was laid. Noble families survived the revolutionary and Napoleonic period with surprisingly little loss of real wealth, and they retained throughout the nineteenth century an unquestioned social primacy.

The third fundamental change concerned the peasant. Before the Revolution he had been acquiring land; during it the wealthier peasant acquired more and the less wealthy, freed of the economic burden of manorial dues (abolished between 1789 and 1793), concentrated on building up the family small-holding. They possessed their land with a bitter passion. No government that failed to guarantee them the unfettered enjoyment of their gains could hope to survive in post-revolutionary France. It was this that helped to give nineteenth-century France her distinctly conservative flavour. The land settlement of the Revolution was the guarantee of political (and to a great extent social) stability, and in this sense Napoleon, as he said himself, 'was more the Emperor of the peasants of France than of the soldiers'. This strengthening of peasant proprietorship meant also that the changes that at this time were transforming much of British agriculture were delayed in France until the middle of our own century, perhaps until the impact of the Marshall Plan in the 1950s. French rural society remained solidly unprogressive. Share-cropping (*métayage*) continued, rural poverty was widespread and poor relief remained ill organised, declining during the Directory and Consulate until it was regulated during the Empire.

French urban society was more volatile. It was by capitalising on the grievances of the urban poor that the bourgeoisie had been able to effect the political changes of 1789. This alliance between bourgeois and poor provided the motor power for the Jacobin Terror in which all energies were concentrated on national defence. In the towns the major burden of these efforts was borne by the popular movement, led by the *sans-culottes*, with whom the bourgeoisie made common cause. But the social programme of the *sans-culottes* openly threatened the sanctity of private property and, once the perils of the nation that had made the Terror of 1793–4 a necessity had receded, the bourgeoisie assumed complete control, destroying at the same time the power of the Robespierrists and the hopes of the *sans-culottes* in the great crisis of Thermidor (1794).

The Thermidorian Reaction (1794–5) was led by men whose prime motive was personal survival, not social regeneration. They had achieved power by securing the inactivity of the *sans-culottes* at the moment of Robespierre's fall. The *sans-culottes*, for their part, exhausted by their exertions during the Terror, their numbers diminished by volunteering, decimated by epidemics and starved in the frightful winter of 1795–6, remained the dupes of Thermidor to be destroyed as a political movement in the crisis of Prairial (1795). Yet men continued to fear them because of the power they had exercised during the Terror and bourgeois politicians were anxious that they should not rise again. The *loi le chapelier* prevented their combining, and since their leaders were well known to the police they were under constant surveillance. Some two hundred of the extreme left were repeatedly arrested between 1795 and 1800 for their past record alone – thus the police 'decapitated the democratic movement' (Cobb). Napoleon was not to relax vigilance towards them, although (the bad year of 1812 apart) they benefited from rising standards of living. Their left-wing allies, and the surviving Robespierrist Jacobins, were equally suspect. One of the motives behind the coup of Brumaire (1799) was the fear of the bogey of expropriation of property raised by the Jacobin revival of 1798–9.

On the social front, therefore, Napoleon inherited a disturbed situation. His answer was to pursue a well-defined policy that guaranteed the position of peasant and bourgeoisie by avoiding on the one hand the Charybdis of reaction and on the other the Scylla of social revolution. But his impact was so forceful that he brought a new unity to France built upon that administrative unity which the Revolution had achieved. It was a unity that seemed to end a decade of uncertainty and to seal off the deep social divisions that the Terror and its suppression had opened. These divisions were to erupt during the following century in the Lyons riots of 1833, the June Days in Paris in 1848 and again in the Commune of 1871, and in the complexities of the Dreyfus Affair at the end of the century. That he gave Frenchmen unity, that he spoke for France, is one of the keys to the secret of Napoleon's greatness.

A feature of that unity was the Concordat that Napoleon negotiated with the Church. The religious question lay at the root of a good deal of the disruption of the revolutionary decade. The Revolution was anti-clerical, not anti-religious, but in the tumult of the times the distinction seemed too fine to draw. The Constituent Assembly had deprived the Church of its primacy and much of its wealth. The Jacobins, during the Terror, had secularised the State: unbelief, once the licence of the wealthy, had gone deep into the life of society, and the Church, siding with counter-revolution, had become a political party. It could no longer speak for France. Its rural parishes were less affected, but in the towns the parishes were disrupted – although in the wealthier quarters non-juring priests exercised considerable influence. As early as 1795 the Directory had been fully aware of the need for a new Concordat: a religious peace was necessary for the maintenance of internal security.

On the industrial front there was plenty of movement, but, despite the incredible efforts during the Terror, the structure of industry remained basically unchanged. As yet, economic conditions did not favour the development of large-scale units which were already beginning to appear in Britain's cotton and iron industries. The Directory began the practice of holding industrial exhibitions for the purpose of encouraging industrialists and inventors, and Napoleon continued the practice, but, despite efforts to harness pure science to the service of industry, the pace of industrialisation was not greatly increased. The Revolution had released the spirit of *laissez-faire*, but political disruption, the ravages of inflation in the 1790s, and an extended economic warfare under the Directory (especially with the draconian law of Nivôse 1798, see page 152) damaged commerce and foreign trade. The consequence was the strengthening of the position of the small masters, economically retrogressive in outlook, but, like the peasant, devoted to their gains from the Revolution.

During the Thermidorian Reaction Paris had witnessed the relaxation and indulgence of the *nouveaux riches*, who were now free of the threat of the guillotine and able to keep the workers in their place. In the streets the *jeunesse dorée* domineered and the extremes of fashionable dress earned the names *incroyable* and *merveilleuse*. The Thermidorians themselves, with their corruption, levity and lechery, typified by the scantiness of the clothing about Mme Tallien, Fortunée Hamelin and Joséphine de Beauharnais, presented a demoralised 'society' that could speak only for themselves, not for France. Among those scratching for a living in Paris, observing the excesses of war profiteers, was Napoleon himself. His opportunity to join the successful was shortly to come through his action in the crisis of Vendémiarie (see page 75) and his subsequent marriage to Joséphine de Beauharnais. Meanwhile, the Thermidorians existed in a power vacuum that helps to explain the political instability of the Directory that succeeded them.

Abroad was the army, once the repository of true Republicanism, now becoming steadily more professional and more independent, the commanders becoming more conscious of the personal advantages to be gained from successful campaigns and from political intrigue. Increasingly, the politicians in Paris recognised that their fate hinged on the reliability of local commanders whose activities lay behind the coups that disturbed the Directory. At home, much remained to be completed in the field of reform: but the Directory had always to steer a precarious course between the threat of a coup from the left or from the right. Brumaire was the last of these coups. That it brought stability and a strong régime behind which Frenchmen could willingly unite, made it possible for Brumaire to speak for France. But there was nothing in the planning of the coup, nor in its execution, that gave it any different quality from previous attempts to overthrow the Directory. Only the evident success of the Consulate guaranteed its future: it was only then that Napoleon came to personify France.

[3] THE DIRECTORY

Its achievements at home

The establishment of the Directory was far from propitious. Its constitution was that of Year III (1795) confining the political classes to a narrowly based property-owning oligarchy of bourgeois notables. But the Thermidorians, fearful that the first elections would produce a royalist majority, passed the Law of Two Thirds, requiring that two-thirds of the deputies be former members of the Convention. This provoked the wealthy areas of Paris to rise. They were defeated by Barras with the help of Napoleon's 'whiff of grapeshot' in the crisis of Vendémiaire (1795). Thereafter, the royalists and the right wing were reduced to persistent but vain plotting. On the other hand, the Directory was determined that the left wing should be as powerless. There was no attempt to build a social republic, for not only were the poor excluded from the political classes by the high property qualifications, but the vigorous suppression of Babeuf's Conspiracy of Equals (1796) confirmed their disqualification.

Between these two extremes, neither of which could command sufficient political support to assert itself effectively, the Directory pursued an uneven course, stepping from one expedient to the next, and descending to a series of more or less violent purges in order to preserve itself from political enemies on its flanks. These purges involved an increasing reliance on military force: if the civilians could not govern, the army would take control. There was nothing remarkable in foreseeing the emergence of a Cromwell to lead the nation, but among the several aspirants to this heroic rôle, Napoleon, even in 1797, did not rank especially high.

Considering the unstable political situation with which it struggled, the Directory's achievements have received too little credit. The Constitution denied the Directors vigorous executive powers, and the principle of annual election institutionalised instability and endangered continuity – for half the municipalities, a third of the Council and a fifth of the Directors were annually elected. Yet it provided no mean inheritance for the Consulate – a stable administration and revised taxation system, an increasingly prosperous country with a stable metallic currency, new law courts and a new education system. The disorder of the Thermidorian Reaction was gone, the extreme left was destroyed and the royalists made no progress – William Wickham, disbursing Pitt's gold from Switzerland, failed to rouse much feeling for the pretender, Louis 'XVIII'. Abroad, counter-revolutionaries might preach uncompromising hostility, but diplomats urged accommodation with a régime that seemed to have returned France to sanity after the excesses of the Revolution. Even Pope Pius VI advised French catholics to accept the Republic in the *Pastoralis sollicitudo* (1796), and modern papal diplomacy, not distinguishing between Christian and non-Christian states, dates from the Treaty of Tolentino (1797) negotiated through Napoleon's elder brother Joseph.

At home a new administrative machine was built up, providing a new avenue of advancement for talent among the relatively poor. The secretariat, inherited from the Committee of Public Safety, became the *Secrétairerie d'Etat* of Napoleon, and Ramel's financial reforms in 1798 established a pattern that lasted a hundred years. The *liquidation Ramel* (September 1797), liquidating some two-thirds of the government debt, helped to stabilise an impossible situation and gave a lead to the Consulate, which completed the work by the further liquidation of 1801. The Consulate was thus able to extend its popularity by ending the run-away inflation and Treasury bankruptcy. In November 1797, an *agence des contributions directes* was established in each department staffed by civil servants to assess and collect taxes, providing a group of trained officials whose work Napoleon was to extend. In the Autumn of 1798 the new staff were able to reorganise existing taxes and improve the efficiency of collection. This was quiet, administrative work that passed largely unnoticed, but it was upon such reforms that the stability of the Consulate was built. The historian ignores the complexities of administration at his peril. Yet, for all its increasing efficiency, the Directory remained at the mercy of financiers, and corruption was endemic to such a degree that even Napoleon's régime could not stamp it out.

In education, Condorcet's hope that –

an ever-increasing progress of enlightenment may open an inexhaustible source of aid according to our needs, of remedies according to our ills, of means to individual happiness and common prosperity [in order to] contribute to this general and gradual improvement of the human race ... the ultimate aim towards which every social institution must be directed

– was carried forward at a creditable rate, the more so as France was still at war, as well as struggling for political and economic survival. François Neufchâteau was in charge of the Ministry of the Interior, and his work consolidated the reforms begun under the Constituent Assembly at the beginning of the Revolution. The National Museum of Natural History and a system of national primary schools had been begun by the Jacobins, despite lack of money and the strain of the Terror and war. The Thermidorians hoped to provide a school and a state-paid schoolmaster in each commune – although lack of funds curtailed their efforts. Three medical schools, veterinary schools and an Institute for the Instruction of Deaf Mutes were founded. The Academy was revived, and a Bureau of Longitude, a School of Oriental Languages, a Conservatoire of Music and of Arts and Crafts were opened under the Directory. Each department was to have a Central School for secondary education (although it was not free). In 1795 came the School of Mines and the Central School of Public Works (to become the *École Polytechnique*).

Such reforms were a generation ahead of the achievement of other countries and went far towards realising Condorcet's schemes, even if it was not intended to extend them to all children in France. Inflation, however, took its toll and primary education ceased to be free (with deleterious effects on working class children in particular). But the intention was there: the Directory continued the policy of its predecessors and Napoleon had merely to crown the edifice.

The economic situation was bad in the 1790s, and the depression did not lift until the end of the decade. The improved economic outlook coincided with the Consulate and Empire, during which rent rolls rose by 50 per cent and wages by 25 per cent. In contrast, the Directory has been condemned as a period of economic doldrums. The evidence is too ambiguous to permit so forthright a judgment. Encouragement of commerce and industry was a concern of the Directory: it was Neufchâteau, for example, who organised in August of 1798 the first national exhibition on the Champ-de-Mars. Napoleon was to hold a succession of similar shows to encourage trade and industry. But industrial production remained at a relatively low level, and the continued war did not help, particularly as it confined foreign trade. The bad harvest in 1796 also had its effect. Neufchâteau set up *bureaux de bienfaisance* in each commune to improve the administration of poor relief. The Directory was not indifferent to its social responsibilities, although it was burdened with an inflationary spiral and compelled to continue the war, as much to employ the army as to gain the bullion necessary for the metallic currency. Until 1797, defeated countries paid heavily – the army extracted some 10 million francs from the Rhenish lands and some 51 million from Italy in 1796–7. But, when 1799 brought heavier taxation and threat of invasion by the Second Coalition, the Directory's surviving support collapsed.

[4] ITS POLITICAL INSTABILITY

It is too naïve to think of the Directory as careering from crisis to crisis until Napoleon ended its course at Brumaire. There was nothing inevitable about a soldier seizing control, although the possibility could easily have been foreseen. Given greater executive power and more common aims among its leaders, the Directory might well have survived and Napoleon been no more than a very successful general. But a military coup became the more likely the longer the Directors failed to establish their personal ascendancy. The descent into dictatorship can clearly be traced through the successive crises of Fructidor, Year V (1797), Floréal, Year VI (1798) and Brumaire, Year VIII (1799). From an early stage Napoleon was concerned with the first (see page 79) and he became caught up with the last at a fairly late stage. But it would be to disparage the great Englishman to liken him to Cromwell: great ambition burned in both men, but Napoleon was no reluctant ruler. Indeed, for all the Roman symbolism of the period, civic virtue was not Napoleon's first attribute: darker, more elemental passions made him hero of France.

The Crisis of Fructidor (1797) was a tangled skein. The elections of April 1797 brought a royalist landslide, and two Directors, Carnot and Barthélemy, were prepared to side with the right wing in an effort to end political instability. Royalist agents had for some time been in direct communication with generals at the various fronts – Moreau's lack of progress across the Rhine may have this simple political explanation. But their greatest catch was General Pichegru who became President of the Council of Five Hundred. Napoleon, commanding in Italy, gained some papers that indicated Pichegru's complicity and he sent Augereau to Paris to defend the Republic (as much as to preserve his own command). Whilst the right hesitated, as was their wont, Barras and the other Directors acted quickly and in the crisis of Fructidor arrested Pichegru and Barthélemy. Carnot escaped (as did Pichegru). A purge of a hundred and seventy-seven deputies followed. Thus, at the price of dependence on the army, a revised Directory had defeated the political right wing.

The next danger came from the left, for the elections of 1798 returned so many democrats and Jacobins that the Directors quashed 106 returns in the coup of Floréal, fearful of the rumours of plots to replace the régime which emanated from such varied sources as Siéyès, Talleyrand, Benjamin Constant and Mme de Staël. Politically, the Directory now stood alone, 'a kind of dictatorship without the usual advantages of dictators: it had little prestige or charisma' (Palmer). Yet it held France together in the dangerous months of 1799, when the victorious Second Coalition was about to invade, and a revived outbreak in La Vendée threatened from the rear.

This was its most serious crisis yet. The right had grouped behind Louis 'XVIII' and, with Britain actively helping the Vendéans, a restoration was confidently expected. But, as always, the royalists were ill-organised. The 1799 elections returned a strong Jacobin vote in response to the threat to the Revolution. The régime now depended on the army, but the Directors had offended many of the leading generals, men like Bernadotte, Brune, Masséna and Joubert – they were about to court-martial Championnet.

In May, Sieyès (although a noted opponent of the régime) became a Director and began, with the aid of Barras, to plot another coup. Meanwhile there was an active revival of Jacobinism, both to combat royalist plotting and to save France from invasion. Bernadotte and Lindet (once an important member of the Committee of Public Safety in 1793–4) became ministers and a return to Jacobin methods was presaged by Jourdan's conscription law (June), increased taxes on the rich and the Law of Hostages (July), directed against suspect right wing families. But the atmosphere was no longer that of 1793, and these measures were widely resented and gave rise to fears that the social order might be imperilled. This was a sign that Napoleon read correctly: Jacobinism was not to be the way of the future. In August, the Manège Club, where surviving Babouvists met, was forcibly closed by Fouché, now Minister of Police. When Jourdan demanded an appeal to the spirit of 1793 by declaring 'the country in danger', he was countered by Lucien Bonaparte in the Council of Five Hundred demanding a strengthening of the existing executive. Too many feared the spirit of 1793: this was another sign that Napoleon was to read correctly.

Meanwhile, Sieyès, helped by Barras and Talleyrand, was working to secure his future. The plotters concealed their fear of royalists by

attacking the Jacobins. But they had to have the army on their side –
their first choice as military puppet was Joubert, but he was killed at
the battle of Novi in August. Fortunately for them victories came –
Masséna defeated the Russians at Zurich and Brune the British and
Russians in Holland, forcing their withdrawal at the Convention of
Alkmaar (October). Barras could now afford to scoff at Jourdan's
outworn cry of '93, and Bernadotte was dismissed lest he carry out a
Jacobin coup. The enemy without had been repelled: the enemy
within still threatened, for if Jacobinism had been openly attacked,
there yet remained the royalists. The revisionists dared not risk wait-
ing for the 1800 elections: they set to work quickly with Napoleon,
newly returned from Egypt, as their general. The coup of Brumaire
began as another attempt to preserve the Republic against the rival
threats of left and right. Since Fructidor, Year V, the Directors had
been in the hands of the army, but had managed to control it: with
such aides as Barras, Fouché, and Talleyrand, Siéyès may be forgiven
for imagining he could continue to control it. He seems to have been
genuinely surprised at Napoleon's seizure of power at the coup of
Brumaire which he had devised.

[5] ITS FOREIGN POLICY

By 1795 the incredible exertions of 1793 through which the Jacobins
had saved the Revolution and begun the defeat of the *ancien régime*
had already begun to seem aberrationist. Counter-revolutionaries
might preach a crusade against the Revolution, 'the terror and dismay
of the world', but by 1795 a strong element of realism had entered
France's relations with Europe. The mad head-long rush across the
frontiers had quietened to a more traditional war of limited ends to
achieve the left bank of the Rhine and gain security for the future.
In short, the Directory sought a *modus vivendi* with Europe and the
appointment of Talleyrand as Foreign Minister (1797) was a sign of
a new era.

There were many factors encouraging this change of attitude: the
strain of war could not be borne at the pressure required by the Terror,
the Constitution of Year III, with its strong emphasis on property
rights offered the opportunity of a détente with Europe, the danger of
royalist efforts to subvert local commanders in the field, all argued for
a policy of co-existence with the *ancien régime* on the basis of natural
frontiers. To press beyond the Rhine meant perpetual war, and after

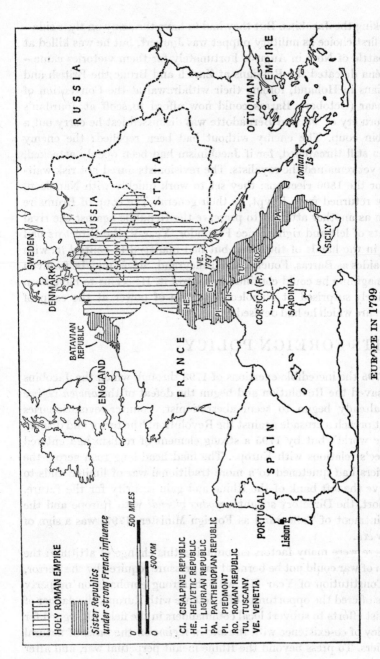

EUROPE IN 1799

Note the extension of French influence beyond the natural frontiers apparent in the sister Republics.
The expansionist policy was beginning under the Directory.

CI. CISALPINE REPUBLIC
HE. HELVETIC REPUBLIC
LI. LIGURIAN REPUBLIC
PA. PARTHENOPIAN REPUBLIC
PI. PIEDMONT
RO. ROMAN REPUBLIC
TU. TUSCANY
VE. VENETIA

HOLY ROMAN EMPIRE

Sister Republics
under strong French influence

1795 only Britain and Austria remained out of the principal powers of the First Coalition. Peace could be achieved if the natural frontiers could be guaranteed.

The Directory required three things for this: to exert a degree of control beyond the natural frontiers, preferably through sister republics, to reconcile Britain to French control of the Channel coast from Brest to the Texel, and to persuade Austria to surrender Belgium. For the sake of the last point, the Directory was happy to play the game of eighteenth-century diplomacy. After all, Poland had in 1795 just been annihilated by agreement between Russia, Prussia and Austria. In order to limit the war, Austria would be willing to exchange Belgium for some significant province – she had tried to exchange it for Bavaria in 1785. Everything hinged upon an agreed realignment of frontiers. But this concerned the Holy Roman Empire as well, and if Austria was nominally head of the Empire, she exercised small authority in it.

However, there were advantages in a limited war with Austria. Not only was it necessary to the Directory to retain the support of the contractors who made fortunes out of supplying the forces, but it was too dangerous to bring home the army without a full settlement with Europe. Generals who might be troublesome at home were employed at the front, and the armies brought in bullion for the metallic currency, as well as gained useful pawns for the diplomatic game of exchange to secure the Rhine frontier. It was this, indeed, that was Carnot's object in launching the offensive of 1796. The principal attack was to be made across the Rhine towards Vienna by Jourdan and Moreau, whilst a limited flank campaign in Piedmont was entrusted to Kellermann and a minor diversion was to be mounted under Shérer in Italy in order to engage Austrian reinforcements. South Germany was a good choice, for students there were active in demanding republics formed by *das freie Volk*, and the democrats of Mainz were calling for a Cisrhenane Republic stretching from Holland to Alsace. The Directory preferred the more modest line of annexing all lands west of the Rhine, a policy endorsed by the Consulate.

Carnot, however, was attracted by a campaign plan of the young Napoleon to seize Lombardy and so threaten Austria from the south. Accordingly, Napoleon superseded Shérer (1796) – but in making this change, the Directory did not envisage a reversal of their diplomacy, they merely hoped to offer Austria a mulcted Northern Italy as compensation for their Rhine frontier. Within a year Napoleon was to convert what had been intended as a side show into a reforging of the balance of power in Western Europe.

In Germany the 1796 campaign made little progress, for Jourdan was at odds with his staff and Moreau was in treasonable communication with the enemy. Britain, fearful of a French invasion of Ireland and of impending bankruptcy, sent Malmesbury to Lille in October to negotiate peace. The campaign in Italy went very well, and the Directory hoped for a general pacification by exchanging gains in Italy. Here Napoleon forced their hand. First he promoted the declaration of a republic in Milan, thereby securing his own continued employment and forcing the Directory into an Italian policy. Then he began a looting of Italy, requisitioning supplies for his army, and enforcing demands for troops, bullion and art treasures. Napoleon himself made a fortune, his generals did well and the morale of his troops increased as they were paid in coin. Risings against the French were not infrequent and they were violently suppressed. However, the 'looting of Italy' has been overdone by propagandists – after the French privations there seems to have been a great deal left for the Austrian and Russian armies of the Second Coalition in 1799.

When Carnot secretly proposed the exchange of Lombardy for Austrian recognition of a French Rhineland, Napoleon once more seized the initiative in a series of major battles leading to the capture of Mantua (February 1797). Fearing the rapid advance of fresh Austrian reinforcements to threaten his extended forces, Napoleon hastened to open preliminaries of peace at Leoben (April), offering (without consulting the Directors) his own scheme for frontier readjustments – Austria to exchange Belgium (which France already occupied) for Venetia (as yet independent and at peace) and Lombardy to remain a French-dominated republic. This was eighteenth-century diplomacy on a grand scale – the Partitions of Poland brought to the West. And it was diplomacy by a young general who had no authority whatever to make such proposals. Moreau might sign an armistice without permission, but these proposals were a direct challenge to the Directory. In the event, the Directory had to accept them as the best bargain, although they involved pushing the direct influence of France far beyond the natural frontiers into the heart of Italy. To appease an ambitious young general, the Directory had entered upon an expansionist policy. The peace proposals were the first public indication that in Napoleon France had found more than a successful young general. Skilfully he spread the news of the preliminary peace negotiations through the armies in Italy and on the Rhine before the Directory was informed. The Directors capitulated, and the Cisalpine Republic was created and Genoa became the Ligurian Republic, while the ancient Republic of Venice was destroyed by French troops in order that it might be given to Austria in exchange for Belgium.

Meanwhile, Britain, faced with mutinies in the fleet and a financial crisis, had resumed negotiations at Lille, while the appointment of Talleyrand (1797) seemed to augur well for a general peace. But this was also the moment of the Fructidor crisis, and, dependent now entirely on the army, the revised Directory planned a new push into Germany, both to keep the army occupied and to regain the initiative. Britain withdrew from her negotiations. In Italy Napoleon hastened to sign the peace of Campo Formio (October 1797), by which Austria received Venetia in return for recognising the Rhine frontier and agreed to the calling of a Diet at Rastadt to complete the dismemberment of the Holy Roman Empire.

Once more the Directors capitulated to this young general who had shown himself the equal of diplomats and politicians alike. He had now no obvious rival on the military front, for Hoche was dead, Pichegru in exile, Moreau in disgrace, and Bernadotte lacked Napoleon's victories and Jourdan was no politician. It is a tribute to his perspicacity that he did not attempt a coup at this auspicious moment. But the Directory had now to defend its Rhine frontier, and it created a 'cordon sanitaire' of sister republics. To the Batavian Republic (1795), the Ligurian and Cisalpine Republics (1797) were added the Helvetic Republic and the Roman Republic (1798) and, after an ill-advised attack on Rome by the Bourbons of Naples, the Parthenopean Republic (January 1799). Thus the Directory no longer limited itself to French territory but, if only the better to secure the natural frontiers, controlled areas beyond, against the likelihood of future attack. In this respect the Directory, though on a limited stage, was already coming to anticipate the expansionism of the Empire.

In 1797 England alone resisted the Directory. A bid was made to regain control of the seas by uniting the Spanish and Dutch fleets: both were defeated and attempts to help the United Irishmen proved ineffective. On the economic front, in a surprising anticipation of the Continental System (see page 152), the Directory passed the draconian Law of 29 Nivôse, Year VI (January 1798) authorising the seizure of any vessel having anything of English origin aboard (even the chrono-meter). Meanwhile Napoleon was put in charge of the Army of Eng-land, but advised against invasion, preferring an expedition to Egypt. This provided an opportunity for glory; it was also a continua-tion of the eighteenth-century maritime war with Britain for empire – a chance, even, of reversing the position of 1763 and regaining India, for Tippu Sahib was proving a good ally and a tough antagonist to Wellesley. Almost inevitably, in fighting Britain, the Directory was adopting a world-wide policy: in some respects it seemed to anticipate some of the policies of the Empire. Napoleon, within a week of the Floréal coup, sailed for Egypt and might have changed the whole future of the Near East, if not of India, had not Nelson destroyed his fleet in Aboukir Bay (1798) and Sir Sydney Smith prevented his taking Acre (1799).

But the Directory was the victim of its own policy, for the sister republics had to be defended to secure the natural frontiers and Austria, for her part, could not allow their expansion if she were to retain her influence in Italy and Germany. It was partly because of Austrian frustration at making no further gains that the campaigns of the Second Coalition were fought. The Directory's initial success against the Bourbons of Naples, the creation of the Parthenopean Republic and the absorption of Piedmont were followed by defeats for France on all fronts. The Directory, having provoked the war by attacking Malta and Egypt, could not sustain a series of defeats on her own frontiers, while the rising in La Vendée and in the South was a further cause of weakness. But France was once again saved by the disunity of her allies and Masséna's victory in Switzerland and Brune's in Holland precipitated Russia's withdrawal from the coalition. The victories did not save the Directory, for the final coup was already in preparation. However, when Napoleon landed at Fréjus in October, he did not come to save the Republic. This had already been done. But he did bring a revived sense of security and achievement. And after the coup of Brumaire he maintained the basis of the foreign policy of the Directory. As with home policy, so in foreign affairs, there was no sudden change with the coming of the Consulate. That change came with the Empire.

Further Reading

For the Revolution itself, so many books are available that no short list would be adequate. The principal volumes of consequence are cited in Jones, *French Revolution* (University of London Press, 1967) which covers the revolutionary period to 1799. Lefebvre's *The Thermidorians* and *The Directory* have been translated into English (Routledge and Kegan Paul, 1966), and the first chapter of his *Napoleon* (tr. H. F. Stockhold, Routledge and Kegan Paul, 1969) deals with the revolutionary background. M. Reinhard's *La France du Directoire* (2 vols., Paris 1956) should be consulted for its thorough coverage. Soboul's *La Directoire et le Consulat* (Paris 1967, in the *Que sais-je* series) is brief but penetrating. Several of the essays in *French Government and Society, 1500–1850*, edited by J. F. Bosher (Athlone Press, 1973) are particularly valuable. K. D. Tönnesson, *La Défaite des Sans-Culottes* (Paris 1959) is useful for the popular movement and his article on Babeuf in *Past and Present*, 1962, number 22, is useful. See also an article by A. Daline on Napoleon and the Babouvists in *Annales historiques de la Révolution française*, No. 201, 1970. Richard Cobb, *The Police and the People* (Oxford University Press, 1970) is an invaluable survey of police methods with regard to the poor for the period 1789 to 1820. L. Chevalier, *Les Parisiens* (Paris 1967) is a fine and humane treatment of the problem of the poor – a neglected aspect of the Napoleonic era. I. Woloch, *Jacobin Legacy* (Princeton University Press, 1970) offers some interesting ideas. On the European front, R. R. Palmer, *The Age of the Democratic Revolution*, Vol. II (Oxford University Press, 1964) will serve as happy supplement to the *New Cambridge Modern History*, Vol. IX (Cambridge University Press, 1965).

[6] REACTION AGAINST THE REVOLUTION

The joy and enthusiasm with which Europe had greeted the French Revolution within a few years turned to hostility. This was not merely a matter of the emotional recantations of the young (like Coleridge or Wordsworth), but also of a wide range of Europe's intellectual leaders, among whom, in far off Königsberg, Immanuel Kant, once an apostle of Revolution, had now become the first German revisionist. The Napoleonic era grew out of this rejection of the ideas and practice of revolution.

It was the war, and especially the Terror that provoked the condemnation and wrath of the rest of Europe against Revolutionary France. By the end of the century, the Revolution and all its works was already castigated as the prevailing of the works of darkness which all good Christian men should labour to destroy. But the Revolution was hydra-headed: it is important to grasp what was being condemned. The political and administrative reforms of the Constituent Assembly were generally welcomed. It was the Terror, which characterised the Jacobin dictatorship, that was rejected. The Terror was explicable in terms of the vigorous paramilitary measures necessary to preserve the Revolution, but it was easily and widely misrepresented as a bloodbath of nobles, as an anti-christian movement, as an attack on property rights, implicit in the political strength of the *sans-culottes*. But, after it had been ended by the Thermidorian Reaction, there came the Directory, during which those excesses that had characterised a government in a state of siege were replaced by a genuine attempt to establish a stable new social order based on a hierarchy of wealth and respect for private property. This was as much a part of the Revolution as was the Jacobin Terror; yet, by 1797, the *ancien régime* was fast approaching an accommodation with the former whilst so vilifying the latter that it seemed to have grown the more horrid in recollection.

This distinction between the constructive reforms of the Revolution and Jacobinism is vital for the understanding of the situation to which Napoleon was heir. Generally, he was welcomed as much for being the guardian of the new order in France, a society with which the *ancien régime* could comfortably coexist, as for being the guarantee against Jacobinism. It was only later, after the victory at Austerlitz, that he came to be classed along with Jacobinism as the public enemy of Europe. There is here a crucial distinction. Napoleon, secure at home and abroad, represented the constructive reform that socially advanced Europe would accept – and this helped to create the stability of the Consulate. But the Napoleonic Empire meant continued and immoderate aggression against the Great Powers and had therefore to be defeated and contained.

In welcoming Napoleon as Consul, Europe was seeking order and stability from a volatile France. In condemning Napoleon as Emperor, Europe was seeking the security of a balance of power within her own frontiers. The more violent of his opponents sought to link his name with the general vilification of Jacobinism in order to strengthen the opposition to him. This confusion of nomenclature is understandable: yet in defeating Napoleon, Europe did not rise against the French Revolution, but against the imposition of a French Imperium. De Maistre, among Napoleon's most effective opponents, justly commented:

> Louis XVIII has not been restored to the throne of his ancestors: he has simply ascended the throne of Bonaparte.

Napoleon was the heir to the Revolution, and his career was possible solely because of it: yet he represented only a part of that gigantic movement. He did not so much fulfil the Revolution as ossify it, guaranteeing one part of the revolutionary achievement – political equality, the career open to talent, and the land settlement. It was as much as French society could then encompass, for it was still agricultural based, lacking concentrated urban industrial centres. A future generation would need to wrestle further with the problem of social equality that had emerged momentarily under the Jacobin Terror, and horrified Europe with the spectre of the *loi agraire*, the threat of a redistribution of property.

Napoleon, then, at least as Consul, personified the triumph of a new bourgeois social order which was intent on preventing the Revolution from travelling further along the road to equality. It is ironic, indeed, that Napoleon, a friend of Augustin Robespierre and imprisoned after Thermidor as a Robespierrist, should achieve power as the guardian of the social order and the oppressor of Jacobinism. This was partly because the Jacobins, in their struggle to attain and strengthen their power during the Terror, had been forced into a *mariage de convenance* with the *sans-culottes* and this had left them suspected of threatening property rights. Napoleon was not going to repeat this mistake. Nor did he, a successful general, stand in need of the support of the urban proletariat. He could well afford to continue their subjection. That new-style antagonism of 1793 of poor against rich, that was to emerge fully as socialism and to dominate the politics of the second half of the nineteenth century, had no place in the Napoleonic order of things. He was prepared to be paternalistic towards the urban proletariat, but not to admit them to any vestige of political power: instead, workers were issued with an identity card (*un livret*, see page 113) by which their movements were controlled, and the *Loi le Chapelier* remained in force, making trade unions illegal. For half a century, they remained the 'dupes of Thermidor' (see Jones, *French Revolution* p. 164).

[7] DICTATORSHIP FROM THE RIGHT

But if Napoleon rejected the nascent social democracy implicit in the economic measures of the Terror, he built upon the political unity that the Jacobins had forged to produce a totalitarian state of great significance for the future.

De Tocqueville, with his usual percipience, recognised a quite new force emerging in politics:

> From the eighteenth century and the Revolution, as from a common source, two rivers flow: the first bears men towards free institutions, whilst the second draws them towards absolute power.

This new force was given one of its sharpest delineations early in the Revolution by Sieyès – 'the Nation exists before all things and is the origin of all things . . . its will is always the supreme law'. It was this new dogma of popular sovereignty that inspired the Jacobin Terror to establish a vigorous dictatorship in which ruler and ruled were so closely identified that Robespierre could, in effect, assert that his opponents were guilty of *lèse-nation* (treason, in effect). Once citizens and government are regarded as synonymous, the individual loses his rights, and, not unnaturally, Burke condemned this view of popular sovereignty as the end of political liberty. Nevertheless, it was a view of which Napoleon made full use, and which has appeared in exaggerated forms in our own century.

Professor Talmon's brilliant analysis of the period has traced a line of development that can throw a great deal of light upon the emergence of the Napoleonic régime from the Revolution. Two new political movements appeared during the Revolution (those two rivers to which de Tocqueville referred): liberal democracy and totalitarian democracy. Both spring from the intellectual background of eighteenth-century rationalism. Both are idealist concepts seeking to establish a moral and equitable society. But in their approach to politics they are fundamentally opposed to each other, for liberal democracy is empirical, depending on human spontaneity, whilst totalitarian democracy seeks to achieve its aim though the medium of an all-embracing state. It is the latter that triumphed in the Terror, culminating in that excess of *civisme* associated with Robespierre, and requiring the exercise of coercion in order to hasten the hoped-for social harmony, as much as to save France from defeat and the Revolution from destruction. It is this use of active coercion that

divided the liberal from the totalitarian. But totalitarian democracy is
itself divided into two wings – the left wing (of which Robespierre is
an example), believing in the ultimate perfectibility of man, and the
right wing, believing man to be weak and corrupt and in need of the
coercive power of the state in order to establish and maintain an
organised social harmony. It is from this latter source that twentieth
century fascism comes. Yet the origin of both wings is the direction of
the physical and moral forces of the nation towards a life of civic
virtue. Now Napoleon, whether by accident or design, or simply by
dint of hard practical experience, emerged as the prototype leader of
right wing totalitarian social democracy.

He inherited a France in which not only had there been created the
elements of a strong administration, but also a new phenomenon, a
state inspired by a patriotism that looked beyond its frontiers to carry
its message into foreign lands. In 1796 Burke had shuddered at the
sight of aggressive revolutionary France,

> struck out at a heat … it has unity and consistency in perfection
> … Individuality is left out of their scheme of government. The
> State is all in all.

But Napoleon, keenly aware of the instability of the Directory he
had replaced, had no wish to become entangled in frustrating constitutional wranglings and had come to believe that men in the mass
preferred vigorous leadership to parliamentary debate. And to
complete the circle, he had recourse to a democratic weapon, which
was to be used extensively by later dictators – the plebiscite, the
massive popular vote that gave a specious air of legality to major
constitutional changes.

Representing victory abroad, prosperity and good order at home,
he was certain of massive support. As the prosperity and victory
continued, that support survived the transformation of a policy well
suited to France's interests, into one of Caesarist expansionism under
the Empire. Throughout, his régime rested upon dictatorship shorn
up by popular enthusiasm inspired by success.

He was the strong man who had come to end anarchy: he was more
than this – to the generation upturned by the Revolution and buffeted
by the growing storms of Romanticism, he was a veritable 'Zeitgeist on
horseback'. Earlier in the century, Vico had suggested that legendary
heroes were the personification of ideal human qualities: in the days
of his success, men of his generation (and of later generations, too)

looked to him as if to a hero of old – and beyond this, even, they saw in him the particular personification of moral and political virtue. To Michelet, he was the mouthpiece of '*conscience populaire*'. To Saint-Simon, he was the great architect and scientific legislator of mankind. To Mickiewicz, the Polish patriot, he was the organ of God's revelation, the precursor of another and greater Messiah –

> Napoleon carried in his soul the entire past of Christianity and realised it in his person ... Napoleon has begun an evolution in Christianity.

This Messianism, partly a reflection of the ideas of the time, partly an aspect of the charisma that pervaded the successful Napoleon, is indicative not only of his individual greatness, but of his capacity to speak for his generation, indeed for mankind.

It is a very great and unusual gift: but it is also exceedingly dangerous, for in this uncharted world where the real and the spiritual merge, there can be no certainty either of fame or of condemnation, nor can there be any certainty that honour and glory will be maintained. And where the career of one man is so intimately connected with the history of a country, there can be no guarantee that his policies are not dictated by purely personal ambition and conceit, with no real attention paid to the permanent interests of the country he serves.

Appearing at a moment of immense social and political upheaval (for the French Revolution made its American predecessor look like a change of ministry), when the political ideas of men were graced with a seemingly absolute significance, Napoleon gave the impression of carrying all before him. But the very arrogance of the claims of the Revolution had provoked Burke to challenge man's presumption in seeking himself his own salvation; and the combined impact of the Revolution and Napoleon drove Joseph de Maistre and Louis de Bonald, in reaction, to assert the principle of a theocratic absolutism. Wittingly or no, Napoleon had trespassed into the preserves of the spiritual world, and in the van of the reaction which eventually destroyed him rode the agents of that remarkable religious revival of the period. Hailed in 1800 as the precursor of the social order, within a decade he was to be vilified as Antichrist.

[8] ROMANTICISM

The Revolutionary and Napoleonic eras coincided with the blossoming of the Romantic Movement, an immense cultural revolution that added vast areas of spiritual and aesthetic experience, and dominated European culture for at least a hundred years. Efforts to define and explain Romanticism have proved as difficult as those seeking to evaluate the impact of particular great men, but, within a generation of the Revolution, Romanticism came to pervade the whole attitude and outlook of the young.

It was compounded of many things, not the least among which was a vigorous intellectual reaction against the rationalism that had dominated eighteenth-century thought. This reaction was more than a change in intellectual fashion: it was as much a psychological rejection of the force of human intellect, as an appeal to human emotions; a sense of security beyond what cartesianism could give.

It is as if, at high noon of the Enlightenment, at the hour of the Siesta when everything seems so quiet and secure all about, one were suddenly aware of a short, sharp slipping of the foundations, a faint far-off tremor running underneath the solid ground of common sense. (Becker)

Rationalism had found neither a satisfactory sanction for morality, nor a safe haven for the emotions. Kant's attempt at a synthesis of rationalist and empiricist views, *Critique of Pure Reason* (1781), did not satisfy the new generation, and the bloodshed of the Terror seemed an awful warning of the limitations implicit in seeking the perfection of man by the force of ideas. From a different source, too, came further evidence that man was not master of his destiny: in 1798 the Reverend Dr Malthus produced his *Essay on Population* which, its argument vulgarised by publicists, pointed to the uncertainties of a future threatened by the growth of population, and seemed to declare that the notion of unlimited human progress was a wild fancy.

If Romanticism had merely castigated Rationalism as the sin of pride, it would have been understandable – and of no great consequence. But, with a splendid disregard for logic and consistency, it proceeded, through an excess of sensibility, to glory in the achievement of particular men who had triumphed over apparently insuperable barriers. The Romantic Hero was a superman personifying a great range of human emotions and pursuing a moral purpose in which, the ennoblement of life was implicit. He was not the 'angry young man', like Shelley or Byron, but a man with years of solid achievement behind him to add lustre to his genius. In music, Beethoven saw himself as such a figure. And Napoleon, inspired by the rumoured vision of his destiny vouchsafed him on the bridge at Lodi in 1796, was the Romantic Hero par excellence; a myth hero, enshrining the unspoken desires of the human psyche, trespassing beyond the ordinary limits of life. (Hobsbawm). In him are combined the history of ideas and the management of politics: by restoring law and order, he re-forged the promethean chains that youthful romantics had sought to break and provided a goal for the now aimless Revolution – namely, the co-ordination of national energies by an efficient, centralised and secular state. Whatever idealists hoped for in 1800, however much his genera-tion rejected his imperial ventures, posterity has endorsed his choice for France. At the time when there was wholesale apostasy among the young intellectuals of Europe who once had rejoiced in the fall of the Bastille; when the youth of France either entered the service of the Revolution or joined the *émigrés*, Napoleon, capturing their imagina-tion through success in war, was, as Lefebvre has put it, a romantic poet turned man of action. It was a metamorphosis which the carping Chateaubriand, for all his efforts, failed to make. Napoleon's mind was classical in mould, so that precision and good order characterised his administration, yet the insatiable and irrational pursuit of power and glory marks him as a romantic. Janus-like, mirroring the achieve-ments of a past age yet looking forward upon those of an age to come, he stands

in his energy and his thirst for the unattainable, the most perfect historical expression of a dynamic and Faustian culture. (Bruun)

With its anti-rationalist roots, its emphasis upon emotion and intuition, Romanticism tended to favour totalitarian solutions to political problems. But the totalitarianism was not the cosmopoli-tanism of Napoleon's Empire, rather it was the individual finding his freedom in a cheerful submission to the collective 'national' identity. It was agreed that the individualist liberal ideas of 1789 had led, in the Terror, to a destruction of the social order hitherto deemed essential to civilisation. This had caused a loss of faith in man's capacity to change society by himself, and in reaction, there developed an appeal to a misty, unhistorical medievalism in which was perceived an ideal society based on social duties and respect for established authority. Its influence is to be seen in the popular historical novels of the period, in the gothic revival, and, in England particularly, among proponents of reform who viewed with fear and hatred the social as well as the aesthetic effects of industrial change. But, at the time of Napoleon, it was chiefly important, on the one hand for adding weight to the arguments of Burke in favour of 'organic' rather than radical change, and to Herder's ideas of a *Volksgeist* dominating the history of a people, and to the 'historical school' of jurists, led by the German Savigny; and, on the other hand, in promoting the religious revival that aided the rising tide of reactionary opinion with de Maistre and de Bonald at its head. It was also to help the advocates of a 'people's war' against Napoleon, for it was particularly strong in Germany, where ideas of a mythical German *Volk* were already gaining currency. The distinction between these cloudy romantic impressions and the classical precision of the Napoleonic Code throw these co-existing intellectual worlds into sharp relief.

Germany was the acknowledged centre of Romanticism: it was also where the religious revival was most vocal. Together, these cultural movements were to strengthen the cause of reaction and to destroy Napoleon. But the story is no simple one, and German romanticism was not always hostile to Napoleon – at first he was mistaken for the incarnation of a new European Hero by cosmopolitan intellectuals like Goethe who had responded to the Revolution's call of Liberty; and Hegel thought of him as an embodiment of State force. But the exactions of French imperialism coincided with the growing strength of a peculiarly German form of romanticism so that resentment at French 'cultural imperialism' increased opposition and led rapidly to that patriotic resistance that Turnvater Jahn in 1810 called the *Volkstum*, whilst Savigny and Eichhorn condemned the Napoleonic Code as an arbitrary product of human intellect, inappropriate to countries beyond the frontiers of France since it was not founded on their customs.

The religious revival helped to turn many former supporters of the Revolution into reactionaries, the more so as the revival aided chiefly Roman Catholicism – as early as 1799 in *Christenheit oder Europa*, Novalis, though remaining a Protestant, had extolled Christian unity and composed a Hymn to the Virgin. But mysticism was in vogue, too, with Swedenborg, Pasqualis and Saint-Martin, the 'Unknown Philosopher', culminating, perhaps, in Madame de Krudener who sought political influence through it with the Tsar Alexander I. Apocalyptic writings achieved remarkable currency: Jung Stilling was preaching in Baden that there would be one come out of the North to overthrow Napoleon the Antichrist (an appeal that was not lost on the Tsar). Such preachifying inspired Schleiermacher, whose *Address on Religion to the Educated who Despise It* (1799) had helped to make religion once more popular among the intellectuals, and who was soon to be a dominant force in the patriotic German movement against Napoleon.

In France, also, despite the reconciliation achieved by the Concordat, pietism was a growing movement, potentially hostile to Napoleon – the more so as his relations with the Papacy deteriorated. Chateaubriand, in whom the Revolution and the Counter-revolution were to be in some measure fused, had written to his sister, in 1798, '*Ma conviction est sortie du cœur; j'ai pleuré et j'ai cru*'. In 1802 his *Génie du Christianisme* recruited the forces of sentiment not for the Consulate, as Napoleon had hoped, but for Reaction. By 1805 he had joined the growing ranks of publicists who once were supporters of the Revolution, but now, by their apostasy, had come to strengthen the reactionaries against Napoleon.

However, the impact of Romanticism on public opinion as a whole should not be exaggerated. Leading publicists might well have been inspired by philosophic motives, but most of the opponents of the Revolution, and later of Napoleon, were inspired by self-interest, and if they felt a need for a nobler motive they found it in a religious revival that was anterior to the Revolution itself. The nobles who rallied to throne and altar, and obediently believed that the Devil was the first Jacobin, had a weather eye for the safe roads leading to a harbour. And the inert mass of popular opinion that overtly or tacitly joined in the attack on Napoleon was untouched by philosophy or the changes in aesthetic fashion.

[9] REACTION

The movement of counter-revolution which grew in size and significance with the coming of the Empire, when it was absorbed into the opposition to Napoleon, was composed of two very definite groups. On the one hand, an important group of intellectuals established the philosophic basis for the reaction that was to dominate the Europe of Metternich during the following generation (see Andrew Milne,

Metternich, University of London Press, 1975). On the other, émigré
nobles and their friends, some actively engaged in widespread plots,
waited and worked for a Restoration that would grant them both
revenge and the return of their property. A veritable constellation of
different motives moved around each group: the Reactionaries were
never a cohesive body of men united upon common aims.

The theorists were not averse to reform, provided it came from
above and preserved the existing nature of society. Burke, the greatest
of them, had little impact in France, but his views swept Germany
when Frederick von Gentz (the future secretary to Metternich)
produced in 1791 a translation of his *Reflections on the Revolution in
France*. In Switzerland it inspired Mallet du Pan, a journalist of
genius, to join the reactionaries, urging that since the Jacobins were
organising anarchy, their opponents must now organise order. In
Piedmont it inspired Joseph de Maistre, soon to be the leading
theocratic writer and to wield considerable political influence in St
Petersburg. It inspired Louis de Bonald, another leading theocrat, to
produce his *Théorie du pouvoir politique et réligieux* (1796) that was to
provide the required philosophic basis for absolutism. Man, he argued,
is naturally bad but made good by society: this society must be a
pyramid in form, composed at its base of subjects willingly submis-
sive to the authority of the king. 'Others have defended the religion of
man; I defend the religion of society.'

To this, de Maistre added the overriding need of an independent
Church to provide the necessary social cement. 'The greatest crime a
nobleman can commit is to attack the Christian dogmas', he asserted
in *Considérations sur la France* (1796), and he went on to claim that
the satanic power of the revolution was a divine punishment for
impiety. Later, in *Du Pape* (1817), he was to advocate the immanent
power of the Papacy over the politics of Europe. Such emphasis by the
leading theorists of reaction upon the social function of organised
religion strengthened the bond between noble and clergy, both of
whom had suffered at the hands of the Revolution. Gentz, it was said,
seemed to feel more strongly about the social value of religion than
about religion itself.

But for all their activity, the theocratic writers had their greatest
influence in the years following Napoleon's fall. They were not
concerned with espionage, nor with the actual overthrow of the
tyrant. When he fell, it was because of a successful diplomatic and
military attack (see Part VIII). Yet the religious revival had played its

part, not only in inspiring popular resistance, but also, even more important, in helping to convert counter-revolution from a blind and vengeful hatred of the Revolution into a movement that had accepted and absorbed many of the major reforms of the Revolution. For this reason it was possible for Louis XVIII to be restored to a throne that was similar to that of Napoleon.

The *émigré* nobles who worked for the Restoration through the many different plots between 1795 and 1804 (and beyond), were in pursuit of lost privileges and sinecures. They were happy enough to make use of the growing religious revival, but their motivation was purely secular. Their intrigues and plots, sometimes affecting the course of European diplomacy, reached a climax in the conspiracy that ended with the execution of the Duc d'Enghien (see page 170). With this violent act Napoleon slammed the door on their hopes of a Restoration, for, if on a less significant plane than the execution of Louis XVI, it nevertheless ensured the continuance of a revolutionary régime and hastened the declaration of the Empire.

The decade after 1805 had a different atmosphere. On the one hand the political dogmas of the Revolution were not absorbed by the rest of Europe as they had been in France, so that there was no longer a fear of widespread revolution. On the other, the great powers were gradually brought to a recognition of the necessity for co-operation to defeat the French Empire, if not to destroy Napoleon. The ideological conflict had changed. It was no longer a case of a new social order threatening the privilege of the *ancien régime*, but of a great power dominating Europe – a situation that could be handled simply in military and diplomatic terms. Yet, as the scale of the wars and of the losses increased, 'the churchyard assumed the rôle of the preacher', and, when a wave of pietism was sweeping Europe, it was not to be wondered at that Napoleon, the Romantic Hero once hailed as the guardian of the social order, should be declared Antichrist.

So tremendous a change in popular opinion is itself a tribute to the charisma of the man. Even in defeat he remained a secular myth, explicable as much by his victories and propaganda as by his remarkable career. Born a poor noble, this 'little corporal' rose to rule a continent: henceforth his name would be an inspiration that would plague writers, generals, politicians in the succeeding generations, and make the prosperous bourgeois, who had done well out of the Revolution and the Empire, tremble. More than this, against the German romantic who, in the name of the *Volksgeist*, condemned

Napoleon for riding rough-shod over the traditions of Europe, this remarkable man raised the vision of a European synthesis, a grandiose scheme for creating a European society subject to the harmonious rule of universal laws and single institutions. In the years of exile at St Helena, reinterpreting his career for publication, he created a legend that was to reverberate through the courts of Europe for a hundred years (see page 213). Perceiving, among the bourgeois of central Europe, the birth of a new idea of nationalism (however weak the movement), he claimed to have been the defender of *peoples* against dynasties that regarded them as merely subjects. These seeds of a new cultural nationalism were to blossom after 1848 and to yield their bitter fruits in our own century.

In a quite different world, Lenin, a greater revolutionary and a far greater theorist, once wrote,

It is not enough to be a revolutionary ... it is also necessary to know at every moment how to find the particular link in the chain which must be grasped with all one's strength in order to keep the whole chain in place and prepare to move on resolutely to the next link.

Napoleon, a trained soldier, was too practical to be anything more than pragmatic in his approach to politics: nevertheless, there is a sense in which this quotation is profoundly true of his career.

Further Reading

The contemporary literature is too vast to be listed here: the principal works are quoted, or referred to, in most good history books of the period, and they have inspired a number of penetrative studies. Among the latter is Professor Talmon's outstanding synthesis contained in *The Origins of Totalitarian Democracy* (Secker and Warburg, 1952) and *Political Messianism: The Romantic Phase* (Secker and Warburg, 1960). Then there is Dr Schenk's brilliant study, *The Mind of the European Romantics* (Constable, 1966), and his *The Aftermath of the Napoleonic Wars* (Routledge and Kegan Paul, 1947) is also useful. Jacques Godechot's *La Contre-Révolution, 1789–1804* (Paris 1961) is an invaluable study. Some thought-provoking works are H. Laski, *Authority in the Modern State* (Yale University Press, 1919) – for the theocrats – Mosca, *The Ruling Class* (tr. Kahn, McGraw, New York 1939), J. Nef, *War and Human Progress* (1950),

N.—2*

and C. L. Becker, *The Heavenly City of the Eighteenth-Century Philosophers* (Yale University Press, 1932). Isaiah Berlin's *The Hedgehog and the Fox* (Weidenfeld and Nicolson, 1953) contains useful hints about de Maistre within a fine essay on Tolstoy's *War and Peace* and historiography. A. Cobban, *In Search of Humanity* (N. Kaye, London 1960), differs from Talmon. Among books dealing more specifically with political history, G. Bruun, *Europe and the French Imperium* (Harper, new ed. 1963), Hobsbawn, *The Age of Revolution* (Weidenfeld and Nicolson, 1962) and R. R. Palmer, *The Age of the Democratic Revolution*, Vol. II (Oxford University Press, 1964) are useful.

Plamenatz, *The Revolutionary Movement in France* (Longman, 1965), and Talmon, *Romanticism and Revolt, Europe, 1815–1848*, (Thames and Hudson, 1967) also offer some fruitful lines of thought. The first lecture of George Steiner's *In Bluebeard's Castle* (*The Listener*, 1971) also has some pertinent comment.

PRINCIPAL EVENTS, 1787–99

France	*Abroad*
1787 Assembly of Notables	
1789 Constituent Assembly 'Abolition' of feudalism	
1790 Breach in French Church over Civil Constitution	
1791 *Loi le Chapelier* Monarchical Constitution	
1792 Girondin ministry Declaration of war against Austria Fall of monarchy in France Republic declared (September)	**1792** Battle of Valmy
1793 Jacobins in control The Terror (August '93–July 1794)	**1793** Second partition of Poland
1794 Thermidor crisis – fall of Robespierre Thermidorian Reaction (July–October 1795)	**1794** Battle of Fleurus, end of foreign threat
1795	**1795** Third Partition of Poland Prussia makes peace (April)
Prairial crisis (May) (*Sans-culottes* defeated)	
	Spain makes peace (July)
Constitution of the Year III Vendémiaire crisis The Directory (October)	Belgium annexed Batavian Republic formed Pichegru makes armistice with Austrians (December)
1796 Carnot's plan to attack Austria Napoleon succeeds Schérer (March)	

France	*Abroad*
	1796
	Jourdan and Moreau attack across
	Rhine. Little progress
10 May. Babeuf Conspiracy	10 May. Bonaparte defeats Austrians
destroyed	at Lodi
	Pastoralis sollicitudo (Papacy)
1797	**1797**
	14 January. Napoleon defeats
	Austrians at Rivoli
	14 February. Jervis defeats Spanish
	fleet at St Vincent
	Treaty of Tolentino with Papacy
	April. Preliminaries of peace at
	Leoben
	April. Venice occupied
	June. Ligurian Republic
July. Talleyrand foreign minister	July. Cisalpine Republic
4 September. Coup of 18 Fructidor	
preserves Directory	
30 September. *Liquidation Ramel*	
('bankruptcy of the two-thirds')	
	October. Duncan defeats Dutch fleet
	at Camperdown
	Malmesbury at Lille
	18 October. Napoleon makes Treaty of
	Campo Formio
November. Ramel's *agence des*	
contributions directes (tax reform)	
1798	**1798**
January. Draconian Law of Nivôse	
against British commerce	
	February. Roman Republic
	April. Helvetic Republic
11 May. Coup of 22 Floréal saves	
Directory from the left	
	18 May. Napoleon departs for Egypt,
Ramel's *bureaux de bienfaisance*	taking Malta *en route*
(poor relief)	
August. Neufchâteau's Industrial	August. Battle of Nile
Exhibition	Second Coalition
	November. Naples attacks Roman
	Republic
	1799
	January. Naples occupied and
	proclaimed the Parthenopean Republic

France

1799

Rising in la Vendée and in southern France

Danger of invasion

20 May. Sieyès joins Directory

'Jacobin' measures to meet serious foreign threat

12 July. Law of Hostages

August. Fouché closes the Manège Club, 'Jacobins' begin to lose power

9 October. Napoleon lands at Fréjus

9 November. Coup d'état of 18 Brumaire

Consulate

Abroad

March. Jourdan forced back across Rhine

March–May. Napoleon vainly besieges Acre

15 August. Suvarov defeats and kills Joubert at Novi

27 August. Duke of York lands in Holland

26 September. Masséna victorious at Zurich

18 October. Convention of Alkmaar

22 October. Tsar Paul withdraws from Second Coalition

PART II
Napoleon's Armed Forces

[10] THE WEAPONS AVAILABLE

To the junior officer and the common soldier, the principal feature of a Napoleonic battle must have been the confusion confounded by the smoke and noise of artillery. To command such a battle, when vast numbers of men were involved over a wide area, and when the fastest means of communicating specific orders was a horse-rider, demanded a technical skill of more than ordinary quality. Napoleon commanded at sixty such battles within twenty years. This is a military achievement without equal. Yet historians have been unable to isolate the essential quality of his military genius.

Few have possessed a charisma like Napoleon's, whether it was for the common soldier or the Nation; yet, leadership by itself is not a sufficient answer. Inspired courage is of no avail before a superior bombardment, as the French armies, for all their Napoleonic *élan*, discovered in 1914. It was not merely leadership, but the intimate knowledge of his own trade as soldier that gave Napoleon victory. This victory was ensured by three coincidental factors: first, a political situation favourable to France in that the Revolution had made her vigorous in a totally new way whilst the rest of Europe was weak and divided. Secondly, the brilliant organisational work of Carnot and his helpers during the Revolution that had created a magnificent military machine on foundations laid since the reforms of the 1770s. Thirdly, Napoleon's own capacity as a general, and his skill at using tactics based upon strategic conceptions with which any officer of his age would have been familiar.

All generals are dependent upon the resources available. If these resources include new weapons or a quite new technique of fighting, they are lucky. Napoleon was not lucky in this respect. He was no innovator in the weapons he used because technology did not produce effective new weapons during his period of power: he was no innovator in tactics, for he applied, with consummate skill, the ideas of the leading theorists of his age. The brilliant, lightning, knock-out blow bringing a rapid end to a victorious campaign – his *Blitzkrieg* effect – was merely the characteristic of Napoleon's campaigns: he did not invent the method.

During Napoleon's lifetime, the Industrial Revolution was preparing the basis for the great achievements of the nineteenth century but it came too late really to affect the Napoleonic Wars. Not until the Crimean War (1854–6) were armies refitted with really new and improved weapons. Until then they managed with those already in production in the 1770s. Napoleon cannot be blamed for the failure of technology to keep pace with the demands of warfare.

Armies depended heavily on infantry (the cavalry playing something of a secondary rôle) and their principal weapon was the musket. The French model of 1777 modified in Year XI remained in use until 1840 – a tribute to its designers. But it was heavy and inefficient, smooth-bored, muzzle-loaded, with flintlock and usually with a fitted bayonet. The flints wore out, the barrel was frequently fouled by coarse powder, and if the powder got wet the musket might not fire at all. Highly skilled troops could fire no more than three rounds in two minutes because of the loading and priming operations, and the range and accuracy were so poor that it was not effective at much more than a hundred metres. Infantry were trained to hold their fire until the very last moment. A volley fired at a hundred metres would severely maul attackers but leave no time for reloading before bayonet work began. Thus the range of tactics available to the infantry was confined by the shortcomings of the musket (and commanders were quite happy to walk or ride openly among their men ready positioned for battle).

The rifle was already recognised as a superior weapon, being accurate to three hundred metres; but the narrow rifled barrel made loading difficult and Ferguson's breach-loading device (1775) was not taken up. Its rate of fire was necessarily slow, and the barrel was too weak to carry a fixed bayonet; furthermore, the dense clouds of smoke that enveloped eighteenth-century battlefields made it difficult to see the movement of whole bodies of troops, let alone individual targets. (The rifle had to await portable, smokeless ammunition before it could replace the musket.) Groups of snipers (like the Croats of the Austrian army) were useful both in harassing the enemy and in supplying information about their disposition, but they could not play any really vital part in a full-scale battle.

The French artillery had been transformed into the best in the world by the efforts of Gribeauval in the 1770s, who standardised the field pieces into three sizes (twelve-, eight- and four-pounders, although the four-pounders were not too successful) and made them lighter and more easily manoeuvrable. Horses replaced bullocks as draught animals so that the artillery could keep pace with infantry and even cavalry. It was now possible to move cannon frequently in the course of a battle and a standard unit of eight guns with 150 mm howitzers for each infantry division was recommended. Cannon were expensive, so that artillery remained for the most part supplementary to infantry. The average in 1805 was twelve pieces per division and even when more were available, after 1808, there were rarely more than three per thousand men.

A twelve-pounder's effective range was 1,800 metres, but much shorter ranges, down to 400 metres, were common. Better shot and Belidor's pre-packed powder charge made fairly rapid fire possible, but the use of canister shot, Shrapnel's explosive shells (1787) and Congreve's rockets were confined in all armies because of the unreliability of the early models. In fact, Napoleon could add little to Gribeauval's work. However, in 1802 he ordered Marmont to recast the ordnance. Had this been achieved, a major step forward in military techniques might have been made. But, although coke smelting made iron guns both lighter and cheaper than bronze, industry was not yet capable of producing the guns at the speed and in the quantities required: there was a lack of tools, a shortage of transport, carriages and horses and of ammunition. The ten years of war that began in 1805 ended any hope of completing the order given in 1802. It is not surprising that Napoleon, himself an artillery man, was no innovator in this arm of the services: time and technology were against him. Certainly, he would have welcomed more and better guns with which to exploit new methods, but they were not available:

It is a principle of war [he said] that when it is possible to make use of thunderbolts, they should be preferred to cannon.

Gribeauval's reforms had inspired the Chevalier du Teil's *De l'usage de l'artillerie dans la guerre de campagne* (1778). The young Napoleon read this at the artillery school of Auxonne. Du Teil envisaged the complementary use of artillery and infantry, the cannon being drawn to within 1000 metres of the enemy before firing on the flank (more men were killed by firing down the line than through it). In this way the artillery would change from simply harassing the enemy to providing a concentration of fire-power that would seriously weaken the enemy line before a charge. Massed guns also compensated for inaccuracy and slowness of fire. Napoleon put du Teil's ideas to good effect, but lack of guns and ammunition prevented him from developing the 'creeping barrage' technique of 1914–18.

The emigration of royalist officers during the Revolution had seriously weakened the French cavalry, although the Directory did much to restore its strength. However, despite the brilliance of Murat and other commanders, the nature of the tactics used meant that cavalry played a subordinate rôle. Apart from set charges and the pursuit of a defeated enemy (never properly effected), it was used for reconnaissance, protecting the army's flanks and providing cover for an advance. The great loss of horses in the 1812 Russian campaign was a very serious disability for the French, for cavalry was a vital arm of the army, especially for reconnaissance. Eylau, Wagram and Waterloo were exceptional as battles in which cavalry played a major rôle.

[11] STRATEGY AND TACTICS

Just as Napoleonic armies used on a grand scale the weapons developed in the previous generation, so they brought that generation's tactics to a fine art. For the previous fifty years opinion had been swinging in favour of more fluid battle formations, one of the principal points of dispute being whether to attack with an advancing disciplined line of infantry, or with a dense column of men whose impact would be greater and less vulnerable to an enemy volley at short range. The Comte de Guibert favoured the latter, urging that once superior fire-power had seriously weakened the enemy line, a vigorously pressed charge on that point would break the line and secure victory. His *Essai général de Tactique* (1772) became the established textbook in the French military academies where Napoleon learnt his craft. However, as Guibert was prepared to leave to the general in charge the decision as to which method to employ, the idea of combining both line and column movements was developed, *l'ordre mixte*,

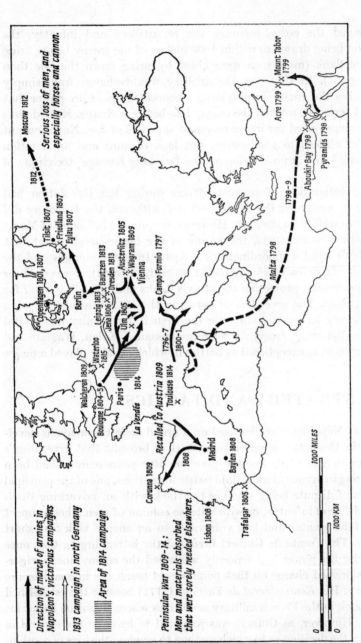

PRINCIPAL CAMPAIGNS OF NAPOLEON

Direction of march of armies in
Napoleon's victorious campaigns

1813 campaign in north Germany

Area of 1814 campaign

Peninsular War 1809–14:
Men and materials absorbed
that were sorely needed elsewhere.

Serious loss of men, and
especially horses and cannon.

Moscow 1812

Tilsit 1807
Friedland 1807
Eylau 1807

Copenhagen 1801, 1807

Berlin

Walcheren 1809

Boulogne 1804–5

Waterloo 1815

Paris

1814

La Vendée

Recalled to Austria 1809

1808

Coruña 1809

Lisbon 1808

Madrid

Baylen 1808

Trafalgar 1805

Toulouse 1814

1796–7

1800–1

Campo Formio 1797

Vienna

Ulm 1805

Jena 1806

Leipzig 1813

Bautzen 1813

Dresden 1813

Austerlitz 1805

Wagram 1809

Malta 1798

1798–9

Aboukir Bay 1798

Pyramids 1798

Acre 1799

Mount Tabor 1799

0   1000 MILES

0   1000 KM

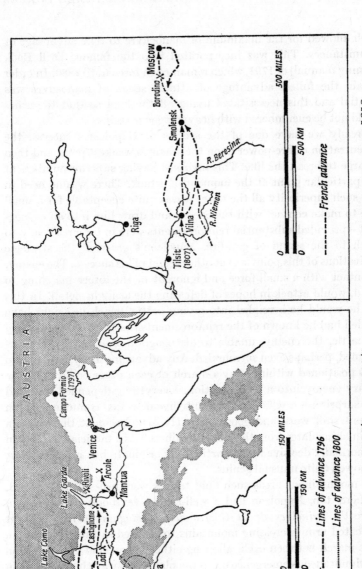

NORTH ITALIAN CAMPAIGNS 1796/7 AND 1800/1

- - - Lines of advance 1796
······· Lines of advance 1800

MOSCOW CAMPAIGN 1812

- - - French advance

which allowed for the maximum of manoeuvre to take advantage of circumstances. This was incorporated into the famous Drill Book (training manual) of 1791, which remained in force until 1830. In order to gain the fullest advantage of attack, speed of manoeuvre was essential and this necessitated living off the land so that the army should not be encumbered with heavy baggage trains.

Already we have one of the secrets of Napoleon's success, the concentration of fire-power upon the enemy's weakest point and then a charge to break the line. This involved having superior numbers at that particular point at the moment of attack. There was no need to have such superiority all the time; it was quite acceptable for a small force to make contact with the enemy and draw him into an engagement – provided substantial reinforcements were in the area ready to march to the sound of gun-fire. Napoleon's grasp of the strategic implications of this point was another secret of his success. The enemy, in contact with a small force and ignorant of the forces marching to its aid, would attack in hopes of defeating the army in detail. In this way he would be inveigled into giving battle, which he might have avoided had he known of the reinforcements. As these arrived during the battle, the enemy, unable to disengage himself, would be overwhelmed, perhaps even surrounded. Any advancing army divided into corps positioned within a day's march of each other could draw the unwary enemy into a fatal position. Everything depended on speed and surprise, on efficient and intelligent corps commanders, on efficient staff work and good maps. (It is no accident that modern map-making dates from the time of Guibert.) As a tactician, Napoleon was normally decisive if not particularly original; but as a strategist he showed quite unusual genius.

In mountainous areas such fluid tactics were necessarily confined, but here, too, Napoleon had a well-known textbook to guide him, Bourcet's *Principes de la Guerre des Montagnes* (1771). Bourcet advocated armies crossing mountains to proceed in three columns, a day's march between each, allowing either for a rapid concentration or a simultaneous emergence on to the plains in a way that would gain tactical mastery. Napoleon was to put this into effect at the beginning of the Italian campaign in 1796.

Clearly, the basis of Napoleon's tactics was the common training of all young officers at the end of the *ancien régime*. It is not to criticise Napoleon to say that he owed much to his teachers; rather it is to enlarge his genius, for his success was achieved with methods available to any general. Frederick the Great, another formative influence, had written in his *Secret Instruction* (1748),

> Our wars should be short and lively, for it is not in our interests to protract matters.

Napoleon fully understood this and he gradually perfected that *Blitzkrieg* effect that was seen at its best in the 1805 campaign. In 1797 he declared:

> There are in Europe many good generals, but they see too many things at once. I see one thing, namely the enemy's main body. I try to crush it, confident that secondary matters will then settle themselves.

But Napoleon owed yet one more debt, a very great one indeed, to 'iron Carnot' and his helpers who had devised the conscript armies capable of supplying that concentrated mass of troops his methods required.

[12] CONSCRIPTION

Clausewitz was convinced that the only radically new aspect of the wars between 1792 and 1815 was the appearance of 'the nation in arms'. This changed the eighteenth-century pattern of limited warfare as 'the sport of kings', and meant massive armies that could be maintained only by conscription.

When the Revolution was in dire peril, it had resorted to national conscription with Carnot's *levée en masse* (23 August 1793), and by the spring of 1794 had an army of 750,000 men supported by an incredible war effort that justly earned the name, 'the nation in arms'. France was saved. But discipline and training presented a problem until the raw recruits and the veterans were combined by Carnot's *amalgame* (see Jones, *French Revolution*, p. 149).

The passionate intensity of this national effort was never repeated. Milder methods were used when France faced another invasion. Jourdan's conscription law (1798), not fully codified until 1811, supplied the armies needed for the defeat of the Second Coalition (see page 22), and the subsequent armies of Napoleon. All men between 20 and 25 were liable unless they had dependents, were married, or were priests. From the first, however, it was possible to pay for a substitute to take one's place (this was legalised in May 1802), and, in any case, until the last desperate years of the Empire, it was normal to call only a proportion of those liable for service – it was cheaper to do so, and it disrupted local employment less. The conscript numbers were supplemented by drafts from France's allies.

The conscription system was wide open to abuse. At first the Legislature approved the size of each Department's draft, but each municipality decided who should go. Napoleon tried to reduce obvious corruption by bringing the system under central control and by 1805 the Prefect was in full command, and Napoleon himself determined the size of each Department's draft. Conscripts were selected by lot, but 'replacements' were allowed, at a price (in the Côte d'Or it cost 2000 francs after 1805). Thus the poor bore the brunt of conscription.

[13] THE ARMY OF THE EMPIRE

Conscription became progressively more burdensome as campaign followed campaign and the popular image of glory tarnished. Heavy losses meant that recruits remained with the colours, and quotas were anticipated repeatedly, so that by 1813 youths not yet eighteen were called up. The wealthy found that their exemptions were not permanent, and from 1812 the previous enlistment classes were combed to catch those still eligible. Few defaulted before 1812, for they were hunted down by the gendarmerie and National Guard, and their families were fined. Yet conscription was not onerous as compared with 1794. Over two million Frenchmen were called up between 1804 and 1815, but even in the hour of defeat (1814) only some forty-one per cent of those eligible were conscripted. Growing public resentment at so mild a conscription reflected growing weariness of war: there was to be no *levée en masse* in 1814, and the Charter which Louis XVIII granted (see page 194) specifically abolished conscription.

However, a conscript army was essential to Napoleonic battles. The size of armies continued to increase, and the losses were so severe that whole divisions of raw troops had to be formed as early as 1809. In the Italian campaign, Napoleon had 35,000 men, on the Marengo campaign, 50,000, in the Austerlitz campaign, 200,000. His enemies kept pace. He maintained his numbers by drawing increasingly upon subject lands. Swiss and Polish regiments were formed in 1803, Hanoverian and Irish Legions by 1805: by 1812 Frenchmen were in a minority and the national character of the French army was thereby destroyed.

As more and more raw recruits entered the army, sophisticated manoeuvres became increasingly difficult to execute simply because of lack of experience and training (indeed, the declining quality of recruit may have played an important part in Napoleon's final defeat). With one obvious exception, the new infantry divisions came to be treated simply as cannon fodder. After 1806, drilling was neglected and some eight days in a training camp came to be thought adequate training for recruits to supplement the needs of hard-pressed armies. Battle proved an excellent training ground, and the troops learnt quickly from veterans under fire.

In such conditions, the Napoleonic soldier remained something of a warrior. He obeyed under fire, but refused iron discipline after battle. Insubordination was fairly common – even small-scale mutinies – but Napoleon was tolerant so long as the troops were ready for battle and they repaid him by maintaining the *élan* of their attacks to the end. The Grand Army that invaded Russia was different: it was un-manageably large and contained so many divergent elements that ill-discipline and desertion were common from the very beginning of the disastrous campaign.

The exception was the Imperial Guard. Formed on the tenth anniversary of Robespierre's death (29 July 1804), it was the *élite* corps. It was intended to have two-thirds veterans, but losses reduced this proportion; it was originally composed of 5,000 foot, 2,800 cavalry, a unit of light artillery and the only supply train in the entire army. In training discipline and *esprit de corps* it had no equal in its day: but the care that was lavished upon it contrasted ill with the treatment of other regiments. It has been argued that the Guard's expansion in 1810 (up to 80,000 men) was intended as the first stage of a complete army reorganisation, cut short by the losses sustained in 1812. If this had been the case, then the reorganised army would have been unbeatable: but, in fact, continual losses meant deteriorating and make-shift line regiments. There was no time for extensive innova-tion in military organisation.

But Napoleon was keenly aware of the value of symbols in maintain-ing an army's morale. The Eagles were chosen for their Roman over-tones and Napoleon was lavish in giving decorations. New dress uniforms were frequently being chosen (a common dress was normal in battle). The ragged army that saved France at Wattignies and Fleurus was the army of the people in arms: that of the Empire had become the Praetorian Guard of a new social order. It was also a career open to talent – prowess on the battlefield was the normal criterion for promotion. This did not necessarily produce the best generals; indeed, Napoleon's Marshals, daring and skilful in manoeuvre, were not always effective when left to devise their own tactics (Davout was exceptional here.)

Napoleon himself must bear a principal responsibility here, for his insistence on directing campaigns himself left local army commanders little opportunity for initiative. He neither bequeathed to France a staff tradition, nor developed a Staff College. No doubt he believed battle the best training ground, but it meant that many likely young officers died before mastering the art of generalship. Napoleonic methods were self-destructive: they could not outlast Napoleon. The Prussians, preferring organisation to the mystique of personal leadership, knew better: after their military reforms of 1808–13, the future lay with them.

Historians have excused Napoleon on grounds of lack of time and the constant activity and fighting that consumed his period. Yet his handling of his Staff makes one question whether he was psychologically able to give them the opportunities they needed to have become generals in their own right. He was no generalissimo: he could neither share a command nor delegate sufficiently. He managed his Staff by keeping them in a state of jealous dependence scrabbling for signs of favour. As the size of his armies increased, he continued to use men who had risen with him, whose bravery was never in question but whose ability as independent commanders was (Ney is the obvious example). It seems almost as though his judgment of men declined as his power grew: it cannot merely have been lack of suitable officers that caused him to continue as generals men whom he knew to be inadequate. (For example, Junot and Marmont in the Peninsula). Again, Bernadotte, Joseph Bonaparte's brother-in-law, and a man who knew much about those few years of his own rise to power, continued to serve as Marshal although Napoleon had said in 1809,

> Bernadotte is an intriguer whom I cannot trust. He nearly lost me the battle of Jena, he was mediocre at Wagram, he never turned up at Eylau when he could have, and he did not do what he might have done at Austerlitz.

As the wars continued the Marshals showed increasing signs of weariness and a desire to retire to enjoy their wealth and honours. Had things gone otherwise, Napoleon might have encouraged this, for he was clearly anxious to create a military aristocracy, as witness the creation of Princes and Dukes of the Empire; the Prytanée (military academy for sons of officers); the school of cavalry at Saint-Germain and of cadets at Fontainebleau (moved to Saint Cyr in 1808); and the local 'guards of honour' drawn from well-born members of the National Guard.

[14] THE PROBLEM OF SUPPLIES

The armies of the Revolution lived off the country – it was cheaper and allowed speedy movements. Napoleon continued this tradition. He had no idea of self-sufficiency: Napoleonic France was never a country organised in all its sinews for war. Contractors made fortunes because Napoleon rejected the alternative of the totalitarian measures of the Jacobin Terror (see Jones, *French Revolution*, p. 142): as a result he never got honest service, despite his own personal checking of many contractors' accounts, the creation of a separate army treasury and a Ministry of Military Affairs under Dejean in Year X. In May 1808 he was still complaining, 'They make me pay all the dead soldiers'. This failure to create a powerful enough administration to give immediate and corruptionless service was a serious fault in a country committed to war.

The supply problem grew with the size of the armies. Shortage of cash made it impossible to accumulate sufficient stores for a campaign in advance, so that food and clothing had to be sacrificed to weapons and ammunition. Pay was often overdue and quantities of weapons were lost – there seems to have been no systematic attempt to recover muskets from battlefields after a victory. The artillery was surprisingly badly supplied, and ammunition had to be used sparingly. French industry seemed unable to provide for the demands of sustained war on a massive scale. (Britain, for all her industrial potential, suffered a 'shell crisis' in 1915, so one should not blame Napoleon too easily here.) The other major shortage was in transport vehicles and draught animals (conquered countries were drained of horses). Napoleonic warfare demanded the backing of a developed industry and railway transport, and neither was available for at least a generation after Waterloo. It is incredible that so much was achieved by living off the country through which armies marched. Berthier wrote to Marmont in October 1805:

In a war of energetic offensives, such as the Emperor wages, store houses do not exist. It is up to the commanders-in-chief of the army corps to obtain for themselves the means of subsistence in the countries they overrun.

In a campaign of lightning marches there was no time to build up a series of supply depots. But this was Napoleon's way: he counted on winning the critical victory at the outset of the campaign before the need for extensive supply work became desperate. If roads were poor and bridges lacking, or if the country were infertile or ravaged, or if that lightning victory eluded them, his armies faced the real peril of famine. What was successful in the fertile plains of Northern Italy, did not succeed in Russia. That the ordinary soldier suffered did not trouble the generals much (Davout, again, was exceptional in this). He was left to forage for himself, which was inefficient and bad for discipline. Medical services were quite neglected, the doctors requisitioning supplies from the locality after a battle. Only a fraction of the final casualties were killed in battle: the rest died of wounds, disease or exhaustion. That this was common to all armies of the time perhaps explains why the common soldier maintained his morale.

The problem of supplies was fundamental to military victory – Berthier, the Chief of Staff (aged forty-two, he had joined the twenty-six-year-old Napoleon in Italy), did much to overcome the problem. When he went sick after 1812, his absence was all too obvious. The problem was vital, too, to the political relations with conquered countries which had to supply money, men and goods. As this burden increased, so did resentment at the French occupation.

[15] NAPOLEON'S TACTICS

In war Napoleon was 'an incorrigible improviser'. His genius lay both in his overall conception of a campaign and in the recognition and immediate exploitation of his enemy's weak point. Consequently there was no set pattern to a Napoleonic campaign or battle. Yet he derived his tactics from books available to every soldier, and there was truth in his remark at St Helena, 'I have fought sixty battles, and I have learnt nothing which I did not know in the beginning. His methods were already formulated by 1796: thereafter he merely perfected them on a grander scale. He always sought battle, even when using his troops defensively, as at Leipzig 1813, or at La Rothière and Arcis, 1814.

From Guibert and Bourcet he took the idea of dividing his army into corps each complete with cavalry and artillery, a day's march from each other (see *History Today*, 1965). This *batallion carré* technique had numerous advantages, from speed of advance and greater opportunity of making contact with the enemy, to enticing him into an ill-conceived battle against one corps, whilst the others converged to envelop him. At Eylau, 1807, Napoleon almost managed a double envelopment, for whilst Murat, despite the snow, led the most famous cavalry charge of the century through and through the Russian centre, Ney and Davout were converging from north and south: but Eylau proved to be no Cannae, for the brilliant strategic conception failed in the event.

Napoleon's strategy demanded exceptional staff work and more than efficient local commanders. Rarely did he achieve the full realisation of his plans, but his skill in combining his various army corps was such that the enemy found it impossible to avoid action, unless they withdrew, as in the Russian campaign of 1812. Once a fatal weakness of line or disposition of troops appeared, Napoleon was ready, stopwatch in hand, to order his troops forward at precisely the right moment. Unlimbered horse artillery would be rushed forward for a surprise bombardment, followed by a bayonet charge in *ordre mixte*. Heavy losses would be sustained in this charge but the enemy line would be broken and the battle won.

In theory, the light cavalry should then initiate a vigorous pursuit of the routed enemy; but rarely were there sufficient fresh troops for this final stage of the battle. Only at Rivoli, 1797, Austerlitz, 1805, Jena, 1806, and Eckmühl, 1809, was the pursuit really carried out. Before him, Frederick the Great had never been able to complete a rout with a pursuit: indeed it was something of a novelty, serving as the culmination of a complex strategy achieved at the breathtaking speed of a *blitzkrieg* carried out by marching men.

Speed was the essence of a Napoleonic campaign. But speed meant depending on a quality of command and troops that were not always there. His strategy involved taking incredible risks, trusting that divisions were at a vital point at exactly the right moment. A skilful enemy might take advantage of a temporary weakness in the French position and threaten Napoleon himself with that very defeat he had planned for another – as at Marengo, 1800 (see *History Today*, 1967) when Napoleon was saved only by the fortuitous return of Desaix, who was killed in the charge.

As the wars continued the risks grew greater, for the persistent losses meant relying on raw troops who had to be sent into attack in column, thus giving the enemy a temporary advantage of fire-power. As his strategic concepts became more complex, army commanders might not grasp the tactical significance of what they were required to do, and so ruin the final manoeuvre; like Ney, who failed to penetrate the enemy rear at Bautzen, 1813, thus spoiling a perfect battle plan. Enemy commanders in time learnt how to deal with Napoleon's methods and used them effectively against his Marshals, when he was elsewhere. Perhaps the greatest weakness of all was that each campaign depended fundamentally on Napoleon, and there was no one to take his place.

The 1815 campaign well illustrates this: it began with speed and brilliance, but ended at Waterloo, 'the classic case of the biter bit', where brilliant tactics failed through errors of timing and where Blücher appeared on the French flank instead of Grouchy rolling up the British line. Napoleon was caught in the very trap he had prepared for Wellington.

Basically, his tactics at Waterloo were to force a gap in the British centre by massive concentrated attacks, so that he could hold one wing of the divided British army with a small force, while concentrating upon the other with superior numbers. It was a technique he used increasingly in the latter days of the Empire. If a breach were made Napoleon would enjoy short lines of communications between his two fronts, while the enemy was divided. The principal weakness, even if a breach were made, was that the enemy could withdraw rapidly and escape, as at Arcola, 1796.

A development of this technique, but on a vastly extended scale, aimed to burst through a poorly held defensive position and to penetrate deeply into the interior in order to seize an effective base for a campaign and oblige the enemy to fall back. At the beginning of the 1796 Italian campaign, he had used this method to divide the Austrian forces and to gain the initiative in the Po valley. He had hoped to use it in 1814 when he contemplated penetrating into Alsace in order to relieve the threat to Paris by cutting the Prussians' communications and threatening the Austrian flank. Perhaps the best examples come from the Russian campaign of 1812, at Vilna and at Smolensk, when he drove forward in a vain attempt to engage the main Russian forces, but his commanders failed to trap them.

In his major battles, Napoleon frequently adopted manoeuvres

from several different battle plans. A simple frontal attack rarely led
to decisive results, especially as losses were likely to be fearful. He
would use it to exploit an enemy's weak position, as at Friedland,
1807, or when forced into it at Leipzig, the Battle of the Nations,
1813, or when he felt compelled to give battle to prevent the enemy
withdrawing and lacked the necessary numerical superiority to
manoeuvre, as at Borodino, 1812. Normally, Napoleon preferred more
subtle methods, for example, the so-called 'double battle' as at
Austerlitz, where the main forces were engaged on one front and a
secondary battle was fought on the wing, three miles away; or a
frontal attack combined with a surprise attack on the flank, the
psychological effect of which would be tremendous. This was a
favourite technique of Frederick the Great, which Bourcet had
praised in his textbook.

None of these strategic manoeuvres was original, but Napoleon
showed his genius by combining different tactics as the occasion
arose, and thus preserving the essential element of surprise. Much
depended, of course, on his knowing the precise position of the enemy
forces before battle-contact was made, and this meant not only keen
map work, but combing through newspapers and any other source of
information, from diplomats to spies, prisoners and the local people.
He also attempted to mislead the enemy by circulating false information as to his own position.

Early in his career the battle of Castiglione, August 1796, showed
that the twenty-seven-year-old general was a military genius with few
equals. With him were several corps commanders who were to become
Marshals, Augereau (created Duke of Castiglione, 1808), Masséna and
Marmont. The tactics were sophisticated to a degree – so much so that
the corps commanders spoilt the final victory by attacking too soon
in the last stage of the battle. Two Austrian armies were held apart,
the main one drawn into action, anticipating support from the other,
until the sudden arrival of fresh French troops from the south,
combined with French reinforcements in place of the expected
Austrians, forced the defeated enemy to retire. Napoleon wrote to
the Directory:

I ordered a retrograde movement of the whole army in order to
draw the enemy after us – and thus occupy the time it would take
Sérurier's division (which I was expecting – from the south – every
second) to come up from Marcaria (about 25 kilometres away), and

thereafter turn Würmser's left. This move had at least part of its intended effect.

Such sophisticated tactics, better understood and executed, were to carry the Eagles to victory at Austerlitz and Bautzen. Napoleon's favourite strategy, capable of many variations, was his *manoeuvre sur les derrières* (advance by envelopment of the enemy). A feint attack would engage the enemy and lead him to commit his principal forces in order to gain immediate numerical superiority: meanwhile, the French main force, concealed by a screen of cavalry or any natural cover, would make a surprise attack on the flank or rear, thus isolating the enemy and leaving him the alternatives of surrender or fighting to the last man. This was first used to defeat the Piedmontese before the Armistice of Cherasco, 1796, then, with much less success, at the Bridge of Lodi, 1796, where the main Austrian force escaped (indeed, this battle scarcely deserves its place in the popular mind). By 1805, the technique had been perfected and was brilliantly illustrated at Ulm, where Mack, the Austrian commander, surrendered. So startling were the effects of strategy on so magnificent a scale that it took the Allies nearly a decade to learn how to deal with it. But by 1814, conscious of their numerical superiority and the likely capitulation of Paris, they chose to ignore the threat of Napoleon in their rear and marched on the capital, thus preventing his seizing perhaps another victory. Although Napoleon used this technique frequently, winning fifteen major battles with it, both Frederick the Great and Bourcet had advocated it in theory, and Jourdan had made use of it (albeit accidentally) in the manoeuvring preceding the battle of Fleurus, 1794. This underlines Napoleon's lack of innovation in tactics, and his genius in so consistently defeating generals who were as aware as he of the source of his tactics.

[16] HIS DECLINING MILITARY POWERS

From many points of view it is satisfying to explain Napoleon's downfall in terms largely of failing military powers after, say, 1807. It heightens the dramatic nature of events; it partly excuses the collapse of the colossus (without adding to the credit of the victors); it adds an appropriate touch of morality – exile in St Helena as the just retribution for overweening ambition; and as an explanation of a great event it is sufficiently human and traditional to be immediately

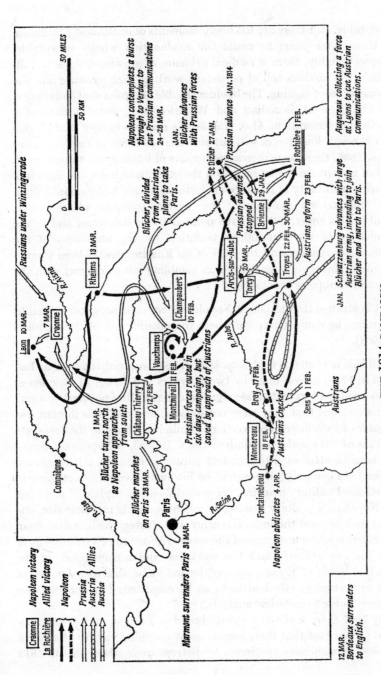

THE 1814 CAMPAIGN

Note the speed and area of Napoleon's movements and the succession of victories, 27 January to 4 April.

Key (legend):
Craonne — Napoleon victory
La Rothière — Allied victory
Napoleon
Prussia
Austria
Russia — Allies

Russians under Winzingarode

Napoleon contemplates a burst through to Verdun to cut Prussian communications 24–28 MAR.

JAN. Blücher advances with Prussian forces

JAN. 1814 Prussian advance

Blücher, divided from Austrians, plans to take Paris.

Prussian advance stopped

St Dizier 27 JAN.

Brienne 29 JAN.

La Rothière 1 FEB.

Rheims 13 MAR.

7 MAR. Craonne

Laon 10 MAR.

10 MAR.

Compiègne

R. Oise

Champaubert 10 FEB.

Arcis-sur-Aube 20 MAR.

Torcy

Troyes 22 FEB. 30 MAR.

Austrians reform 23 FEB.

R. Aube

1 MAR. Blücher turns north as Napoleon approaches from south

Blücher marches on Paris 28 MAR.

Vauchamps 14 FEB.

Montmirail 11 FEB.

Château Thierry 12 FEB.

R. Aube

Prussian forces routed in six days campaign, but saved by approach of Austrians

Bray 17 FEB.

Montereau 18 FEB.

Sens 1 FEB.

Austrians checked

Austrians

R. Seine

Paris

Fontainebleau 4 APR.

Napoleon abdicates 4 APR.

Marmont surrenders Paris 31 MAR.

Paris 31 MAR.

Augereau collecting a force at Lyons to cut Austrian communications.

JAN. Schwarzenburg advances with large Austrian army, intending to join Blücher and march to Paris.

12 MAR. Bordeaux surrenders to English.

50 MILES

50 KM

acceptable. But there are too many moments of outstanding brilliance in these later years to make the explanation wholly acceptable. Unquestionably, there is medical evidence of growing fatigue and ill-health, the obvious toll of persistent work at high pressure and the rigours of campaigning. The bladder trouble and piles that so damaged his efficiency at Borodino and Waterloo are clear evidence of a physical deterioration. Also, Napoleon's nervous energy that carried him through long hours without rest showed signs of flagging: after Jena, 1806, there were increasing periods of lethargy on the one hand and of violent emotional scenes on the other, which may be signs of a growing instability of mind. Some historians have laid emphasis upon the 'conqueror's syndrome', the hystero-epileptic attacks, that troubled his court. Others have pointed to his delusions, and to the tarnishing of the Republican tradition by the ambitions of the Bonaparte dynasty and the idea of an Empire greater than Charlemagne's. Napoleon is portrayed as gambling with Fortune, with the peace of Europe as the stakes.

It is strange that although Napoleon's common sense amounted to genius, he could never see where the possible left off [was Molé's view].

All this is evidence that Napoleon in 1815 was not the man he had been in 1796: he was older by twenty years and an age of experience. Who would not expect to see signs of deteriorating physical powers? The wonder is that they were not greater, and that this ill man was capable of such incredible exertions of mind and body in the desperate months of 1814 and the Hundred Days. Indeed, if Napoleon's downfall is to be attributed to incipient paranoia, then the clear planning of the 1815 campaign, dependent on his own powers and not those of a well-oiled military machine, becomes difficult to explain. To account for Napoleon's military demise, as much as for his meteoric rise, one must look beyond the man. His army and strategy he inherited from the reforms of the last years of the *ancien régime*: the Revolution gave him his opportunity, and the weakness and intransigence of the crowned heads of Europe ensured he would be able to make use of that opportunity. (He had luck, as he admitted: but chance is an unlikely guide to historical analysis.)

By 1807 there was a new spirit abroad in Europe, measured somewhat by the fact that there was no great sweeping victory after Jena in 1806. His enemies continued to distrust each other, but by 1812 they had come to work together. They showed a greater awareness by then of the patriotic resistance to the invader by the people. Here was a difference of atmosphere from that of the eighteenth century; one that checked the impact of French ideas. It is seen most clearly in Prussia, despite the loss of morale after Jena, and in the winter campaign against Russia in 1807, which brought the stalemate of Eylau, when Napoleon's own men called for peace and bread.

The message of Eylau that Napoleon might not be invincible rang through Europe as clearly as the joy at Dupont's capitulation at Baylen was to do in 1808. Napoleon was now fighting different types of armies, so that in the 1809 Austrian campaign he had to risk speedy and costly battle at Aspern and Essling, lest Prussia re-enter the war. The campaign ended at Wagram, the biggest artillery battle of the war so far; but victory did not crush resistance. Three years later he faced at both extremes of his Empire, Spain and Russia, the type of guerrilla warfare against which organised armies have always been helpless, whether one thinks of Hannibal in Italy or the Americans in Vietnam. In this changed situation, carrying with it the need for persistent vigilance and continual fighting, may be found one key to Napoleon's military collapse.

The Moscow campaign of 1812 has been roundly condemned as 'madness'. Yet he had not underestimated the geographical difficulty involved, for the supplies he built up for his Grand Army were more than adequate for the campaign he envisaged. But the Russian army continued to withdraw and denied him the engagement he sought. The strategy he employed to trap his enemy showed no loss of brilliance; but the battle of Borodino was a different matter. Had the rest of the campaign proved as unsubtle as his tactics at Borodino, there would be some truth in the charge of declining military powers. Yet, in retreat, screened by Cossacks, and pursued by a Russian army enlarged with irregular volunteers, his brilliance shone through. The Russian Partisan, Davydov, commented on his escape from the engagement at Krasnoi, 'The Guard and Napoleon passed through our Cossacks like a hundred-gun ship through a fishing fleet'; and, as Clausewitz said, at the crossing of the Berezina, Napoleon 'not only completely saved his honour, but acquired new glory'.

The fabulous losses of this campaign, especially in guns and cavalry (the arm he so sorely lacked in 1813), lengthened the odds against him. His enemies fielded armies well led and swollen with volunteers: what France had produced against Europe in the 1790s,

Europe was now bringing, albeit to a lesser degree, against France. Yet, for all their advantages, the Allies did not enter France until 1814.

The French army itself had changed. In 1805 it had reached a peak in terms of equipment, organisation and training that enabled it to conquer Europe within eighteen months. But by that time its huge losses had had to be made good by conscripts who never had the chance to train, and thereafter the French armies, whether in Spain or Central Europe, became increasingly crude and ill-equipped facing allied armies which after 1812 were confident of ultimate victory. By 1814, superior numbers, especially in cavalry, gave the allies a tremendous advantage.

Even so, the conduct of the 1814 campaign in France testifies to Napoleon's continuing brilliance. It was a hopeless struggle, the more so as he refused to call for a *levée en masse* (as much for fear of unleashing Jacobinism, as in recognition of France's refusal to respond). He relied on veterans and young recruits, the *Marie-Louises*, daily to perform incredible feats of arms, and hoped for equally incredible errors of command and coordination among the allies. The army performed those incredible feats at Brienne, Vauchamps, Soissons, Craonne and Laon. But each engagement meant loss of valuable troops: there were not enough trained soldiers to supply the need for NCOs, and the Marshals themselves were war-weary and unequal to the excessive demands made on them. By April the 1814 campaign was over: France would not rise for him. Yet he had once more shown his magnificence as a leader and strategist.

The Waterloo campaign itself began as though Napoleon with a makeshift army had regained the impetus of 1805: it was only in the last two days that things went wrong. Much has been written about his last battle, and many excuses made. Berthier was dead and Soult was not a good choice as Chief of Staff; neither Ney nor Grouchy was capable of grasping the intricacies of the strategy that should have reached a climax on 17 or 18 June, as their conduct at Waterloo showed. But in that final battle, Napoleon had lost his touch: the unaccustomed hesitation in his decisions amounted almost to absent-mindedness. Blücher, who was also tired and ill, was a striking contrast to Napoleon. And Waterloo broke Napoleon's spirit. Soult rallied a sizeable force at Philippeville, but he had no will to continue the struggle. Because there was no military sequel to Waterloo we shall never know whether he could have reversed that decision.

[17] THE NAVY

Like the Army, the Navy had benefited from reforms during the last twenty years of the *ancien régime*; indeed, during the Maritime War (1778–83) it had gained the mastery of the seas. French battleships were better built than British (a captured one was immediately commissioned as a British flagship) and they shot heavier broadsides. But the British were better at short range, for they aimed for the hull, causing greater damage, whilst the French aimed for the rigging hoping to immobilise the ship.

But the Navy suffered badly during the Revolution, for the officers, whose technical knowledge could not easily be improvised, were largely royalists and aristocrats who emigrated rather than serve under the Republic. This, more than the loss of twenty-six ships of the line at Toulon in 1793, made it impossible for the French Navy ever to show much success against the seamanship and fine leadership of that 'band of brothers', Nelson's captains. Out of the chaos and bad morale, Jeanbon Saint-André managed to re-form a self-respecting navy whose valour was demonstrated at the Glorious First of June, 1794. The Directory continued his methods and centralised the naval administration. Former officers were attracted back, and Napoleon continued this policy, adding a military flavour by organising the sailors into battalions and broadening the basis for commissions. For all that the fleets were more frequently in harbour than out of it; training continued vigorously, but intensive drill could not compensate for lack of experience at sea and in action, and here, too, the French remained at a decided disadvantage to the British. However, training ships for boy recruits were opened in 1810, so that the future of the Service was guaranteed.

Decrès, Minister of Marine 1801–14, proved unenterprising (perhaps as well, considering the disadvantages the Navy suffered, kept short of funds and of men). He sought to preserve his fleets by avoiding offensive action that he knew would lead to disaster. For this reason, Napoleon was justified in complaining that his admirals feared to risk a major action lest they lose a vessel or two. But Decrès argued that Britain's naval power would be more surely worn down by being constantly at sea whilst France kept her 'fleet in being' and added to it by a huge building programme and combining with other fleets to give superiority of vessels. It comes as no surprise to learn that with such a minister Shrapnel's shells and Congreve's rockets were not widely used, and that the submarine, torpedo and steamship remained un-developed (though it is only fair to add that the British scorned these new weapons just as much). All these had been toyed with by the French and British between 1803 and 1815.

Since the French remained in harbour, the British were compelled to blockade. This imposed an intolerable burden and vast expense. There were two methods, that favoured by Howe and Nelson, the 'open blockade', which was cheaper and easier, where the roads were patrolled intermittently (thus allowing whole fleets to slip out, as in 1798 to Egypt and 1805 to the West Indies); and that favoured by St Vincent, Cornwallis and Collingwood, the 'close blockade', involv-ing the continual presence of the blockading fleet. This was expensive in blockade ships and their support, it required enormous endurance – but it decided victory in the end, as Mahan put it,

> these far distant, storm-beaten ships, upon which the Grand Army never looked, which stood between it and the dominion of the world.

When Napoleon closed the Baltic thus cutting off timber supplies and naval stores, the Admiralty was hard put to it to find alternative supplies and had to seek them in Canada and India.

Throughout the war years from 1793 French privateering wrought havoc among British and neutral shipping, despite Britain's control of the seas. In 1798 a Convoy Act sought to reduce this threat and gradually, as the convoy system grew, privateering became less profitable, but it was never eradicated. Nor could the blockade indefinitely confine a fleet to harbour. There had been the Egyptian campaign, where a huge fleet crossed the Mediterranean. There had been various attempts under the Directory to invade Ireland and Britain, attempts foiled by storm rather than blockade. Napoleon inherited the invasion plan of 1798 and by 1805 had gathered 2,343 boats capable of transporting 167,590 men at Boulogne and other Channel ports. Well might Britain fear invasion. Already in 1802 a French fleet had crossed the Atlantic to regain control of some French colonies in the West Indies, in particular Haiti, where Toussaint Louverture had established a republic.

The 1805 invasion scheme was brilliant in conception, and came closer to some degree of success than the final outcome suggests. There is some evidence for saying that Napoleon failed to understand the nature of sea power: he certainly knew nothing of the technical aspects of seamanship, for he once ordered a review in the teeth of a storm, losing eight vessels and over a hundred men. But he understood enough to realise the vulnerability of a fleet as a means of defence. 'Let us be masters of the Straits for six hours, and we shall be masters of the world', he had written to Admiral Latouche-Tréville – but the admiral died in 1804 and his scheme for evading Nelson and joining the other fleets had to be shelved. In 1805 the situation was favourable for Spain had joined the war. Villeneuve was to evade the Toulon blockade, pick up the Spanish fleet and rendezvous at Martinique with Gauteaume leading the combined Brest, Rochefort and Ferrol squadrons. The British fleet would pursue them as much for battle as to defend the West Indies, and Villeneuve, evading them once more, would return temporarily to control the Channel and so secure the invasion.

Between March and August Villeneuve was in the Atlantic. The plan misfired, Gauteaume failed to break the blockade and Villeneuve was forced into Ferrol and then Corunna. Putting out again, he mistook the Rochefort squadron for the British fleet – a piece of good fortune for Britain, for he turned to Cadiz for shelter. Ten days later, Napoleon ordered the Boulogne camp to be struck in order to attack the Third Coalition in Central Europe. The invasion threat was over for the moment. Trafalgar merely confirmed this: indeed, Villeneuve emerged from Cadiz in response to Napoleon's taunts, in order to intercept an Anglo-Russian expedition in the Mediterranean which threatened the flank of the Grand Army, not to capture the Channel. Villeneuve's comment on his fleet was 'bad masts, bad sails and rigging, bad sailors and officers, grown inexpert at too long a blockade; a couple of squalls crippled us'. It was too harsh. Neither Britain nor Napoleon recognised Trafalgar as the end of the road. In the first instance, Napoleon turned to the Continental System, determined to ruin Britain economically as well as to control the sources of timber and naval stores she needed, and close as many European ports as possible; in the second he began to rebuild his shattered fleet and to absorb the fleets of his allies. If the Continental System was, as he wrote to his brother Louis, 'to conquer the sea by the land', he clearly intended to re-create a huge navy to ensure success.

By secret clauses of the Treaty of Tilsit, 1807, Napoleon aimed to unite all European fleets to overwhelm the British. The British intelligence services must have been excellent, for they rapidly had wind of this (perhaps Talleyrand had passed on the information). They moved quickly, invading Denmark and after a bombardment removing 17 Danish battleships from Copenhagen, 1807, and blockading the Baltic. The Portuguese preferred to surrender their ships to Sir Sidney Smith, rather than to Junot, who arrived at Lisbon just too late. The following year the Spanish revolt meant the loss of twenty-four Spanish battleships and of six French vessels sheltering at Cadiz and Vigo. This ruined Napoleon's immediate plans, but it did not stop him embarking on a stupendous naval building programme, with maritime conscription (so much more effective than the British press gang methods) to man the vessels. Docks were enlarged and new ones constructed, with shifts working round the clock, and battleships and frigates were built in the leading ports of the Empire, from Hamburg to Venice. On 30 June 1811 a communiqué confidently declared:

> We shall be able to make peace with safety when we shall have 150 ships of the line – and in spite of the obstacles of war, such is the state of the Empire that we shall shortly have that number.

This was no idle boast, and it reckoned on a superiority of perhaps fifty over the British to compensate for lack of experience at sea. Fortunately for Britain, the Moscow campaign and the War of Liberation checked the building programme, so that by 1814 there were only 80 battleships against 99 British ships of the line (although the French probably had superiority in fire-power).

The Royal Navy was stretched to its limits, and the First Lord of the Admiralty, Melville, admitted in 1814 that Napoleon would have outstripped the Navy in ships if the war had not finished. The fact that Britain was fighting U.S.A. at this time (1812–14) added to the strain; indeed, Madison based his policy on the assumption that the French would soon defeat the British, the more so as, for all the blockading, French fleets put out both in the Mediterranean and the Atlantic in 1808, 1809, and 1812. It seems that the Moscow campaign not only saved Europe, but also Britain, from French domination especially as Napoleon was concentrating his naval activity in these years in the Mediterranean, where there was less fear of British attack, good harbours and good opportunities for gaining that experience in seamanship they would need when they once more met the British Fleet. Clearly, the story of Napoleon's naval dealings is by no means as simple and one-sided as might be supposed.

Further Reading

For those particularly taken with military history, Clausewitz, *On War* (available as a Pelican) is essential. Perhaps the most readable volume on the campaigns which gives precise details is David Chandler, *The Campaigns of Napoleon* (Weidenfeld and Nicolson, 1967), whilst R. F. Delderfield's *The March of the Twenty-Six* (Hodder and Stoughton, 1962) and his *Imperial Sunset* (Hodder and Stoughton 1968) are good but less detailed. Caulincourt's *Memoirs* (3 vols, Paris 1933; 1950) are good for the later period and for 1812 see Tarlé, *Napoleon's Invasion of Russia* (Allen and Unwin, 1942). The *New Cambridge Modern History*, Vols. VIII and IX (Cambridge University Press, 1965) is invaluable. So is Liddell Hart, *The Strategy of the Indirect Approach* (Faber, 1951). For Waterloo see J. Naylor, *Waterloo* (Pan Books, 1960) and Anthony Brett-James, *The Hundred Days* (Macmillan, 1964). An excellent series of military memoirs has appeared recently, published by Longmans, on *Charles Parquin* (1969), *Edward Costello* (1967) and *Thomas Morris* (1969). See also Liddell Hart, *Sergeant Wheeler* (Boston 1951).

The Navy is rather less well served, but see N. Hampson, *La Marine de L'An II* (Paris 1959); M. Lewis, *A Social History of the Navy* (Hodder and Stoughton, 1960); *The New Cambridge Modern History;* A. T. Mahan's classic, *The Influence of Sea-Power in the War of the French Revolution* (Brown, Boston 1893); and an excellent article in the *Journal of Modern History* (1967) by D. Glover on the French Fleet, 1807/15.

PART III
Napoleon: Soldier and Consul

[18] HIS RISE TO POWER

Fortune smiled upon the young Napoleon. Time and again in his early years luck was on his side – he acknowledged that this was an essential ingredient in his career. Occasionally the good fortune was fortuitous, but as he rose in rank his luck held so consistently as to lead one to the conclusion that it was so because he had a capacity for deriving the maximum benefit from a situation. It was a sign of his genius.

Much has been made of his Corsican birth, the more so as the disordered politics of the island clouded the progress of his first years as an officer. But after 1793 Corsica ceased to disturb him, save as a strategic problem. The closeness of his family ties has also been traced to a Mediterranean background; but this is to put too great an emphasis upon the accident of birth. Letizia Buonaparte was a dominating woman who would have wielded powerful influence on any family: her daughters became women of decided accomplishments who might well have gone unrecorded had they lived as obscure lesser nobility, but in cosmopolitan circles of wealth and power they shone deservedly. Napoleon's two close brothers, Joseph, the elder, and Lucien, had by 1799 already begun to climb the ladder of success albeit with some assistance from Napoleon. It was not merely family feeling that led him to lean on his brothers during the Empire. Nor is it only a Mediterranean trait to seek to further the career and fortune of one's close relations if it is within one's power. A brief glance at eighteenth-century England would show nepotism to a profound degree – and no one in England ever had the opportunities for patronage that Napoleon enjoyed. His court has been scoffed at as a court of upstarts and *nouveaux riches*, yet there was a good leavening of old aristocracy about it. The attempt to categorise Napoleon as some ill-trained colonial, unlessoned in the social graces, dependent, peasant-like, upon his immediate family, does no justice to the remarkable man who, for a few brief years, dominated the history of a continent.

Corsica had been acquired by France in 1768, the year before Napoleon's birth, and it was merely because his father chose to remain whilst Paoli, the Corsican patriot, went into exile, that Napoleon was admitted into the French noblesse. His mother's friendship with Marbeuf, the French governor of the island, gave him the chance of a professional training at Brienne, one of the twelve royal schools for sons of nobles, founded in 1776 by Saint-Germain, Louis XVI's minister of war. His academic abilities, especially in mathematics, secured him a place in the Paris École Militaire, where he trained for the artillery. It was a sensible choice, for it was a crack regiment that insisted on having officers of real ability; consequently it was un-fashionable, and only the lesser nobles chose it. Even so, there would have been little opportunity of rising far in the regiment unless one had connexions at court. Without the Revolution to release the senior officer posts from the strangle-hold of the upper nobility, and without the emigration of officers that left so many places to fill, we might well not have heard of Napoleon.

At the École Militaire Napoleon's performance was outstanding: he remembered his teachers and rewarded them later. He remembered, too, the slights he suffered as a poor scholar, at the hands of wealthier and more privileged – if less gifted – pupils. Commissioned in 1785, he spent a year at Valence before returning on leave to Corsica. In 1788 he was posted to the artillery school at Auxonne, where Maréchal du Teil selected him to write reports upon the current experiments with guns and explosive shells – experiments that were not altogether successful. The Revolution made no great rift at Auxonne, where the *petite noblesse* predominated, and hoped to benefit from it. Returning to Corsica, he found the island scarcely touched by the political excitement of France, and promptly organised a Jacobin movement that brought Paoli back as popular leader of the island. Then came the first rift of consequence. The flight to Varennes, 1791, made Napoleon a republican: Paoli, and the Buonaparte family friend, Pozzo di Borgo, took the royalist side. Hitherto, Napoleon had idolised Paoli: the Revolution was changing things.

When war was declared and France invaded, Napoleon was back in Paris to witness the fall of the throne in August and the September

Massacres (1792). His contempt for Louis's inadequacies in the crisis was revealing: the defences of the Tuileries were good; it required only vigorous action and the *menu peuple* who besieged the palace would have fled. If he sided with the Robespierrist Jacobins in politics, he did not share their concern for the human condition of the poor. In March 1793, he returned to Corsica. Paoli's arrest was decreed because of his royalist and pro-British sympathies. Salicetti, another friend of the Buonaparte family, was sent as *représentant en mission* to secure the authority of the Convention. A civil war broke out, resulting in Napoleon being exiled with his family, and Paoli delivering up the island to the British, who occupied it until 1796. Napoleon ceased to concern himself with the island: Pozzo di Borgo, his former friend, now a royalist, maintained a vendetta against him for the rest of his life.

The summer of 1793 was a perilous time for the Republic, for not only was there threat of invasion, but in various departments the Girondins had begun federalist revolts. One of these had opened the great naval base of Toulon to the British. Napoleon produced a dialogue, *Le Souper de Beaucaire,* denouncing the Girondins: it may well have helped to strengthen his connexion with the Jacobins. On mission with Carteaux's army, to which Napoleon was attached, was Salicetti, who pressed the appointment of the young man to succeed the artillery commander at the siege of Toulon. This was a stroke of good fortune. Barras, the other deputy on mission, despaired of the situation and suggested abandoning the whole of Provence, but Salicetti sent Napoleon's plan for handling the artillery at Toulon to Paris, where Carnot himself endorsed it.

In December, the port was re-taken and Napoleon promoted brigadier general at the age of twenty-four. Youth was being recognised. As his aides he chose Murat and Junot, future marshals. He had proved his worth and attracted the attention of Augustin, the brother of Maximilien Robespierre. In consequence, he became operational planner to the Army of Italy and his suggested scheme of attack, already foreshadowing the Italian campaign of 1796, was carried to Paris by Augustin Robespierre himself. But in Paris the Robespierre brothers and their Jacobin supporters were executed in the coup of Thermidor, and Napoleon, as an associate of Augustin, was imprisoned. He was lucky to get away with his life, but Salicetti, again, was able to help by getting him cleared and released in August to continue staff work on the campaigns in the Alps.

His work contributed directly to some minor victories over the Piedmontese, but the principal aim was to invade Italy and for this purpose Corsica would have to be retaken. The attempt failed in 1795, but, with Spain joining France, Britain withdrew from the Mediterranean temporarily in 1796, thus securing the lines of sea communication for the coming Italian campaign. But Napoleon had been recalled to Paris to be placed in charge of an infantry brigade to defeat the civil war in La Vendée. Wisely, he resigned the commission, and existed through the summer of 1795 in Paris with scarcely any money. He suffered, as did all the poor, but what he chiefly felt was not so much the hunger but the slights he received at the hands of indifferent *muscadins*, the well-to-do youths of Paris who evaded military service. A different type of person would have been led to the idealism of the Jacobins or of Babeuf by these experiences – particularly one who had formerly been associated with the Robespierrists. Indeed, Napoleon was never able to throw off the idea that he was of Jacobin sympathies, until he turned on the surviving Jacobins when he was Consul.

Fortunately, he secured employment in the Topographical Bureau and in July submitted a memorandum suggesting an attack against Austria with a battalion moving in from North Italy and another from across the Rhine, the two converging in Bavaria through the Alpine passes. By August he was back in favour, at the moment when the new régime was most in need of help. A new Constitution had been declared, but, fearful of royalist gains at the elections, the Law of Two-thirds had been passed, securing the return of a big majority of Thermidorians. The wealthy sections of Paris were in ferment at the law and a coup by the right wing and royalists was expected. Barras was appointed to defend Paris and, among other generals, called upon Napoleon. The latter sent Murat to fetch cannon and in the crisis of Vendémiaire (October 1795) he destroyed the right wing's effort to seize control. He did so, however, as a soldier and not as a politician. In the crisis of Vendémiaire it was the wealthy who suffered, but this did not make Napoleon a Jacobin.

Instead he became the soldier of the new Directory, and Barras was one of the Directors. His association with this venal man brought him marriage to Joséphine (Barras's former mistress), a love marriage on Napoleon's part, a cool acceptance of a securer future for an ageing courtesan on Joséphine's part. For the next four years Joséphine continued to have lovers with no great regard for discretion. Her infidelities may have wounded Napoleon's susceptibilities at the moment when his heart was first opened to deep human love. Mme de Rémusat commented, 'he might have been a better man if he had been more and better loved'. When she was the wife of the First Consul, and as Empress, she gave up her lovers and brought a touch of dignity to Napoleon's court: but by that time it was too late for their marriage.

His association with Barras – as well as the knowledge that Carnot, another Director, had of his abilities and plans – brought him command of the Army of Italy, in succession to the cautious Schérer. Napoleon had arrived. He dropped the 'u' from his surname.

[19] NAPOLEON IN ITALY

The Italian campaign was the real beginning of Napoleon's public career. Hitherto he had acted as a successful servant, whether at Toulon in 1793 or Paris in 1795; now he had an independent command and the use he made of it changed the course of the Revolutionary War. The dramatic change he wrought has tended to exaggerate his achievement in Italy, great as it was. He was already familiar with the plans of campaign for the Alps and known to most of the senior officers through his staff work. He was more than fortunate to find in Berthier a remarkable Chief of Staff (who stayed with him until 1814), and lucky, again, that it was Salicetti who was civil commissioner with the Army. In addition, the principal Austrian concern was for the Rhenish front.

However, the personal nature of his achievement in 1796 must be admitted. The army he found was dispirited and discontented. 'One battalion has mutinied on the ground that it had neither boots nor pay', he wrote to the Directors in March 1796, 'I will restore order or I will give up the command of these brigands'. He did; and he also increased the fighting strength of the field divisions by combing out some 8,000 men from the rear formations. The army was not quite so badly equipped as later legend suggests, but what mattered was the new sense of urgency and victory that Napoleon instilled and the vigour of his movements that not only amazed his enemies, but gave tremendous spirit to the men. By May he was paying his troops regularly in coin, instead of in *assignats* and had already begun to send back that flood of art treasures and cash that was to raise his reputation in Paris.

Large parts of the Riviera and the principal passes into Piedmont were already occupied when he assumed command, but by exploiting the lack of cooperation between the Austrians and Piedmontese, he succeeded in forcing the former to withdraw and obliged the latter to sign the armistice of Cherasco (28 April). The Directory politely snubbed him by approving the terms of the armistice, so long as they were approved by Salicetti,

> for urgent transactions of this kind, about which the Director cannot be consulted, fall specifically within the sphere of the government commissioners attached to the armies.

It was a warning the young general was prepared to disregard – after all, by the formal peace treaty in August Piedmont ceded Savoy and Nice to France.

Boldly seizing the initiative, Napoleon marched upon the Austrians as soon as his lines of communication were secure. On 10 May he forced the bridge at Lodi in a confused but celebrated charge when he claimed, later, to have had a sudden revelation of his future glory. He was in Milan by 14 May. But the Austrian commander, Beaulieu, extricated himself in good order.

Napoleon demonstrated his independence by allowing a Jacobin Club and National Guard to be formed in Milan and a new tricolor to be acknowledged. Such action, on a diplomatic level, was provocative in the extreme, suggesting the Directory intended to extend their influence over Italy. He also imposed heavy taxes and lived off the country and when revolts occurred, whether provoked by counter-revolution or the exactions of the French, he repressed them severely – at Pavia in May, and at Lugo and Emilia in June.

Before they had news of his later victories in May, the Directory had determined to clip his wings by transferring the command of the army in north Italy to Kellermann and sending Napoleon off on an expedition of plunder into the peninsula. He protested vigorously, appealing personally to Carnot against dividing the command and diverting the campaign from the principal aim of attacking Austria. It was perhaps this argument, rather than his threat of resignation, that decided the Directory to capitulate and allow him to continue as sole commander in Italy. They were already losing control of their generals. By the end of the year, on the demand of the generals at the front, the civil commissioners were withdrawn.

Napoleon knew that his success in Italy and his hope of crossing the Tyrol to threaten Vienna depended on Jourdan and Moreau maintaining pressure on the Rhine. To divert troops into the peninsula would have weakened his own position against Austrian troops who were far from beaten. However, the Directory needed money, and so, in a lightning campaign between June and July, he penetrated as far as the Papal States, bringing two-thirds of Italy under French control.

His principal concern remained the Austrian forces which had received reinforcements under Würmser in order to break out of the Brenner pass and regain Lombardy. There followed the four pitched battles of Castiglione (August), Bassano (September), Arcola (November), and Rivoli (January 1797) which destroyed Austrian hopes and led to the surrender of Mantua in February 1797. On marched Napoleon, now reinforced with some fresh troops, to Klagenfurt. But he was nervous of Austrian concentrations, especially as Moreau remained suspiciously inactive on the Rhine. Consequently, at Leoben, within a hundred miles of Vienna, he opened preliminary peace negotiations in April. (In fact, Moreau crossed the Rhine that month – had Napoleon maintained his march he might even have taken Vienna. The chance of final victory escaped him by a matter of days.)

He returned to Milan where, in the palace of Mombello, he lived in regal style, and Joséphine, summoned from Paris, and wearing a necklace presented by the Pope, assumed the rôle of queen of a republican court. Miot de Merito described Napoleon at this stage,

> He was no longer the general of a triumphant Republic, but a conqueror on his own account, imposing his laws on the vanquished.

Already, in February, Joseph Bonaparte had negotiated the Treaty of Tolentino with the Papacy. The Pope remained in Rome and Napoleon was keen not to interfere with religious affairs, but a revised pro-French government was imposed and the Papal States paid a heavy indemnity. In May Napoleon formed the Cisalpine Republic, once more dragging the diplomacy of the Directory into direct involvement in Italy. And his own version of diplomacy led him to attack Venice. At Leoben he had not secured Austrian acceptance of the French possession of the left bank of the Rhine: he hoped by taking Venice to provide a useful bribe to gain this recognition, as well as to gain the wealth, commerce and strategic position of Venice herself. Venetian guns firing upon a French ship and the anti-French riot at Verona provided the excuse and by mid-May he had taken the ancient Republic. He had now the prize with which to bribe Austria. Even so negotiations were protracted and it was not until the failure of the royalist coup at Fructidor and the breaking off of negotiations between Britain and France, that peace was signed at Campo Formio.

The royalist plot that was nipped in the bud in the coup of Fructidor was complicated and may have involved Napoleon more than he was prepared to admit. For some time royalist agents had been in communication with generals at the front. They were in contact with Moreau, but their biggest success was the man whom he superseded, Pichegru, the general who had defeated the rising of the *sans-culottes* in Germinal (April 1795). Napoleon's staff, and perhaps Napoleon himself, were not without contact with royalist agents, of whom the Comte d'Antraigues was one, whose papers were captured when Venice was invaded. Napoleon sent to Paris only those extracts that proved the treasonable relations of Pichegru. No doubt there was professional jealousy here, for Pichegru had been elected President of the Council and was in close contact with the royalist Clichy Club, while the pro-royalist Director, Barthélemy, aided by Carnot who was interested solely in strong government, was preparing to seize control preparatory to a possible restoration.

Napoleon may well have been approached to assist the Bourbons to return to their throne, but there was no doubt in his mind that he had to back the Republican Directors for the sake of his own future. Miot de Melito reports him saying,

> Do you think that I triumph in Italy for the Carnots, Barras etc? I do not want peace. A party is in favour of the Bourbons. I wish to undermine the Republican Party, but only for my own profit and not that of the ancient dynasty.

He sent to Barras the papers incriminating Pichegru and despatched that rough Jacobin soldier Augereau to Paris to ensure that the royalists were defeated. Barthélemy was arrested, and so was Pichegru (who escaped later). Carnot, forewarned, slipped out of Paris. The plot had failed, the surviving Directors were more than ever dependent on the army. Napoleon's place was assured, and he proceeded to sign the Treaty of Campo Formio in October.

[20] THE EGYPTIAN CAMPAIGN

By this treaty France secured the Rhine frontier, with a promise of Austrian support at a diet of German states to be summoned to recognise the acquisition. In return Austria gained Venetia, but when

the Austrian troops arrived in the city in January 1798, they found
the French troops had taken almost everything of value. France
acquired also the Ionian islands and Venetian Albania, both to
control the Adriatic and to expand French commerce into the Balkans
and beyond to the Levant. Already on 16 August he had written to the
Directors suggesting seizing Corfu and the Ionian islands for trade –
Napoleon was no mere soldier of fortune:

> The islands of Corfu, Zante and Cephalonia matter more to us than
> all the rest of Italy put together. I believe that if we had to choose
> it would be better to restore Italy to the Emperor, and to keep the
> four islands. They are vital to the wealth and prosperity of our
> commerce. The Turkish empire is breaking up everyday. If we held
> these islands we should be in a position either to bolster it up as long
> as possible or to take what part of it we want. It will not be long
> before we realise that, if we are effectively to destroy England, we
> must get hold of Egypt.

Earlier, in May 1797, he had written suggesting seizing Malta in order
to secure control of the Mediterranean, since the British had temporarily been obliged to withdraw to Gibraltar. General Gentile was
despatched in Venetian vessels to take Corfu and to appeal to Greek
national spirit to rise against Turkey with French support.

Napoleon consulted Talleyrand in September about an Eastern
Expedition, and Talleyrand was much in favour, seeking to compensate France with gains in the Levant for her losses in the Caribbean.
The Egyptian Campaign in 1798 was no aberration or romantic
dream: it made sound sense and had been thought about actively for
at least a year.

> Through Egypt we shall reach India, we shall re-establish the old
> route through Suez and cause the route by the Cape of Good Hope
> to be abandoned,

he wrote in his copy of Volney's *Considérations sur la guerre actuelle
des Turcs* (1788). And since 1795 Magallon, the former French consul
in Egypt, had been urging an attack on India via Egypt.

First, however, upon his triumphal return to Paris in December
1797, he was appointed commander of the Army of England already
preparing for a direct invasion across the Channel. The all-out attempt
to defeat England was understandable enough: she was France's
surviving enemy. Whilst an invasion army assembled, the Directory

passed the Nivôse Law (January 1798) to cripple British commerce. Napoleon's careful survey of the Channel ports, however, led him to recommend striking at Britain through Egypt, and he had the active support of Talleyrand in pressing this advice.

The Directory, for their part, were persuaded as much by strategic argument and hope of commercial gain as by the imminence of the elections, for they were quite uncertain of Napoleon's ambitions and an expedition to Egypt would remove an obvious focus for a coup. It marked also a turning point in the war: the Directory were no longer contemplating a European balance, but striking beyond Europe to defeat Britain and regain some of France's lost colonies. The association with Tippu Sahib in India was no wild venture. The consequences of thus enlarging the war – even if it could be argued that it was now against England, not Europe, was the recharging of diplomatic moves against France which were to lead to the Second Coalition.

The resources diverted to the expedition were considerable and, in May 1798, 35,000 troops in nearly 400 transports escorted by thirteen ships of the line left Toulon, incredibly enough evading Nelson. There seems to have been little fear of British naval power in the Mediterranean, for the British navy had been withdrawn to Gibraltar in 1796, and with Corfu and Malta in French hands, there was no great reason to fear Britain. Malta was captured in June and the civil administration completely revised within a week. Napoleon was applying to politics that speed that distinguished his campaigns. Then he departed for Egypt, a destination his troops now learnt for the first time – it had been a well kept official secret, even though there travelled with the expedition a group of prominent academicians, including Monge, Berthollert and Fourier, together with libraries and instruments. Clearly, this was to be more than a military venture. In July he had defeated the Mamelukes and occupied Cairo, but on 1 August, after much searching, Nelson came on the French battle fleet at Aboukir Bay and destroyed it. The Sultan then declared war on France – French hopes of an alliance with Turkey through the defeat of the Mamelukes had not materialised.

The squalor of Egypt, as much as the heat, badly affected morale and there were difficulties over discipline. Napoleon respected Mohammedan customs and sought to present himself as a liberator against Mameluke tyranny. The government was reorganised on a representative basis, with Monge and Berthollert as French commissioners. The institutions he was applying were French in nature and were to be applied in France under the Consulate. In August an Institute of Egypt was founded under Monge and a series of archaeological surveys made. Later Champollion was to decipher Egyptian hieroglyphics from the Rosetta Stone.

However, there was much uncertainty of the French strength in Egypt, despite Napoleon's vigorous propaganda, and ill feeling promoted by forced loans culminated in a rising in Cairo in October. It was vigorously suppressed, but it underlined the insecurity of the French forces, isolated as they were. The decision to attack Syria was not so that he might march across desert to India, for he had not the resources for so dangerous an enterprise now that he was cut off from reinforcements. The purpose was to stop a Turkish attack on Egypt: there was no question of his 'missing his destiny' in Syria. He might write to Tippu Sahib of his wish to deliver him 'from the iron yoke of England', but he took only 13,000 troops to Syria. Aboukir Bay had ended the immediate dream of an Eastern Empire.

Jaffa fell quickly, but Acre resisted because it was supplied by sea by Sir Sidney Smith. The expected Turkish advance was defeated at Mount Tabor in April 1799, and so the siege was abandoned in May as being militarily unnecessary and strategically dangerous, for news of a threatened Turkish invasion of Egypt required the concentration of all available troops. The march back to Egypt was a hard one, made worse by plague, but the expected Turkish force was annihilated in July when it landed at Aboukir Bay.

It was then that Napoleon received, via Sir Sidney Smith, French papers for June telling of the loss of Italy, and of Jourdan's defeat on the Rhine. In great secrecy, accompanied by some generals and scientists, he left Egypt on 24 August 1799. The secrecy was essential, not only for the maintenance of morale, but in order to evade once more the British blockade – for the British now controlled the Mediterranean (they were to capture Malta in September 1800). He left Kléber in command of the dispirited troops in Egypt, and Kléber learnt of his promotion only after Napoleon had left. He was very bitter, complaining that Napoleon had 'fled in order to escape the catastrophe of surrender'. But Napoleon probably hoped to be able to retain his conquest: the Directory had moved the Brest Fleet to Toulon (another shrewd comment on the effectiveness of the British blockade) but the Spanish fleet had not managed to arrive there. Clearly, reinforcements would come to Egypt once victory was assured in Europe: Napoleon was more useful in Europe than in

Egypt, for he hoped to give France that victory – and thus ensure his own future. It was not so much flight from an untenable position, as a strategic reallocation of resources. Admiral Ganteaume brought him safely to France on 9 October – but by that time the situation had changed.

[21] BRUMAIRE

There was no mistaking the hero's welcome he gained in France – news of his victory over the Turks at Aboukir Bay had just arrived. If France was already saved, she nevertheless received him as the bringer of victories. There could be no question of arresting him for deserting his command – as Bernadotte suggested – however much the politicians feared his intentions.

The political situation was confused and rumours of imminent coups were in the air. There was a good deal of plotting going on. The royalists wondered if Napoleon would play the part of General Monk on behalf of Louis XVIII. Some hoped he might seize power and then prepare for a restoration once Louis had agreed to accept the principal changes of the Revolution; others hoped to restore Louis-Philippe of Orléans, who was in America, but he wrote back in favour of Louis, when consulted.

But the royalists were not behind the coup of Brumaire. The Jacobins were innocent, also. There had been a time when the Jacobins might have looked to Napoleon as their future general, but as early as the Vendémiaire crisis Babeuf had voiced suspicions of the young soldier, suspicions that were confirmed when Carnot chose him in particular to close the Babouvist Panthéon Club in 1795. Three days later he was given command of the Army of Italy. It was the opinion of Buonarotti, the follower of Babeuf and a former friend of Napoleon who had shared his bed on their last night in Corsica, that the two events were not unconnected.

Later Buonarotti was to condemn Napoleon as the betrayer of the Revolution, false to the principles of Robespierre. But in 1799, the revived Jacobinism had raised the scare of a threat to property, and the leading Jacobin politicians were no longer of the heroic stamp of 1793. Brumaire was as much a defeat for them as for the royalists, and their defeat was obvious even before Napoleon's return to France. When in August, Fouché closed the radical Manège Club, Lindet sadly commented, 'I feel sorry for the orators of the Manège who fashion a republicanism in the manner of 1793 . . . [lest they become] the victims of a new Machiavellism'. His premonition was justified. Yet Napoleon's former Jacobin associations gave him a possible source of political strength.

Siéyès, of course, had been plotting all summer (see page 23), and after Joubert's death at the battle of Novi, he had approached Moreau. The latter had hesitated, perhaps already committed to the royalists, and then had pointed to Napoleon as the general to aid Siéyès. He was soon in contact with Joseph and Lucien Bonaparte and Talleyrand and Fouché were in touch with Joséphine and Napoleon. Napoleon was to be the general to ensure success: his Jacobin past would quieten the left wing, his reputation would gain the support of the peasants and of the propertied classes, who feared a terrorist plot, and thus the right-wing revisionists would accept him. Jourdan, Augereau and Bernadotte were uneasy about the plot, but they were not strong enough to prevent it. Lemercier, President of the Council of Elders, gave his support, and Lucien Bonaparte was elected President of the Council of Five Hundred. On 10 Brumaire Napoleon and Siéyès met: there was no love lost between them, and Siéyès realised he had to accept as the necessary general an ambitious man who demanded conditions – namely a provisional government of three Consuls, Siéyès, Ducos and Napoleon. In the event, having spent a summer planning the coup, Siéyès was to become its dupe.

The actual seizure of power was well enough planned in general terms, but its details were not coordinated and in execution it proved a chapter of accidents. All went well at the start. Siéyès, upon a well prepared rumour spread with the aid of Roederer (a powerful journalist of royalist sympathies), that a Jacobin plot was imminent, secured the removal of the Councils to Saint-Cloud and the appointment of Napoleon to command the Paris garrison. Sebastiani, a fellow Corsican, and Murat were put in charge of the vital regiments, and Roederer looked after the propaganda proclamations. Fouché secured the resignation of Barras and the other Directors on 18 Brumaire, and Napoleon appeared at Saint-Cloud on 19 Brumaire (10 November) to harangue the crowd and then the Council of Elders on the inadequacies of the Directory.

Meanwhile, the Jacobin deputies of the Council of Five Hundred, suspicious of Napoleon's military display in Paris, had secured a motion that all deputies should personally take an oath of loyalty to the constitution. Lucien failed to prevent the move and it caused a great loss of time. Napoleon intervened with a badly delivered speech, which offended the deputies. He retired to receive news from Talleyrand and Fouché in Paris that things must be completed quickly. He intervened again, but the deputies overwhelmed him with protests and he withdrew once more, helped by four grenadiers. Murat now urged the use of troops, but he was unwilling to go to this extreme until there was heard the cry '*hors la loi*', the cry that had echoed round the Convention at the fall of Robespierre. Lucien appeared and, appealing as President of the Council to the guards, spoke of 'certain deputies armed with daggers ... bold brigands ... doubtless in the pay of England'. Rumour rapidly spread that there had been an attempt to assassinate Napoleon, and Murat led a column of troops into the hall. The deputies fled. The Elders decreed a provisional government of the three Consuls, as arranged, and called for a new constitution. Later, Lucien gathered a rump of the Council of Five Hundred to ratify the decision. It was a confused and badly executed coup, scarcely the occasion to usher in so illustrious a period, and not the sort of thing one associated with so careful a planner as Napoleon. The coup of 18-19 Brumaire was the last coup of the Directory, rather than the opening of an era.

[22] PACIFICATION OF EUROPE 1800-3

If the immediate threat to the Republic had been deflected before Napoleon's return from Egypt, there was as yet no chance of peace; further victories would be needed to convince Europe of the strength of France, and Napoleon himself needed such victories to ensure his position. Vigorous planning preceded the campaigns of 1800: Napoleon was anxious to complete things speedily – he was also aware that France was not anxious to bear severe conscription, and that there was not sufficient money to pay for a massive army. He relied upon speed and his own self-confidence (so much so that the army that marched for the second Italian campaign was ill-equipped and in arrears of pay). Furthermore, he knew that Jacobins and some liberals were hoping for his defeat, while the royalists went on plotting as usual and Cadoudal returned to revive *chouannerie* in the West.

Moreau commanded on the Rhine, but proved slow and uncooperative: in any case the principal campaign was reserved for Napoleon in Italy. Crossing the Great St Bernard pass in mid-May 1800, with a weak army, he made for Milan, hoping that so vigorous an advance would disorganise and demoralise the Austrians, despite the danger of his being cut off. His premonition was correct, but even so, in the complex manoeuvring before the battle of Marengo (14 June) Napoleon was put at a distinct disadvantage. Indeed, had not Desaix returned in time, followed by Kellermann with a handful of troops and some guns, Napoleon would probably have been defeated. As it was, Marengo was the culmination of another brilliant campaign, giving him the victory he needed – had he suffered a defeat his career would have ended. Fortune never smiled more kindly on him than at Marengo.

However, Austria was in no hurry to make peace – indeed, Thugut, the Chancellor, resigned rather than consider it. His successor, Cobenzl, was more amenable, but war was resumed in November. Meanwhile Napoleon had increased his army to 180,000 men and hoped to strike with another victory; but the blow was struck by Moreau at Hohenlinden (2 December) – a shattering blow indeed for Austria, for which Napoleon never forgave him! To save Vienna, peace negotiations began and were concluded at Lunéville in February 1801, upon the precise conditions that Napoleon imposed. Austria, on behalf of the Holy Roman Empire, ceded the entire left bank of the Rhine, compensation at the expense of the church being paid to dispossessed princes. The Cisalpine Republic was enlarged in the Po valley and extended to include the Papal Legations, but Austria retained Venetia.

The immediate settlement in Italy was completed by France absorbing Piedmont (1801); by giving Tuscany to the nephew of the Spanish queen in compensation for Spain ceding Louisiana to France in 1800 (the existing Duke of Tuscany, in best eighteenth-century style, was compensated in Germany); and Ferdinand IV of Naples agreed to close his harbours to British ships and allow French garrisons at Otranto and Brindisi (ports of embarkation for Egypt). The Pope, like all Italian princes, lay at Napoleon's feet; and Austria remained in Italy on sufferance. What Hauterive's *The State of France in the Year VIII* had proposed, a league of continental states dominated by France in place of the traditional balance of power principle, was already becoming a possibility.

Turkey made peace in 1801, leaving Britain once more alone as the enemy. Napoleon hoped to use Tsar Paul to build up a coalition against her – the Tsar had developed a pronounced regard for Napoleon. Paul also considered himself the leader of the Baltic States, who

were increasingly resentful of Britain's interference with their shipping
and trade. By December 1800, a Second Armed Neutrality of the
North was formed, closing the Baltic to British ships. In addition the
Danes entered Hamburg and Prussia seized Hanover (lest France
occupy it), and this cut off the German markets from Britain. Napoleon hoped to secure a Franco-Russian agreement that would
dominate Europe (such as was to be achieved at Tilsit in 1807), and
the Tsar obligingly expelled Louis XVIII from Mittau. Other schemes
were discussed; one was for a projected invasion of India, via Egypt
for the French, and across the steppes by Russia – a Russian army
actually started. Another was the partitioning of the Ottoman
Empire – in 1800 Rostopchin had produced a plan giving Austria and
Russia gains in the Balkans, and creating a large pro-Russian Greece,
while compensating Prussia with Hanover and other North German
gains. It was a plan that not entirely pleased Napoleon.

Britain was badly hit commercially by the Armed Neutrality and
with renewed unrest and fears of a further financial crisis, a demand
for peace was rising: Pitt resigned (February 1801) in the midst of the
crisis and this hastened proposals. By spring 1801, Hawkesbury and
Talleyrand were negotiating. Napoleon's hopes of a grand coalition
against Britain were dashed by the murder in March 1801 of the Tsar.
At first he believed it had been plotted by the British in order to save
India. But he failed to interest the new Tsar, Alexander I, in the
scheme. Within a few days of the murder, Sir Hyde Parker and Nelson
had attacked Copenhagen and by May the Armed Neutrality was
ended. Napoleon's schemes had failed. His hopes of reinforcing Egypt
also came to nothing. Kléber, having routed a Turkish army at
Heliopolis (March 1800) had been assassinated and his successor,
Menou, was beaten in the summer of 1801 by a triple invasion of
Turks, a British force and, ironically enough, a contingent of Sepoys
from India, sent by Wellesley, who had defeated and killed Tippu
Sahib.

There seemed no reason to refrain from making peace now, but
negotiations were protracted. Meanwhile France signed commercial
treaties with Naples, Spain, Portugal and Russia (in 1801) and
Turkey (1802). In hopes of regaining something of France's lost
colonial empire, Leclerc (Pauline Bonaparte's husband) was despatched to Santo Domingo where Toussaint Louverture had seized
control. The island was regained by 1802, but the expedition had
underlined the revolutionary situation in Latin America and indi-

cated that Napoleon, whilst not prepared to support independent republics in the Americas, was prepared to compete with Britain for trade. There were plans for a real occupation of Louisiana – legitimate enough, but clearly a matter of concern to Britain. Napoleon was not confining his interests to Europe. Clearly, with schemes for expeditions into Asia and for strengthening American possessions, it would be wrong to think of the Consulate as a short period of stability in diplomacy.

In January 1802, the Cisalpine Republic became the Italian Republic with Napoleon as its president. There was no question of Napoleon confining himself to France's natural frontiers. In the negotiations with Britain, the principal stumbling block was Malta, and the withdrawal of British forces was agreed only upon a string of conditions. It was no surprise that the occupation proved a permanency. The peace was signed at Amiens on 25 March 1802. England agreed to restore colonial gains except for Ceylon and Trinidad, and to restore Malta to the Knights of St John. France agreed to withdraw from Egypt (scarcely a concession) and from Rome and to restore papal possessions. Amiens settled nothing: it was a breathing space, and Napoleon had the advantage on all fronts in 1802.

The cordon of sister republics that the Directory had established was converted into a band of vassal states which continued to be drained of money and to support the armies – Murat was particularly high-handed over this. Despite the reforms that were introduced promoting unity and social equality for the wealthy, Napoleon was never happy dealing with the vassal states. He feared to appeal to democratic elements lest he encourage Jacobins at home, and whilst he had no love for the aristocracy, he recognised that liberals were often too moderate for his wishes. But he realised that the coming of peace required a proper settlement – and it was also necessary to pay the army. He preferred to evacuate Switzerland in order to profit from its neutrality, once the bourgeois notables had defeated the Swiss Jacobins (1801), and in May 1802, he imposed the 'Constitution of Malmaison', allowing a considerable degree of federalism.

In October 1801 Augereau arranged a referendum to accept a new authoritarian constitution for Holland (abstentions were counted with the affirmative votes) and the new government displaced democrats from public offices. In the Ligurian Republic, Salicetti imposed a constitution (June 1802). These constitutions mirrored the trend of events in France, where the bourgeois notables, those who had done well out of the Revolution and were to play so great a part in the confused politics of nineteenth-century France, had seized control of a state thoroughly centralised in the interests of order and stability. Democrats were pushed out of office and efforts were made to reconcile the wealthy and any well-disposed aristocrat with the régime. It was, perhaps, in Italy where Napoleon showed his true colours, for there he acted as master, not as arbiter. These changes within the vassal states did not disturb Europe. It was expected that French troops would be withdrawn: they were withdrawn from Switzerland in July 1802, but other states were less fortunate. If Italian patriots imagined that the Republic of Italy was the initial step to Italian unification, they were soon to be speedily disabused.

Germany also gave an example of the likely trend of events. The settlement that was arrived at meant a reorganisation within Germany, but it also meant a diminution of Austrian power. By 1803 the Consulate had brought peace and laid the basis for much of the diplomacy of the next decade. In Germany, Napoleon deliberately sought both support from the princes and bargaining counters for use with the powers. With Tsar Paul, he had intended a Franco–Russian settlement of Germany at Austrian expense: with Tsar Alexander, he achieved a not dissimilar settlement. Between the two powers lay Prussia, pursuing a policy of 'indecision and feebleness', as Napoleon put it; but Prussia proved a useful addition to strengthen an anti-Austrian settlement.

Clearly, the careful balance of eighteenth-century diplomacy had been set aside, but whereas the French gains in Italy and Germany could be considered as compensation for the gains as the Three Northern Courts in the recent partitions of Poland (1793 and 1795), some recognised basis for a European settlement was necessary if diplomacy were to function with any hope of efficiency.

The Rhine frontier was less a barrier against Europe than an invitation for further aggression, and for this reason Napoleon sought a German settlement that would divide Austria and Prussia and leave him with the initiative. Dreams of a European empire, which became a reality after the victories of 1805, may have been present in Napoleon's mind during the Consulate – but they were not then practical politics and it would be a mistake to suppose that the diplomacy between Marengo and Austerlitz was merely a preparation for world domination. In these years, indeed, he was regarded as the curber of revolution – even by von Gentz.

If the various schemes for partitioning the Ottoman Empire and for expeditions to the Orient were dashed by the murder of Tsar Paul, and not proceeded with by Alexander despite Napoleon sending Duroc to persuade him, at least the temporary isolation of Austria was achieved. The scene was set in Germany, especially with the help of Talleyrand whose familiarity with aristocratic manners, whose skill and whose success Napoleon respected. And Russian support was necessary to ensure success. 'In secret conferences between Markov and Talleyrand, to which the Prussian Lucchesini was at times admitted, the fate of Germany was decided' (Deutsch). What had begun as compensation for those dispossessed by the arrangements of Lunéville became a new settlement for Germany. Talleyrand increased his fortune from the many bribes he received and on 3 June 1803 France and Russia in effect invited the Imperial Diet to ratify the arrangements they had made. Austria's protests were of no avail, and what amounted to a new Imperial Constitution was formally agreed by the Conclusum of 25 February 1803.

By it, ecclesiastical property was abolished largely in favour of Prussia, Bavaria and Baden. Only Dalberg remained of the clerical Electors and since the number of Electors was increased to ten, giving a protestant majority, it was apparent that Austria could no longer anticipate the usual election of Holy Roman Emperor going in her favour. In effect, if not in fact, the Holy Roman Empire ceased in 1803. It was a measure of Napoleon's diplomatic victory over Austria. It was a measure, too, of the defeat of the Roman Church, which lost land, monasteries and influence. The Imperial Knights, who had formerly looked to Austria or the Church for employment, found their future in jeopardy as greedy states, such as Prussia in Franconia, sought to gain the fullest advantage from their new acquisitions. It is hardly surprising that Napoleon was to find among the dispossessed German knights a number of able and bitter opponents, of whom the best known is Stein.

Prussia, for her part, hoping to profit from a general settlement for which she had done no fighting, failed to secure all she desired. She gave up Hanover and weakly turned down the opportunity of a French alliance, lest it offend Britain too much. However, in the course of the multitude of meetings that had preceded the settlement, Tsar Alexander had met Queen Louisa of Prussia and his romantic attachment to her meant a good deal in terms of diplomatic advantage. England, meanwhile, had to look on this new German settlement unable to resist since it was not in contravention of the Treaty of Amiens. Yet she was conscious of the advantages France had secured and she felt the need as much for added security as for compensation.

The Recess, as the German settlement was called, had assured a temporary French hegemony in South Germany, where the princes looked to Napoleon for support, and a French dominance of central Europe which was to be the principal bone of diplomatic contention for the next twelve years, and to set the scene for the diplomacy of the nineteenth century. It was a settlement, be it noted, that was arrived at by eighteenth-century methods and was the concern of princes. The 'people', whoever they might be, were not consulted, nor were they excited by the Recess.

If the changes were in the direction of greater administrative efficiency within Germany, they were not in the direction of nationalism: Napoleon had no interest in raising a rival to France, only in establishing vassal states or allies. The settlement strengthened the particularism of the Princes – the best guarantee against revolutionary ideas. Nor is it without significance that Talleyrand authorised payments to German journals to print French propaganda and represent Napoleonic France as the bringer of order, rather than aggression. And what was true of Germany was even more true of Italy, where Napoleon may have cleared away petty duchies and brought administrative reform, yet he had no interest in Italian unity. In due course northern Italy was to be absorbed into France, and southern Italy made a Bonaparte kingdom: this was not for any wish to recognise national feeling (if any existed outside of intellectual and literary circles) but to ensure the better control of the geographical area. Meanwhile, the pacification of Europe by 1803 had produced what was in effect already a French dominance – a dominance that could only be challenged on the battlefield and at the risk of exchanging French influence for French hegemony.

PRINCIPAL EVENTS, 1768–1803

Napoleon and France

Outside France
1768
Corsica acquired by France

1769
Napoleon born in Corsica

1785
Napoleon commissioned in artillery

1788
Assembly of Notables. Napoleon
posted to Auxonne

1789
Napoleon returns to Corsica

1792
War with Austria and Prussia
Crisis of the first invasion

1792
Napoleon exiled from Corsica

1793
Crisis of second invasion
Jacobin dictatorship. Hood driven
from Toulon by Napoleon
Napoleon a brigadier general at 24

1793
First Coalition

1794
Crisis of Thermidor. Napoleon briefly
imprisoned
July. Constitution of Year III

1794
Invading armies repelled

1796
April. Armistice of Cherasco
(Piedmont makes peace). Savoy and
Nice ceded to France
10 May. Bridge of Lodi victory.
Jourdan and Moreau attack Austria
in South Germany – unsuccessfully

1797
January. Victory at Rivoli
February. Joseph Bonaparte
negotiates Treaty of Tolentino with
Papacy

Napoleon and France
1797

4 September. Coup of 18 Fructidor
saves the Republic
December. Napoleon returns to Paris
in triumph. Napoleon appointed
Commander of Army of England

1798
12 April. Napoleon given command of
Expedition to Egypt
11 May. Coup of 22 Floréal

1799

June. Jacobin measures to meet
invasion threat
12 July. Law of Hostages

August. Fouché closes the radical
Manège Club

October. New *chouannerie* breaks out
in the West
October. Napoleon lands at Fréjus
9 November. Coup of 18 Brumaire
24 December. Constitution of Year III,
Napoleon as First Consul

1800
May. Napoleon leaves for Italy

3 December. Moreau victorious at
Hohenlinden

Outside France
1797
May. Cisalpine Republic formed

October. Treaty of Campo Formio

1798

19 May. Napoleon sails to Egypt
10 June. Malta taken (captured by
British, September 1800)
July. Napoleon in Cairo
August. Nelson's victory at Aboukir
Bay. Sultan joins war against France
December. Second Coalition

1799
April. Turks defeated at Mount Tabor
May. Siege of Acre abandoned

25 July. Turkish invasion of Egypt
defeated at Aboukir Bay
22 August. Napoleon secretly leaves
Egypt
26 September. Masséna victorious at
Zurich, saves France

1800

14 June. Victory at Marengo

26 December. Tsar forms Second
Armed Neutrality of North v. England

Napoleon and France
1801
8 January. Peace of Lunéville

1802
Napoleon President of Italian
Republic
25 March. Treaty of Amiens

Outside France
1801
Spain cedes Louisiana to France
23 March. Assassination of Tsar Paul
September. French capitulate in
Egypt

1802
January–April. Expedition to West
Indies: Leclerc captures Santo
Domingo
May. New constitution for
Switzerland
June. New constitution for Ligurian
Republic
September. Piedmont annexed.
Imperial Diet invited to ratify new
arrangements for Germany

1803
25 February. Recess (Conclusum) –
in effect a new Imperial Constitution,
for Holy Roman Empire

PART IV
Napoleon and France

[23] THE CONSULATE

Peace, prosperity and an administration characterised by vigour and good order are the hallmarks of the Consulate. The contrast with the Directory seems so obvious that historians have been inclined to exaggerate the achievements of the Consulate and of Napoleon, suggesting that the credit lay with him. But Napoleon did not have a prepared programme of reform, and he was as great an improviser in the field of government as he was upon the field of battle. The Consulate owes much to his charisma, but it enjoyed conspicuous advantages. The peace it gained was already upon the horizon before Brumaire; the prosperity had already come; the administrative consolidation that was to establish the basis of French government for a century and a half was rooted in the achievements of the revolutionary decade. Indeed, to a great extent the Consulate was the culmination of that decade.

Yet, in fulfilling the Revolution, Napoleon gave a twist to the Revolutionary tradition, for he moved progressively towards a dictatorship of the political right wing. It was a dictatorship with which contemporary Europe was prepared for coexistence, and France, seduced by victory abroad and prosperity at home, was content. But, if his régime was acceptable to his contemporaries, it nevertheless showed an approach to government and administration that was at once in the tradition of Enlightened Despotism and yet also prefigured the pattern of the twentieth-century fascist state.

The Brumaireans, the upper bourgeoisie, were satisfied with the coup they had been plotting for six months. They were saved from a Jacobin terror, and the Jacobin measures of the summer were repealed. If they were taken aback by the dismissal of Siéyès (who was compensated with an estate worth half a million) and Ducos, they were prepared to let the new government continue, for no one recognised immediately that a new and powerful régime had appeared. For their part, the royalists were prepared to tolerate this revolutionary general in hopes of his playing the part of Monk.

Siéyès had left the details of his projected constitution vague, as might have been expected from his new slogan of direction from above and confidence from below (the people were merely to assent). Napoleon was not opposed when he inserted the names of the new consuls. He chose well – himself as First Consul, then Cambacérès (Minister of Justice under the Directory and responsible for drafting the Convention's revised civil code) and as Third Consul, Lebrun, former secretary to Maupeou, the frustrated reformer of the 1770s. The Constitution of Year VIII was 'short and obscure', but it guaranteed the land settlement of the Revolution.

The First Consul, assisted by his Council of State, was virtually a dictator, although this was at first concealed by the façade of the Assemblies. However, the 300-strong Legislative Body, if it might prosecute ministers, could only record without discussion a negative or affirmative vote in answer to the advice given by the Council of State upon legislation presented by Napoleon. The 100 members of the Tribunate could discuss the legislation – but no more. The Senate contained 60 members, 31 being initially chosen by the Consuls and 29 by the Senators; thereafter recruitment was by co-option.

Manhood suffrage was retained, but the popular voice was easily suppressed by the complex system of secondary voting. Communes chose delegates from an official list of candidates, who themselves voted for candidates at Department level, who in turn voted for national candidates. By this means the Brumaireans maintained their monopoly and the threat of democracy was destroyed. If this was not enough, Napoleon himself appointed the ministers and officials of the centralised bureaucracy that was being formed, right down to the level of justices of the peace (who remained elected). In this way, Napoleon simply by-passed the Brumaireans: he claimed, justifiably, that they represented themselves, but he represented the nation. To demonstrate this, once the Constitution of Year VIII had been safely promulgated, it was submitted to a plebiscite – a device that was to prove useful in the hands of liberals and dictators alike for the next hundred and fifty years – in order to give a spurious air of popular support. This first plebiscite was disappointing – only 3 million votes were cast in favour, with 4 million abstentions and 1,500 dared to vote against the Constitution. The figures are a shrewd comment on the opinion of those who would represent the Consulate as thoroughly popular from the outset, for the government was very active both in propaganda and in controlling the conduct of the plebiscite.

'The Revolution is ended', Napoleon proclaimed at Brumaire. Whoever tampered with the real gains of the Revolution – the land settlement, abolition of feudalism, the career open to talent – would fall (as Charles X discovered). But the Constitution retained only the empty form of popular election and representative assemblies: the spirit of 1789 had expired. Very soon the Council of State gained the right to 'interpret' laws and Napoleon went on to modify laws by decree as the occasion warranted it. There was no question of balanced powers; any opposition in the Senate and Tribune was met with truncation of powers, and the device of Senatus-consultum, to which Napoleon had recourse from January 1801, overruled the assemblies. Through it, Napoleon was able to declare himself Consul for life (1802, the Constitution of Year X). By 1802 he had no need to lean on the politicians, for he controlled the administration which was infinitely superior to the assemblies. He attracted to it both former revolution-aries prepared to forget their past, and *émigrés* prepared to accept the new order. Recruiting the latter helped him towards the Empire (Constitution of Year XII, 1804). In this sequence of events, however, there was no working out of a master plan: he did not necessarily see the Imperial Crown when he snatched the Life Consulship. He was not his nephew: he lacked patience and he did not wait upon events.

Napoleon continued the trend to administrative centralisation that the Revolution had begun. It was accentuated by his personal direc-tion of affairs. On 19 February 1800 he moved into the Tuileries, making his study the nerve centre of France. Only his hard-worked secretaries had access to him – even his ministers had to communicate in writing. Soon these ministers were writing Reports like civil servants and the Directory's Secretariat was retained under Maret to collate them and issue Napoleon's orders, which were as likely to come at night as during the normal working day. Boards were created to supervise specific services like highways, forests and education. They were in the charge of high-powered civil servants (the future *direc-teurs*) and were joined in 1803 by the *auditeurs* of the Council of State, an ideal training ground for senior civil servants. By 1811 they numbered some 300 (requiring a university degree after 1813); in effect they were trainees for the higher civil service, a practice fifty years in advance of any other country. The *auditeurs* tended to be drawn from upper bourgeoisie and younger sons of the nobility. On the other hand, the generals, whose social origins were various, were excluded from administration unless their ability was proven, lest they became too ambitious.

Napoleon himself was less an administrator than a man capable of recognising and using the talents of others, like the twenty-nine members of the Council of State, some of whom were royalist sympathisers whose experience lay in the administration of the *ancien régime* (though this was not deliberate policy – he would have chosen Jacobins had they had time to build up a cadre of skilled personnel). Men like Chaptal, Roederer, Fourcroy, Portalis and Berlier showed the strength of the Council, which came to regulate the whole administrative machine. Not content with so fine an engine, however, Napoleon was continually forming advisory bodies and calling upon provincial officials for personal reports.

The Directory had begun to establish a new bureaucratic organisation, integrating it with the surviving staff of the old ministerial framework (rather like Carnot's Amalgam). Chaptal continued the work by reorganising provincial administration (17 February 1800). Departments were divided into *arrondissements*, cantons and communes and the officials, down to local mayors, were appointed by the central government – this ended the revolutionary tradition of election of officials. Each Department was under a Prefect, most of whom were appointed in March 1800. Lucien Bonaparte as Minister of the Interior drew up the list, over half of whom had served in the Convention or the assemblies of the Directory. They were largely moderate revolutionaries, although Jeanbon Saint-André of the Robespierrist Committee of Public Safety, and Letourneur, a Jacobin activist, were chosen. Their postings were to Departments to which they were strangers and they tended to rely on moderate revolutionaries to fill the junior administrative posts (although it was often a case of having the former *seigneur* at very local level because of the lack of men of education). In their Departments, however, the Prefects were conscious of the limitations imposed on them by the hardening bureaucratic régime.

The police were organised as a national force separate from the administration. Fouché reorganised the Ministry of General Police and appointed a special Prefect of Police for Paris, Dubois, a trusted servant. Separate from and in rivalry with the police was the gendarmerie, and in addition Fouché maintained a complex system of spies and informers drawn from all classes of society, and from the beginning arbitrary arrest was not unknown. Napoleon would have concentrated the police still more, had he not feared Fouché's power, and kept his own check on him by his own system of informers. The ordinary citizen suffered the consequences of rivalry between them.

Reform of the judiciary began in March 1800 by the ending of election of judges – Napoleon now appointed them, although they were irremovable. Twenty-nine courts of appeal were opened for civil cases. Police courts continued to use juries until the Senatus-consultum of 18 October 1802. The office of public prosecutor was reconstituted, and there was a purge of junior officers.

Had the Committee of Public Safety had more time and a less perilous situation, it might well have produced a centralised bureaucracy on this Napoleonic scale. The difference was that Napoleon had made his machine dominate the assemblies. The upper bourgeoisie who had helped him to power had gained office, but some of them resented their exclusion from political power, and among them were such publicists as Mme de Staël and her lover, Benjamin Constant. The threat of a Jacobin terror, removed by the coup of Brumaire, no longer secured their silence.

[24] THE OPPOSITION CRUSHED

Napoleon continued to fear the Jacobins, especially in the towns, and when there was some talk of a plot and some indiscipline in the army in Germinal VIII, he appointed Carnot as Minister of War. He was nervous, too, of the royalists who soon realised Napoleon was no General Monk. He knew of their intrigues. Their agents approached Joséphine, Lebrun and Talleyrand, some had even sounded out Louis Philippe of Orléans, in exile in America, who had declined to be a candidate for king. Then, on 20 February 1800, Louis 'XVIII' wrote personally to Lebrun and to Napoleon,

We can assure tranquillity to France, I say we, because I need Bonaparte and he cannot do without me.

Napoleon did not reply immediately. Instead he appointed a commission to close the official list of *émigrés*, inviting suitable ones to return, and then went off to Italy to gain his vital victory at Marengo. Then he replied (7 September) that if Louis returned to France he would have to march over 100,000 corpses, and he began to negotiate through the Tsar for Louis to renounce the throne.

Meanwhile renewed censorship had stopped sixty of the seventy-three journals in France, and activists turned to violent schemes like the projected royalist rising in 1800 in Provence, while in the West a new *chouannerie* flared up. Brune and Lefebvre crushed it savagely and its leaders signed a pacification in December 1800. The royalists now turned to assassination plots. The best known is that of the 'infernal machine' (24 December 1800), a bomb that caused casualties among the crowd watching Napoleon arrive at the Opéra. With an accustomed eye to the main chance, Napoleon struck against the Jacobins, blaming them for the outrage in order that he might purge France of Jacobin and Babouvist influence. One hundred and thirty were proscribed and a hundred and six transported to the Seychelles or to Cayenne. But not all the Babouvists died in exile, for some were linked with Oudet, founder of the anti-Napoleon Philadelphians. Buonarotti escaped and may well have been linked with Malet's conspiracy of 1812 (see page 185). But by proscribing the Jacobins, Napoleon washed himself free of the stain of a Jacobin past. Fouché, knowing the royalists to be responsible, was unable to prevent the proscriptions; but by April the royalist plot had been uncovered and two of the culprits executed – Cadoudal escaping to England – whilst over a hundred royalists were detained without trial.

In the proscription, Napoleon had not consulted the assemblies, but operated through the Senate. From now on he assumed the right to legislate personally by Senatus-consulta, and was thus able at will to revise the Constitution of Year VIII. Already Roederer and Talleyrand had suggested a monarchy and Lucien Bonaparte had launched a pamphlet (perhaps by Fontanes) *A Comparison between Caesar, Cromwell, Monk and Bonaparte*. But Napoleon thought it premature and dismissed Lucien in favour of Chaptal. Violent repression had 'pacified' La Vendée, but other Departments had to be dealt with less vigorously. There was not only royalist activity, but ordinary brigandage and disorderly vagrancy. Special courts brought order to the countryside in 1801, and consolidated peasant support behind the régime. Military tribunals sat openly, and protests in the Tribunate against the infringement of personal liberty were of no avail. Napoleon knew the parliamentary opposition had little support in the country and replied in the Council of State:

> A Constitution must not interfere with the process of government, nor be written in a way that could force the government to violate it .... Every day brings the necessity to violate constitutional laws; it is the only way, otherwise progress would be impossible.

The year 1801 had begun with the final breach between Napoleon and the Jacobins; it ended with that between Napoleon and the republican bourgeoisie which had helped him to power. As yet, however, he had to secure their approval for the Concordat, without which no genuine social peace was possible. The country seemed to favour it; the assemblies, conscious of their revolutionary past, did not.

[25] THE CONCORDAT

The Constituent Assembly had naïvely raised a hornet's nest when it reorganised the Roman Catholic Church as a French institution. The rift it had innocently provoked accentuated the disruption of the 1790s and drove the non-juring priests into counter-revolution and co-operation with the royalists. Napoleon hoped not only to bring secure social peace by a settlement of the religious problem, but also to gain a powerful social ally in the clergy, whom he intended to control: he also sought the immense popularity of achieving such a solution without infringing the land settlement of the Revolution.

He did not view the situation from any religious point of view: he sought merely security and the cooperation of the priesthood who would consequently cease to be the storm-troopers of counter-revolution, and instead help to induce an atmosphere of social quietism among the populace. An organised church underpinned the stability of a hierarchical society. 'Society cannot exist without inequality of wealth and this cannot exist without religion', he observed in 1800. Six years later he was even more explicit:

> I don't see the mystery of the incarnation, but the mystery of the social order; religion concentrates within Heaven a conception of equality that prevents the rich being massacred by the poor.

There was a further factor in the situation. Europe was experiencing a religious revival (see page 37) especially among the wealthy and nobility. The case for a concordat was strong; it was promoted by royalist publicists (*dévots*) like the Bertin brothers in *Le Journal des Débats* (January 1800), Fontanes in *Mercure de France* (June 1800) and Geoffroy's *L'Année Litteraire* (November 1800). In Paris, Chaptal patronised religious charitable organisations and in 1801 the *Congrégation de la Vièrge* was founded.

Napoleon's own dealings with the Pope (the Treaty of Tolentino, see page 78) contrasted with those of the Directory, and the succession in 1799 of Pius VII, a gentle, amiable scholar who had earned the title of 'Jacobin' bishop of Imola, seemed to augur well for a settlement. On 25 June 1800, following the victory at Marengo, Napoleon opened negotiations. The Pope, however, recognised the difficulty of the situation. The old French episcopate, having sacrificed much, might interpret a rapprochement with Napoleon as a betrayal; the catholic sovereigns of Europe might be alienated; and, despite Marengo, Napoleon's own position was not yet clearly unassailable. Louis 'XVIII''s resentments mattered less to him. But there were conspicuous advantages to the papacy in a settlement, for, not only would it be a great victory, over the Revolution and Gallicanism, but it would also save Rome from despolation by French troops. Accordingly, in November in Paris Cardinal Spina met the Abbé Bernier, the former leader of the Vendéans who had joined Napoleon and was his principal negotiator. In the tortuous discussions, Napoleon showed he was no master-mind, for he would have allowed catholicism as the 'dominant religion'. It was Talleyrand who demonstrated that this would have renounced the two revolutionary gains of liberty of conscience and the secular state. The papal curia dallied, but the conclusive victory at Hohenlinden guaranteed Napoleon's position and the papal Secretary of State, Consalvi, was induced to sign the Concordat on 16 July 1801.

Catholicism was recognised as the religion of most Frenchmen including the Consuls. The Church was to have freedom of public worship and the state was to pay clerical salaries to a maximum of three thousand priests. Cathedral chapters, diocesan seminaries and charitable foundations were allowed, but not maintained. The settlement of the clergy was not easy. The Pope undertook to secure the resignation of the non-juring bishops (his lack of success – thirty-six out of eighty-two refused the Concordat – produced the *Petite Eglise* that appeared in some dioceses). Napoleon secured the resignation of the constitutional bishops more easily. The new bishops were to be installed by the Pope, but nominated by Napoleon. He obliged the Pope to accept twelve former constitutional bishops (Grégoire, the most able and most outspoken was not among them, for Napoleon preferred efficient civil servants to leaders of the Church) and himself accepted sixteen former refractory bishops and thirty-five new appointments. The schism was ended. The bishops' powers were increased beyond the Edict of 1695, but they had to ensure that all clergy took the oath of fidelity and offered public prayers for the Republic during divine service, as well as accepting the land settlement of the Revolution. Through the bishops Napoleon hoped to control the three thousand parish clergy, and his appointment of Portalis as minister of public worship (7 October 1801) showed his leanings towards Gallicanism.

But the Council of State was openly hostile to the Concordat. So were the assemblies. On 22 November the Legislative Body showed its resentment by electing as its president Dupuis, author of the anti-religious *L'Origine de tous les cultes,* and on 30 November, the Senate chose Grégoire to fill a vacancy. The Tribunate also was hostile. Napoleon had never before faced such united opposition. Already he had had to compel Fouché to rescind an order, issued within four days of the signing of the Concordat, requiring the hunting down of refractory priests. More significantly, the attitude of the army was also hostile.

Portalis, however, skilfully argued that the Concordat meant including the Church within the State, and Talleyrand suggested issuing regulations to control its working. These were the Organic Articles which Napoleon added without papal consent and which strengthened the Gallican aspect of the settlement. The Gallican Articles of 1682 were to be learnt by seminarists, civil marriage was to precede the religious ceremony, the publication of Papal Bulls, holding of General Councils, editing of catechisms and a host of minor matters were all subject to the specific agreement of the government. (Protestants gained security under special Articles for Protestants, and their ministers were paid a salary by the state.)

The Legislative Body passed the Concordat on 8 April 1802, and a solemn Te Deum in Notre-Dame celebrated the formal reconciliation of the Revolution and Rome. But in order to secure this greatly modified settlement, Napoleon had to effect another coup – not entirely, of course, for the sake of the religious question.

[26] CONSUL FOR LIFE

In January 1802, Napoleon struck against the opposition by with-drawing all legislation before the assemblies and requiring the Senate to determine how the first fifth of the members of the assemblies should be replaced, as required under the constitution. When the Senate suggested men like Benjamin Constant and M.-J. Chénier they were replaced by civil servants. Carnot remained a Tribunate and was joined by Lucien Bonaparte, determined to play a rôle similar to that at the Brumaire coup. On 1 April 1802, he got the Tribunate to agree to meet in camera and in three divisions, ostensibly to deal with the complexities of the Civil Code. This reduced their effectiveness as a political force.

The Council of State lost its power to control the final draft of laws.

'It is not as a general that I govern [Napoleon told them on 4 May] but because the nation believes that I have the proper civil qualities for government.' He intended to place, without the aid of assemblies, 'blocks of granite' upon the soil of France.

The opposition in the assemblies was ignored and by-passed. But there remained disaffection in the army, whose republicanism distrusted the Concordat. The threat was met partly by despatching an expedition to the West Indies. But the danger of a military coup remained, for the peace left the army unemployed and filled Paris with troops whose arrears of pay had not been met, and whose generals were itching to seize Napoleon's place. Moreau was the principal intriguer, and he was joined by Bernadotte who was very cautious, for the situation was less favourable to him than that in Year VII when he had contemplated seizing control. Fouché squashed the plot by arresting Bernadotte's Chief of Staff and some minor officers on 24 June. But there was no Napoleonic Terror as in January 1801, for Napoleon feared to disrupt the army's morale. He imprisoned the officers without trial and shipped the regiment off to Santo Domingo. General Decaen was sent to the colonies, Lannes to Lisbon and Brune to Constantinople. Bernadotte was saved from proscription by his wife Julie Cary, Napoleon's quondam fiancée, but he was dismissed. Fouché cautioned those politicians who had been associated with the plot, and Mme de Staël hurried off to Switzerland.

Between May and August 1802, a series of decrees transformed the Consulate into an open dictatorship. Napoleon sought to be re-appointed Consul for ten years with the right to appoint his successor.

Opposition from the Senate led him to accept Cambacère's advice and to appeal directly to the people by plebiscite to be declared Consul for Life. Fouché and several councillors absented themselves fom the Council of State when the resolution was passed, but the plebiscite on 2 August showed that France accepted the new dictatorship. On 4 August a new Constitution of Year X confirmed the plebiscite, and the politicians remained the prisoners of the man whom they had brought to power at Brumaire. But the problem of the succession was beginning to worry Napoleon, and, more particularly, Joséphine. Joseph and Lucien openly quarrelled about it.

The new constitution gave the First Consul full powers of peace and war, the exclusive right to designate candidates to the Senate and to interpret the Constitution by Senatus-consultum. He had also the right to suspend the Constitution and dissolve the assemblies, which were now reduced to a nominal position. It was monarchy in all but name, and the republicans who objected suffered. Fouché was dismissed in September and the opposition was forced into weaving plots, both counter-revolutionary and Jacobin. Manhood suffrage was retained, but election was reduced to a minimum and a new system of electoral colleges brought it more closely under Napoleon's control. The Senate was reconstituted and its members suitably rewarded with senior administrative posts and estates in order to tie them to the new régime. The way was open for the Empire.

The Brumaireans had been transformed into a 'mercenary corps of elevated slaves who reacted with all the weight of their moral degradation upon the inert and servile masses' (Nodier). The 'servile masses' failed to protest at Napoleon's overt perversion of democracy – to them effective government was more important than representative government. His ascendancy was possible because he respected the social legislation of the Constituent Assembly and gave victory abroad; this allowed him to plant the seed of a modern state with techniques the twentieth century was to perfect – but his contemporaries saw him as the soldier of the Revolution bringing stability out of strife.

[27] EMPEROR OF THE FRENCH

Napoleon had freed himself of dependence on the politicians; and he increasingly leaned now upon such members of the old nobility – shorn of their privileges – as were prepared to accommodate them-

N.—4*

selves to his régime. This would help the establishment of a Bonaparte monarchy, but it was not essential to it. On 26 April 1802, a
Senatus-consultum granted an amnesty to all émigrés (excepting only
those proscribed in 1800) who returned by 1 Vendémiaire XI (23
September) and swore fealty to the Constitution of Year X. The
decree did not raise the opposition that the Concordat had produced,
but the Assemblies were hostile, even though it was clear that Napoleon was not preparing the way for Louis 'XVIII', and that the
returned émigrés were under police supervision for ten years.

The Legion of Honour (19 May 1802), again, was not conceived as a
necessary step to a monarchy; indeed, if anything it strengthened the
Revolutionary tradition of careers open to talent, for it was an
honorific award for service to the State. There were to be 15 cohorts
numbering 350 legionaries sworn 'to dedicate themselves to the
service of the Republic', chosen by Napoleon from both the military
and civil fields. A grant of 200,000 francs for each cohort gave the
opportunity for gifts and pensions that could change the nature of the
Legion.

At the Tuileries, the manner of former days reappeared (with a
superficial 'respectability' to distinguish it) and Duroc was created
Governor of the Palace. From November 1802, Joséphine was
attended by four ladies-in-waiting of the old nobility. A new splendour
(if a trifle vulgar) appeared in the liveries and costumes at Court.
When General Leclerc, Pauline Bonaparte's husband, died of fever on
active service in Santo Domingo in January 1803, official court
mourning was ordered. From 1802, Napoleon's birthday (15 August)
was celebrated as a feast day, and in 1803 coins were struck with his
head upon them. But it comes as a shock to realise that the great
Revolutionary feasts of 14 July and 1 Vendémiaire (the Republican
calendar) ceased to be celebrated officially after 1804. Even the
Legion of Honour seemed too redolent of the Revolution and Napoleon delayed nominating the full number of legionaries. But as he
moved now to monarchy, France did not stay his hand: the move
might not raise much enthusiasm, but it did not incur opprobrium,
nor make him the less a hero.

Naturally, the royalists and counter-revolutionaries continued
their plotting: to establish a new dynasty might put an end to their
efforts. From 1803 an Anglo-Royalist plot was being woven, covering
a wide loom and involving Artois, Louis's brother, Cadoudal, Pichegru
and Moreau who burned to be in Napoleon's place. One part of the

plot attempted to raise revolt in the Rhineland to prepare for the entry of a corps of émigrés under the Duc d'Enghien. Another was led by Cadoudal, who was in Paris in August 1803, making contact with his Chouans. In January 1804, Pichegru, accompanied by Polignac (who was to be Artois's minister at the time of the 1830 Revolution) met Cadoudal, but the police uncovered the plot, arresting Moreau in February and Cadoudal, Pichegru and Polignac on 9 March. Only the Bourbon Prince who was to lead the revolt had not arrived; and the only likely one on the frontiers was the Duc d'Enghien who was under secret police supervision. Both Fouché and Talleyrand urged his arrest, although he was on neutral territory, and he was arrested on 15 March, taken to Vincennes on 20 March and shot next morning. Talleyrand gave an exceptionally brilliant ball at the Ministry of Foreign Affairs three days later.

Much has been made of this incident. Enghien was innocent of the actual plot, though he may have known something of it: certainly he was engaged in royalist activity against the régime and so was a security risk. When the quite innocent Jacobin victims of 1801 go unrecorded, it is a little puzzling that this death should have caused so much furore. Yet it was then regarded as a deed beyond the bounds of civilised behaviour – clearly, international relations had returned to normality after the experiences of the previous decade. Protests rose throughout Europe, and in France Chateaubriand took this opportunity to quit Napoleon's service – 'Worse than a crime, it's a mistake' was his opinion. Louis 'XVIII' condemned the execution from a boat in the Baltic – oddly enough, for all their opposition, no monarch would let him do so from their own territory. Austria and the minor German courts made no formal protest.

Pichegru died mysteriously in jail in April. To Napoleon's chagrin, Moreau was merely condemned to two years' hard labour, which was commuted to banishment for life instead. He went to America and returned for the War of Liberation to be killed at Leipzig in 1813 (see page 189). Cadoudal was executed in June, but Polignac was pardoned. Napoleon revealed the extent to which British spies were implicated and several were required to leave German states. But within France a new wave of opposition broke:

The hate and vituperation aimed at the government have become as violent and pronounced as ever I saw them in the time before the Revolution [wrote Roederer in June].

The country, however, remained solidly behind Napoleon and on 18 May ratified by plebiscite the Declaration of the Empire (Constitution of the Year XII) by $3\frac{1}{2}$ million votes. The Senate asked for constitutional guarantees against despotism and Fontanes asked that the Legislative Body be given the right of discussion. Both were disappointed and the police were strengthened by the return of Fouché as minister.

The establishing of the Empire not only ended the hopes of the royalists, it also involved creating honorific offices that hastened the appearance of a new nobility which Napoleon openly sought through the Legion of Honour. The Empire was solemnised by a coronation on 2 December 1804. It was a tremendous diplomatic triumph, for the Pope was called to Paris and there, not inappropriately, Napoleon humiliated him by placing the crown himself upon his own head. Popular enthusiasm, however, was conspicuously absent. Although the motto 'République Française' remained officially stamped upon the coinage until 1808, Napoleon and the nation were beginning to go separate ways. 'In those days,' commented Chaptal, 'the history of the Revolution was as remote for us as the history of the Greeks and Romans.'

[28] THE NEW NOBILITY

The Emperor emphasised the personal nature of his government, legislating by decree and Senatus-consulta so that, after the publication of the Codes the Council of State ceased to have significance. Even the great administrators of the Consulate were thrust aside – first Chaptal, then (justifiably) Talleyrand, and then Fouché, while Fourcroy was disappointed of real power. Napoleon preferred now men of less ability – Crétet, Champagny, Savary and Maret. Former royal servants and returned émigrés did well. 'It is only people like that who know how to be servants', he observed. A clique of officials distinguished by their birth and fortune appeared after 1804 – there were over 360 of them by 1811. Already the world of the July Monarchy was apparent. At local level the big proprietors became officials and mayors, and the civisme that had served the Jacobins so well was often absent.

It is difficult to tell how effective in actual practice the bureaucratic centralisation really was. As early as 1803 the Prefects were complaining of delays in referring matters to Paris, of contradictory orders

received and of lack of initiative. Some acted on their own judgment
and Napoleon complained (with unconscious irony) of their playing
the despot. Paris did not always know what was going on in remoter
areas and when Napoleon wanted specific information he generally
passed judgment on his administrative machine by sending out
special commissioners. The Prefects, according to their personalities
and their distance from Paris, acted as they thought fit: as the first
Prefects were promoted or replaced, however, independent action
became less common, for their successors were less capable.

An impression of a diminishing vitality in administration is
strengthened by the creation of the new aristocracy and the concentration upon the outward show of court ceremonial. The Legion of
Honour was transformed into a purely honorific award, going
principally to soldiers. Within the Imperial Court, between 1804 and
1808, a new Imperial nobility was created with curious medieval
titles recalling the Holy Roman Empire – as much a reflection of the
medievalism of the Romantic Revival as of Napoleon's ambitions.
Elaborate procedure and a sizeable organisation was under the
control of M. de Ségur by 1811. A Senatus-consultum of August 1806
allowed Napoleon to grant hereditary fiefs to generals and senior
officials throughout the Empire (he rarely granted them in France
lest revolutionary susceptibilities be hurt). It was a deliberate policy
to raise his marshals and administrators above a petty struggle for
wealth and to bind them the more closely to the régime – in fact it
had the effect of encouraging his marshals to defend their fortunes
rather than Napoleon in 1814. Next came the official title of 'Grand'
conferred upon Napoleon in July 1807 – a title Lous XIV had enjoyed.
Then, in March 1808, the new nobility was formally established. After
the 'royal' family had been swamped with titles as Princes, with
wealth and the opportunity of new kingdoms, came Dukes with
a gift of 200,000 francs and inalienable hereditary lands worth
20,000 francs; Counts with 30,000 francs and land worth 10,000
francs; Barons with 15,000 francs and land at 5,000 francs. Below
came the Knights of the Empire with 3,000 francs but no grants of
land, although they and their sons could be ennobled (Napoleon
hoped the class of Knights would induce social mobility, but this did
not prove to be the case). They were abolished by decree in October
1814 by Louis XVIII. All Legionaries were Knights, so were men like
Joubert, Governor of the Bank of France, and David the Court
painter. There were some 1,600 Knights, about 7 per cent of them

from the old nobility: if any lacked for money, a grant was forth-coming.

Napoleon argued that his new nobility annihilated the old by fusing with it an open aristocracy of talent – and when old general Lefebvre with his washerwoman wife appeared as a Duke, it must have seemed so. Siéyès, author of *Qu'est ce que, le Tiers Etat?* (1789), emerged as a Count. Roederer, Chaptal and Merlin, author of the Law of Suspects (1794), were there, too, and they were joined in 1810 by Quinette, a regicide. Yet old revolutionaries were worried at the numbers of former aristocrats who joined the ranks of the new nobility. True, they gained no seigneurial rights; but they gained big estates – the old nobility recovered perhaps 30 per cent of its patri-mony, sometimes, as in the West, Central Massif and the Midi, recovering the entire estate. Land was a guarantee of social primacy: all social climbers sought it.

The new social system that was emerging rested on three points, the landed notables at the head of a still rural society, and who numbered nearly all the families who were to dominate France in the nineteenth century; the office holders; and the army. The office holders earned high salaries – the Paris Prefect had 30,000 francs, provincial prefects between 8,000 and 24,000. The Inspector of *Ponts et Chaussées* had 12,000 francs, a chief engineer 5,000, an Archbishop, 15,000 francs, a bishop 10,000 (the Church, for salary purposes, rank-ing with the Imperial civil service). Each division wore its own uni-form, and was proud to do so. Progress in careers was slow, but there was an excess of applications – perhaps in hopes of avoiding conscrip-tion! The Army, as always, had the lion's share, but it became more institutionalised under the Empire, so that promotion from the ranks, despite the huge losses, became rare: even after 1812 the opportuni-ties that had given commands of whole armies to young revolution-aries in their twenties did not recur – the campaigns of 1813 and 1814, even the Waterloo campaign, might have had a different outcome if Napoleon had returned to his grass roots in the hour of need. But by then the roots had rotted away. The Marshals did very well – quite apart from their gains by pillage – for they had huge estates granted them all over the Empire: Ney got 800,000 francs and Berthier 300,000 francs. Compardon's official list of Imperial nobility showed 59 per cent were soldiers, 22 per cent higher civil servants, 17 per cent notables and a mere 1·5 per cent from the professions – industry and commerce were scarcely recognised.

It was not enough to establish a new nobility as a *corps d'élite*; Napoleon contemplated grouping his subjects into a hierarchical structure, reviving the old corporations and putting workers under the patriarchal authority of their employers. It proved a dream only, this wish to atomise society, if not to serialise it – but it had its protagonists, and Mussolini was to attempt a similar reorganisation in fascist Italy. Within the Empire, however, the spirit of the Revolution was not dead. The new nobility bit no deeper than the self-interest of the new nobles. Those who rallied to the Empire endured its gaudiness and determined to lose none of their gains, while the returned *émigrés* hopefully awaited Napoleon's fall – some even formed secret societies, like the Congrégation de la Vièrge, to plan for action in favour of a legitimate monarchy. Napoleon had strengthened the old nobility without tying them to his régime: the Brumaireans he had deprived of the power they dreamt of wielding. The régime was losing its breadth of support. The marriage with Marie Louise (1810) and the birth of the King of Rome, heir to a great Empire, was no more than an incident in the Bonapartist calendar, it was not an experience for France such as the *journées* of the Revolution, or even the coup of Brumaire. As war continued, each new campaign repeating the stakes of tremendous triumph or destruction of the régime, a feeling of uncertainty walked abroad. The Lyons Chamber of Commerce boldly asserted:

> France cannot stand up to the all-out effort required by an indefinitely prolonged state of war. The extreme tension resulting from this effort exhausts the energies of the whole of society.

At the moment of its greatest height, the summer of 1812, the Empire was less firmly based than it had been in 1808. There was little likelihood of the nation rallying to this artificial creation in its hour of defeat. It was not to the Empire that France rallied during the Hundred Days.

[29] SOCIAL REFORM

The Codes
In the social reforms of the Consulate the dream of a State organised in a hierarchy of interest groups can dimly be perceived within the scheme of reform that consolidated the gains of the Revolution. The Civil Code (later called the Napoleonic Code) was the cornerstone of

the reforms – it was Napoleonic in name only. The Constituent Assembly had begun active work upon a common legal code in 1791, with the object of unifying and simplifying the French legal system. Five separate drafts had been produced by 1800 – Cambacérès being responsible for that of 1795 with its emphasis on Roman law. Napoleon was merely completing the process when he appointed a committee to prepare a draft code on 12 August 1800. The committee was well chosen; his own interventions in discussions were more publicised than important, save, perhaps, for the inclusion of divorce, the authority of the father and the subjugation of workers to employers. The draft was ready in January 1801, but the conflict with the Assemblies delayed its passage and it was not promulgated until 21 March 1804.

It was a remarkable compilation as a permanent basis for the legal system of France – and of other countries, too. Incredibly enough, it achieved the seemingly impossible task of consecrating the revolutionary achievement at the same time as promoting the authoritarian Napoleonic régime. Its crushing of feudal law and its assertion of the social principles of 1789 permitted it to sweep Europe as a symbol of Revolution and the harbinger of modern law, while it promoted the interests of the State, placing even the family in tutelage and regulating the manner of property inheritance. Bourgeois in outlook, it was generally silent about the poor and in proclaiming freedom of labour it abandoned the wage earner to the hazards of competition, repudiating the Jacobin ideal of 1793 of a citizen's right to a livelihood.

A series of other codes followed concerned with more specific subjects: the Code of Civil Procedure (1806) relying heavily upon the experience of the *ancien régime*; Criminal Procedure (1808) and the Penal Code (1810), both furthering arbitrary rule – the latter restoring the branding iron and collar and the loss of a hand for patricide. The Commercial Code (produced by a commission appointed in 1804) was not well adapted to the future needs of nineteenth-century capitalism, and was not a success. The Rural Code (the commission also appointed in 1804) was published after Napoleon's abdication in 1814 and proved a dead letter, while the Industrial Code was never published. It is as well to recall the other codes, lest a false impression is gained of the excellence of the institutions and methods of Napoleonic France.

The workers

The urban worker had demonstrated his potential political import-
ance among the *sans-culottes* of the Revolution. As yet the problem
of the urban proletariat had not reached the proportions of a genuine
social peril, but memories of the Terror and fears of the mob made an
anti-proletarian policy very acceptable. The *Loi le Chapelier* (1791)
was strengthened in April 1803, and from 1 December 1803 workers
were obliged to carry a *livret*, or work book, without which none could
be re-employed. That this was more suited to the craft tradition of the
eighteenth century than the conditions of nineteenth-century industry, where mobility of labour was more frequent, did not occur to the
administration. The purpose, after all, was partly a matter of public
control.

However, Napoleon was not deliberately hostile to the working
class and the *Conseil des Prud'hommes* (18 March 1806) for arbitration
and conciliation in labour disputes contained both employer and
worker representation. The *conseils* remained a significant part of
French labour law for over a century. Again, Napoleon intervened in
clear cases of exploitation, as in 1813, preventing the employment of
children under ten below ground in coal mines – thirty years before
an equivalent prohibition in England. Normally, however, Napoleon
placed the worker under the supervision of his employer, and the
Penal Code strengthened this policy. The worker himself made little
attempt to resist: he was more concerned to earn sufficient for life and
to avoid conscription. The workers (and the peasants, for that matter)
were the first to be conscripted in each levy. This had the effect of
raising wages in the towns because of consequent labour shortages – it
also resulted in numerous cases of self-mutilation (the common one
being the loss of the fingers of the right hand), especially after 1810.
(Prefects did what they could to keep desertion figures secret, but
they were a testimony to the declining popularity of the régime.) It
was sometimes difficult for employers to find apprentices – but the
livret proved useful in resisting forcible enlistment (Englishmen
preferred liberty – and suffered the brutalities of the press gang!).

Paris, of course, absorbed workers, and wage rates were higher than
elsewhere, rising as the régime continued. A stonemason earned
2.50 francs a day in 1801 and 3.50 in 1810, a locksmith 2.90 francs in
1800 and 4 francs in 1812. Artisans were better fed and dressed
(especially in the prosperous years 1807–10), but very few rose from
their class and all suffered acute distress in the crisis years after 1810,

when unemployment and riots returned and when the slogans of Babeuf reappeared in the streets: the conquest of Europe did not benefit the workers. On occasion (especially in the bad winter of 1811–12) there were whole armies of beggars on the move and Napoleon, who had a real fear of the mob, controlled prices in 1812 and imported quantities of grain from the Empire's European granaries, while the police were severe in repressing disorders, especially around Caen. In the Revolution such disturbances would have had serious political consequences: now they were merely social, for the *sans-culottes* had been destroyed by the Thermidorians, and the Imperial authorities ensured a supply of bread to the poor.

Napoleon made no secret of his fear of the poor, even if his recollection of the 'mob' at the Vendémiaire crisis was somewhat clouded:

> As long as I am here, these dregs of society shall never again be given a chance to stir, because they saw what stuff I am made of on 13 Vendémiaire and they know that I shall always be ready to crush them if I find them up to any tricks.

His followers were quick to take their cue: Réal, a former *enragé*, capped his apostasy by declaring (1812) 'The common people have never been properly put in their place'.

In the countryside, the peasant proprietorship that had been strengthened by the Revolution was guaranteed. Most peasants owned too little land to support themselves, and depended for survival upon customary rights of common pasture and gleaning. The 'agricultural revolution' was prevented. In the relief of poverty, however, there was little progress beyond the machinery set up under the Directory.

Education

Since April 1792, when Condorcet placed before the Legislative Assembly his project for educational reform, there had been much discussion. Some reforms had materialised, but lack of money stopped others. The *Ecoles Centrales* were launched in February 1795, one in each Department, with an original curriculum for secondary schools of the time, combining modern studies with sciences. Their impact, if short-lived, was perhaps as great as that of the Dissenting Academies in Britain. The Convention had provided for tertiary education by the *Grandes Ecoles* and *Ecoles Speciales* (1793) modelled on the *Ecole des ponts et chaussées* and *Ecole des mines* begun under Louis XV. Out of these grew the *Polytechnique* (1794), the *Ecole normale supérieure*, a special school for officers (1799), transferred to Saint-Cyr in 1808, the

Conservatoire, and a series of specialised schools of health, natural history and languages. Already there was in existence a coherent system of education: Napoleon had merely to strengthen and adjust it upon so firm a basis that it remained almost untouched until the riots of 1968.

The educational programme of the Consulate and Empire was outlined in Fourcroy's decree of May 1802. Elementary schools were left to local arrangements (little attention was paid to the schooling of the poor: in Napoleonic France equality did not mean equality of opportunity). Secondary education was closely organised on the basis of the Prytanée (formerly the Collège Louis-le-Grand, which the Revolution had preserved). The curriculum was to be centrally controlled and reverted to classical grammar, mathematics and French literature. The *écoles centrales*, of which Napoleon seems to have disapproved on the grounds that they encouraged independence of thought, were allowed to wither away. From the Year XI, each Appeal Court District was to have a state-supported lycée run on lines of military discipline. There were to be 6,400 bursaries (2,400 for sons of serving officers and administrators, 2,400 for the best pupils of the secondary schools – this excluded most of the poor, but opened a career to talent for the *petite bourgeoisie*). From 1804 the State appointed the teachers. Private seminaries and secondary schools were permitted by special authority; clerical schools were permitted and only restricted when they competed with the lycées.

Napoleon had no illusions about education. He wanted a means of directing the political and moral outlook of the next generation, and of producing the officers and obedient administrators he required (he had no interest in the education of girls beyond training them to be good wives and mothers). Hence his desire to centralise at the expense of academic freedom. Fourcroy himself complained, 'The State cannot form a Nation: it rests on uncertain and vague bases'.

The lycées were slow to open. By 1808 only thirty-seven out of the forty-five planned had opened and they were not popular because of the discipline and the high fees. Clericals opened rival schools which were cheaper. To ensure the government retained a monopoly of education, the Imperial University was established (May 1806, enforced September 1808) to control the whole of French education, schools and teachers. It was, in effect, a ministry of education that controlled all schools except the Collège de France, the great revolutionary institute that preserved its independence.

At the head of the University was a Grand Master who was permitted to correspond directly with the Emperor. Fourcroy was disappointed of his hopes, and saw the clerical Fontanes appointed. The University's authority was not immediately effective – there were not enough inspectors and the University's degrees were not made compulsory for teachers until 1815. Clerical influence grew rapidly – some heads of lycées were priests – and the government was prepared to limit the number of seminaries and require the attendance of children at lycées in 1811 when the conflict with the Pope (see page 120) became a problem. Private schools lost some 5,000 pupils, but the colleges and lycées had only 44,000 in 1813 – a very small proportion of the national age group and a shrewd comment on the contemporary impact of Napoleon's education policy.

In technical education, the creation of the first schools of Arts and Crafts is balanced by the suppression of the Directory's Central Schools. In February 1800, Destutt de Tracy presented a Report urging a two-tier system: primary schools and apprenticeships for working-class children, secondary schools and specialist schools for the professional classes (the system that emerged unplanned in late nineteenth-century Britain). It was this Report that led to the suppression of the Central Schools (1802) and the consequent widening gap between artisans and professional education. The former, however, were not entirely neglected, for Chaptal founded the Society for the Encouragement of National Industry (1801) to assist technical education, and it was supported by some significant citizens like Monge and Neufchâteau. During the Hundred Days (1815) it assisted Carnot, then Minister of the Interior, to establish a commission (27 April 1815) to enquire into new teaching methods and try them out in a special school. The *Société pour l'instruction élémentaire*, formed on the eve of Waterloo, played a big role in nineteenth-century education. The Hundred Days (see page 195) was no simple military parenthesis. There were also schemes to assist technical education in agriculture (Neufchâteau planned an experimental farm in 1801), in chemistry at Lyons, and a college for applied sciences, moved to Châlons in 1808, and another at Beaupréau (1804), moved to Angers during the Hundred Days, which often received special commissions from the Emperor himself to devise new explosives and shells. There were other colleges for civil engineering, art and architecture – but lack of money proved a serious check upon their development.

[30] CENSORSHIP AND PROPAGANDA

No one was more aware than Napoleon of the value of propaganda: the Revolution had demonstrated the power of the press, and Metternich regarded Napoleon's Bulletins to the Grand Army as a new dimension in war, worth an army by themselves. But if Napoleon recognised the utility of propaganda for maintaining morale whether in the army or at home, he was equally well aware of the need to control the press lest Opposition views receive publicity. There was nothing new in censorship, and freedom of the press was already limited at the time of Brumaire. As in other respects, Napoleon was simply perpetuating the existing state of affairs with rather more efficiency.

Anxious that free discussion should not be allowed (for he subscribed to the view that the Revolution had begun in the *salons*), he kept close watch on intellectual circles, especially the Institute, and closed its classes in moral and political science. In the *salons* police informers were active and lawyers were kept under surveillance – they were obliged to register in 1804 and did not regain control of professional discipline until 1810. Some authors were refused permission to publish.

The number of newspapers in Paris was reduced to thirteen under the Consulate, and after August 1801 they were forbidden to comment on religion or on ministerial action. A daily resumé of journals, pamphlets and books was compiled by Ripault after July 1801 for Napoleon's personal use. Censorship extended to the theatre where all presentations had to be officially authorised. In 1807 theatres were reduced to four large and four secondary ones in Paris, all of which had to contribute to the Opéra, five other big towns were allowed two companies and fourteen allowed one, while the rest of the Empire was divided into twenty-five districts each with one or two travelling companies. He was as anxious to use the power of the press himself as to deny its use to others. After 1805 newspapers had to submit their accounts to the police and pay a third of their profits towards the expense of police surveillance. Journals were frequently closed – like *Mercure* in 1807 after one of Châteaubriand's articles – and after 1807 the provincial press had to take its political articles from the official *Moniteur* only, while the police increased their practice of inspiring articles. By 1809 only one journal was permitted per Department.

New restrictions on publishers came in 1805 and Fouché added a special department to his Press Office for censoring books. In 1810, with prefects exercising an official censorship over journals, books and plays, 97 out of the 157 Paris printing houses closed and booksellers had to be licensed – but the censorship proved so prudish and at times silly, that Napoleon himself restricted it to suppressing libels. Napoleon was no blind censor, such as was to be found in Europe at the time; his censorship had a simple political purpose – it extended beyond his frontiers, for he regarded Görres's *Rhenische Merkur* as 'the Fifth Power in Europe' (the victorious Prussians were to suppress it in January 1816). Much has been made of Napoleon's suppression of opinion – especially by those who suffered directly, like Châteaubriand, expelled in 1807, but elected to the Academy in 1811, Mme Recamier and Mme de Staël whose *De L'Allemagne* (1810) was suppressed and who attracted a literary court of her own at Coppet. The censorship, however, was not necessarily worse than elsewhere in Europe.

Whilst suppressing opposition views, Napoleon was active in promoting his own praise. He had begun early, with the *Courier de l'armée d'Italie* (1797), issued without the Directory's permission, which promoted morale as well as republican views at the moment when moderate and royalist views were gaining favour in Paris. Wherever his armies marched a paper appeared – the *Journal de Malte* (1798–1801) and the *Courier de L'Egypte*, for example. Later, the *Moniteur* was sufficient, although he continued irregularly to publish *Bulletins de la Grande Armée* which frequently proved as fine an exercise in the perversion of truth as any piece of propaganda. His technique backfired when Bulletin XXIX (December 1812) actually admitted the collapse of the Moscow campaign, which was thought to be even graver than it was because it was the first reverse that had been reported.

The critical and literary press was much freer, especially the magazines produced for priests and women. Like the Revolution before him, Napoleon made full use of painters, sculptors and architects to add glory to the régime and to present Napoleon as a hero. He was anxious to promote the arts, although later critics have found his taste suspect, accusing him of equating quality with size – however, the decree authorising the Théatre Française was signed in Moscow in 1812. It is still popular to castigate the Napoleonic period in France as one of low achievement in the arts, and to attribute this to censorship: it is well to recall that censorship was present throughout Europe. Napoleon was a keen patron of architecture and town planning. The

Convention had planned commemorative buildings in Paris: Napoleon constructed them, and went far beyond their ideas. In central
Paris the quays were extended and new bridges constructed, open
spaces cleared around Nôtre-Dame, the Chatelet, the Carrousel, and
wide boulevardes were begun for the rue de Rivoli (Percier and
Fontanis were the architects and received great praise – Napoleon
chose well here), the rue de la Paix, and the rue de Castiglione.
Brongniart built the Bourse, and Bélanger Les Halles – a remarkable
and forward-looking building; Pierre Vignon continued the building
of the Madeleine, conceived as a temple of national glory; the Ven-
dôme column was erected and the Arc de Triomphe begun (1806) by
Chalgrin. The period, indeed, was remarkable for its willingness to
experiment with new materials, especially iron, and pointed the way
of the future: there was no lack of invention or inspiration among
architects.

Successful in architecture, Napoleon gathered around him a group
of prominent artists. He lacked the money and the means of twentieth-
century dictators to use art as an extensive propaganda instrument,
although Dinon, Director General of Museums, did his best. Canvases
by David, Gros, Géricault, and Prud'hon testify to the results.
Caricature (as in England) did well, both favourable and hostile to the
Emperor. In sculpture, Canova dominated. In music the Conservatoire under Bernard Samethe, with subsidies for talented pupils, and
the coveted *Prix de Rome* (1803), established France in the forefront,
even if the major European figures were German. If Napoleon's
régime was as artistically sterile as some critics would have us believe,
it is odd that it should have nurtured a composer like Berlioz. There
was a grand decennial award of thirty-five prizes for achievement in
the arts, on 9 November 1810 (the anniversary of Brumaire).

In the arts, generally, the Napoleonic period was one of vitality and
experimentation: paintings owed much to David, the official court
painter, to whom Delacroix could look back as a master in 1860. The
massive canvases of battles, and the propaganda pictures of Napoleon and his family, were to do much for the later Napoleonic Legend.

[31] LATER CONFLICT WITH THE CHURCH

The Concordat worked well enough: there were some problems of
adjustment between the non-jurors and constitutional priests (many
of whom had to suffer frequent social and professional snubs), but no

serious incidents. The position of the lower clergy improved during the Empire, and at the Restoration the Church stood on a strong basis. What provoked dispute was the political position of the Papal States, for within France the Church enjoyed conspicuous advantages, with its own seminaries exempted from conscription and the local clergy and church (from 1810) paid for by the commune. In return the bishops gave good service, and accepted the new catechism of 1806 stressing the duty of obedience to the Emperor and the duty of conscription. The Prefects left them alone, knowing that Portalis and Napoleon himself would probably side with the bishop against the prefect. But a fissure was opened by the Pope's protest at the French occupation of Ancona (1805) to forestall an Austro–Russian landing.

After Austerlitz, Napoleon responded by requiring the Pope to join his system unconditionally, referring specifically to Charlemagne, 'Your Holiness is sovereign of Rome, but I am its Emperor.' Nevertheless, the Pope objected to the Civil Code being enforced in Italy (1806) since it contained civil divorce; relations snapped when Miollis occupied Rome (1808) and the Papal States were annexed (May 1809) in order to enforce the Continental System. The Pope excommunicated Napoleon (June 1809). Napoleon had misjudged his man: Pius VII regarded the Papa lStates as an essential adjunct of the Papacy, and was prepared for martyrdom. Imprisoned at Savona from July 1809, he remained obdurate. The Sacred Council was summoned to Paris, where most cardinals accepted salaries from Napoleon.

The excommunication had no great practical effect – it did not impede the Austrian marriage, for example. But the Pope refused to invest Napoleon's candidates for bishoprics, and there were thirty vacancies by 1809. A bishop was too valuable a civil servant to be lost and Napoleon determined to have no nonsense. In November 1809, Napoleon appointed an Ecclesiastical Commission: he dissolved it (January 1810) when it demanded a General Council of the Church without agreeing to install his candidates. In February 1810 he required by Senatus-consultum all French clergy and each new Pope to acknowledge his power over the Church through the Gallican Articles of 1682. When, in protest, thirteen of the twenty-seven cardinals in Paris refused to attend the marriage with Marie Louise, he exiled them and instructed his nominated bishops to assume their duties.

The bishops were caught between the twin fires of Gallicanism and

Ultramontanism, and in February 1812, Napoleon annulled the Concordat, summoning his prisoner, Pius VII, to Fontainebleau. Bishops who sided with the Pope were required to resign or go into exile, priests lost their stipends, refractory seminarists lost their scholarships and were conscripted and many of the episcopal schools · and minor seminaries were closed. The breach with the Pope now drove the Church once more into the ranks of counter-revolution at the very moment when the campaign to condemn Napoleon as Anti-Christ seemed to be gaining success in Russia. But the régime remained firm: despite clerical revival under the Consulate and Empire, there was not that breach that the Civil Constitution had brought. Many clergy were not prepared to sacrifice their livelihood, and the people, for the most part, remained unmoved.

Returning from Moscow, Napoleon met the Pope at Fontainebleau on 25 January 1813. They agreed upon a new Concordat granting, in effect, Napoleon rights of investiture. It was published without Papal ratification in February. The Pope formally withdrew his consent in March. The breach remained open. But now there was less enthusiasm for Napoleon, even if there was no more for the Pope. The future of the Empire was in the balance. In December, after the Battle of the Nations (Leipzig), Napoleon ruefully offered to restore the Papal States unconditionally, and restored the Pope to Rome, which he entered on 24 May, six weeks after Napoleon's abdication. Napoleon had been defeated in his attempt to convert the Church into a depart-ment of State: it emerged more cohesive and centralised, and much more ultramontane in order to assist the restored Bourbons. But it did not carry public opinion with it.

Napoleon's despotism neither seems to have surprised nor distressed the French people. It was, after all, not out of line with the experience of each of the major contemporary states. It also consolidated the major gains of the Revolution within a basically firm administration. He was able to spread these gains beyond France, although the suppression of feudalism was tempered beyond the Empire by his relations with local nobility – thus the *corvée* remained in South Germany and in the Grand Duchy of Warsaw. The Napoleonic despotism consolidated the new social groupings already emergent in the France of 1799 – a bourgeois and peasant society in which the urban worker had yet to establish his place.

Further Reading

Apart from the general lives of Napoleon, the period of his career outside of France and during the Consulate is also dealt with by Narbonne, *La Diplomatie du Directoire et Bonaparte* (Paris, 1951), Farrero, *The Gamble* (London, 1961) and P. Bessand-Massenet, *Le 18 Brumaire* (Paris, 1965). The domestic policy of Napoleon is studied in Godechot, *Les Institutions de la France sous la Révolution et l'Empire* (2 vols, Paris, 1951); Ponteil, *Napoléon Ier et l'organisation autoritaire de la France* (Paris, 1965); A. Fugier, *La Révolution française et l'Empire napoléonien* (Paris, 1954); J. Bourdon, *La Constitution de l'an VIII* (Paris, 1942) and B. Schwartz (ed.) *The Code Napoléon and the Common Law World* (New York, 1956). The administration in particular is studied in J. Savant, *Les Préfets de Napoléon* (Paris, 1958); P. de Polnay, *Napoleon's Police* (W. H. Allen, London, 1970); R. Cobb, *The Police and the People; French Popular Protest 1789–1820.* (Oxford University Press, 1970); and L. Chevalier, in *Les Parisians* (Paris, 1967) gives a human treatment of the 'Mob'. Social life is also revealed in Robiquet, *La vie quotidienne au temps de Napoléon* (English translation, 1962) and the arts in Hautecoeur, *L'art sous la Révolution et l'Empire* (Paris, 1953). The religious question that featured large in his home and foreign policies, is covered in M. Rheinhard, *Réligion, Révolution et contre-Révolution* (Paris, 1960); H. Walsh, *The Concordat of 1801* (Columbia University Press, 1933); E. E. Y. Hales, *Revolution and Papacy, 1789–1846* (University of Notre Dame Press, New York, 1960) and *Napoleon and the Pope* (Eyre and Spottiswoode, 1962) and A. Latreille, *L'Église catholique et la Révolution française*, Vol II (Paris, 1950).

PRINCIPAL EVENTS, 1799–1815

1799.   (An VIII) 18/19 Brumaire
        December. Promulgation of Constitution of Year VIII
1800.   January. Constitution approved by plebiscite
        March. Reform of Judiciary begun
        August. Committee appointed to prepare final draft of Legal Code
        December. Pacification of La Vendée
        24 December. Assassination attempt on Napoleon, the 'infernal machine'
1801.   January *Senatus-consultum* device to overrule Assemblies. Draft Code
        ready, but not yet published. Society for the Encouragement of National
        Industry (Chaptal)
        July. Consalvi signs the Concordat
        August. Increased censorship of the press
1802.   Central Schools suppressed
        8 April. Legislative body passes Concordat
        26 April. Amnesty for *émigrés*
        May. Fourcroy's decree on education
        19 May. Legion of Honour established
        4 August. Napoleon approved Consul for Life by plebiscite.
        Constitution of Year X
1803.   April. *Loi le Chapelier* strengthened
        1 December. The *livret* enforced. Prix de Rome begun
1804.   21 March. Promulgation of Legal Code. Execution of Duc d'Enghien.
        Commission to produce Rural Code and Commercial Code
        18 May. Declaration of Empire. Constitution of Year XII approved by
        plebiscite
        21 December. Napoleon crowned in Paris. School teachers to be appointed
        by the state
1805.   1 January. Revolutionary calendar abolished. Further censorship of the
        press
        Pope protests at French occupation of Ancona
1806.   18 March. Conseil des Prud'hommes
        May. Imperial University established
        August. Senatus-consultum allows Napoleon to grant hereditary fiefs. Arc
        de Triomphe begun. Code of Civil Procedure
1807.   July. Napoleon has the title Grand conferred upon him. Severe censorship
        of theatres
1808.   March. New Imperial University formally established September. Decrees
        of Imperial University enforced. Code of Criminal Procedure
1809.   May. Breach in relations with Papacy. Papal States annexed
        June. Napoleon excommunicated
        July. Pope imprisoned at Savona
1810.   April. Marriage with Marie Louise. Napoleon assumes right to appoint
        bishops. Further censorship measures. Penal Code issued
1811.   March. Birth of King of Rome. Full censorship and arbitrary arrest
        restored

1812.   Control of food prices
        February. Concordat annulled. Decree establishing Théâtre Française
        issued from Moscow
1813.   January. Concordat of Fontainebleau fails to heal breach with the Pope
        March. Pope formally withdraws consent to new Concordat
        Employment of children under ten below ground declared illegal
1814.   6 April. Napoleon abdicates
        24 May. Pope re-enters Rome
        October. Imperial University abolished by royal decree. Rural Code
        issued
1815.   March–June. The Hundred Days
        June. Society for Instruction in Elementary Education. Degrees of the
        Imperial University (restored) declared an essential qualification for
        schoolmasters

PART V
Caesarism

[32] SCHEMES FOR EXPANSION

The Peace of Amiens in March 1802 was joyfully welcomed: there were, however, among politicians and merchants, many who doubted whether the peace would last for long. Tourists flooded into France, but in Britain particularly dark rumours that Napoleon intended the peace merely to serve as a breathing space before another onslaught were soon current. Merchants found that their entry to the French market was not much eased by the peace and they feared a return of French competition in the colonial markets. Commercial rivalry lay behind much of the struggle between Britain and France since the days of Louis XIV: it lay behind the renewal of the war in 1803. Indeed, it is probably sounder to regard the outbreak of war as a further incident in the struggle for commercial primacy, rather than as a step to world domination by a tyrant consumed by uncontrollable ambition.

For a decade Britain had been unchallenged in the colonial markets: now France could renew her challenge. It was not simply a race to open new markets, for France was determined to re-create her Caribbean empire. Already the West Indies were no longer the principal source of Imperial trade, still Britain remained peculiarly sensitive to any challenge there. Before the peace, General Leclerc had led an expedition to Santo Domingo, where Toussaint L'Ouverture had established a republic in the best traditions of the Revolution. He was arrested in June 1802, and died in France (1803).

That France should seek to recapture her colonies was not un-expected, but Britain feared Napoleon had ideas for a major expansion – an occupation of Louisiana (acquired from Spain), for example.

Rumour had it that Victor's army, now in Holland, was destined for this task. Both Britain and America were alarmed. Fortune favoured them, however, for the renewal of the war in Europe, as well as the cost and distances involved in expeditions to the West Indies and beyond, prevented French colonial schemes from coming to fruition. Yellow fever, which had already decimated the British forces in the 1790s, took a savage toll of French forces in the Caribbean (including Leclerc himself), and the French, in blithe contravention of the principles of 1789, but in response to the demands of planters who found a willing advocate in Joséphine, revived slavery in the colonies (20 May 1802). The immediate revolts in Santo Domingo and Guadaloupe reduced the isolated French forces to a series of wretched besieged garrisons.

Meanwhile, recognising the immediate impossibility of sending Victor, and fearing a juncture of Britain and America against the French, Napoleon decided to sell Louisiana to America in 1803 for 80 million francs. It was a statesmanlike move that opened the possibility of co-operation with America against Britain, and wiped out French debts to America. Louisiana could not be defended. But Napoleon had not given up the idea of a revived French empire in the Americas; it was one of his purposes in securing Spain as a full ally in December 1804. Britain, of course, took full advantage of the situation and gave active help to Miranda and other republican leaders in Latin America, and in 1806 attacked both Venezuela and Buenos Aires.

The Americas were drawn into the Napoleonic struggle. So was the East. One school of historians interpret Napoleon's policy almost in terms of his being mesmerised by the ambition to become an oriental potentate. It is often instanced as evidence for paranoia and for his unrealistic ideas. But it was in line with the best traditions of eighteenth-century imperialism: what the Elder Pitt had achieved, it was not unreasonable for Napoleon to attempt. If the Mediterranean were converted into a French lake, then the prosperous trade of the Levant would be France's, and Britain's position in India would be threatened. It would be naïve to argue that Napoleon was determined to march to India to defeat Britain upon the Ganges because he could not reach the Thames. Similarly, Napoleon remained too much a realist to be seduced by ideas of outshining Alexander the Great. There was great wealth to be had, and the trade was not far beyond his grasp.

His schemes are clearest so far as the Mediterranean is concerned.

A succession of pacts linked the local rulers with France – the Pasha of Tripoli (1801), the Bey of Tunis (1802), the Bey of Algiers (1802) after a series of threats, and in 1802 Turkey made peace, although the Porte continued to be concerned at French intrigue in the Peloponnese and among the Serbs in Jamina. Meanwhile, Ruffin began restoring French trade links with the Levant, and in August 1802 Colonel Sebastiani was sent to Egypt and Syria. Beyond the Mediterranean, Cavaignac was sent to Muscat (Persian Gulf) and Decaen to India (March 1803) where, for four years, as Captain General of French Affairs, he exercised a considerable influence in the East in the best traditions of eighteenth-century empire-builders. Madagascar had already been reconnoitred in 1801.

Naturally, Britain assumed these moves pointed to further conflict over India and she held on to Malta, as much to retain her presence in the Mediterranean as to have a useful bargaining counter. The British press was quite right to be suspicious of Napoleon's intentions: war was coming, it was merely a matter of timing. Napoleon seems to have been thinking in terms of 1804 and it was a mistake to publish in the *Moniteur* (30 January 1803) Sebastiani's report on the situation in Egypt, indicating the ease with which the territory could be recaptured. Britain reacted vigorously to what appeared to be blatant provocation and, more significant from the French point of view, Russia began to show anxiety at a renewed French presence in the Levant.

Already Hawkesbury, the British Foreign Secretary, had approached Russia. 'Our policy must seek to use these aggressions,' he noted, 'to build a defence system of alliance for the future, together with Russia and Austria.' The Tsar agreed to further delay Britain's withdrawal from Malta, the crucial clause of the Treaty of Amiens. Napoleon demanded that Britain evacuate the island, as the Treaty required, and by May 1803, an open breach appeared when Whitworth, the British ambassador, left Paris. There was no formal declaration of war; Britain seized French merchantmen at sea and Napoleon interned Englishmen still in France.

The provocation raised by French policy outside of Europe merely added to similar acts on the continent. Holland remained occupied (ostensibly because Malta was not evacuated), as were Naples and the Papal States. In August 1802 Napoleon annexed Elba; in September, Piedmont; in October, Parma. Switzerland was reoccupied and became a satellite state in 1803. French influence in South Germany was greatly increased by the Imperial Recess of 25 February 1803, and by the spring of 1803, it was already clear that a new struggle was about to be launched, directed more particularly now against Britain. The question of Malta was merely an excuse. But as yet there was no hint that the war would be of a different nature from the Revolutionary Wars that had just ended: Talleyrand, however, was aware of the changing nature of the struggle: 'the first cannon shot could suddenly bring into being a Gallic Empire,' he observed.

The rupture of the Peace of Amiens was deliberately provoked by Napoleon (although it came too soon for his plans). French commercial expansion beyond Europe played a vital rôle in the provocation, and it was clear that Napoleon was challenging Britain's imperial primacy: but Napoleon was too much of a pragmatist to be seduced by dreams of an oriental empire. His policy was realistic; French expansion beyond Europe was to be for the recovery of the empire that Louis XV had lost to Britain. It was still within the tradition of eighteenth-century imperialism.

[33] DESTRUCTION OF THIRD COALITION

The war that now began was to result in a French defeat of Europe within a matter of months and to launch a new pattern in European diplomacy that was to dominate the Great Powers for fifty years.

With Britain, the war dragged on for a couple of years much in the old style, Britain blockading the French ports and recapturing Caribbean islands. Shortage of money partly prevented France retaliating, and Gaudin, Minister of Finance, restored indirect taxes through the Excise Bureau (25 February 1804). The rates were low but there was vigorous opposition for it seemed to be a denial of Revolutionary principle. 'If anyone revolts,' Napoleon remarked, 'I will have five or six rebels hanged, and everyone else will pay.' Several merchant firms were badly caught out by the renewal of war and there were some bankruptcies. Meanwhile, France's allies were called upon for supplies of men and materials, while Mortier seized Hanover and the mouths of the Elbe (May 1803), thereby restricting Britain's trade.

Unable to provoke successful rebellion in Ireland, Napoleon determined on invasion of Britain and assembled a huge army at Boulogne, officially designated the Army of England on 2 December 1803 – although it was always ready to swoop on Europe if necessary.

Napoleon's conception of combined operations revealed that he did not understand the difference between land and sea fighting. He contemplated at first a simple ferrying of the army until he calculated the number of barges needed and discovered that the 1,700 collected at Boulogne would have taken two whole days simply to leave the harbour. Consequently, he was forced into a naval war in order to seize control of the Channel for long enough to cover the transport of the army. Preparations were continually delayed, hindered as much by lack of ships as by the deaths of Bruix and Latouche-Tréville, admirals whom the British had good reason to fear. But the complex series of naval manoeuvres that were to worry the British and to lead to Trafalgar had begun in March 1805. Nelson's destruction of the combined Franco–Spanish fleet on 21 October would have ended the invasion scare had not the Third Coalition obliged Napoleon to adopt a complete change of plan.

Ever since the renewal of war with Britain in 1803, diplomatic activity had been very great. There was no eagerness to resume the struggle, but Napoleon's provocative actions helped to harden opinion and to cement a third coalition, which Pitt endeavoured to consolidate on the basis of British gold. Napoleon's position was critical. At home a rising financial crisis (see page 47) disturbed the régime, and abroad the declaration of the Empire had been badly received. The execution of the Duc d'Enghien had provided a cause about which Europe failed to unite, but the likelihood of a coalition grew as the naval war with Britain dragged on. Napoleon needed an ally in Europe in order to control the situation. For a moment Prussia might have enjoyed this status, but she was so hesitant that the choice passed to Austria or Russia. To divide Europe between France and one of these two now became the object of French policy. Napoleon and Talleyrand disagreed upon which power to choose. Napoleon thought increasingly of a personal domination of the continent – a domination that became a reality after 1805. Talleyrand was more traditional, putting his trust in a balancing of powers in the interests of France. He preferred Austria, for generations a leader of European diplomacy and a centre of culture: Russia was not wholly European and a less familiar figure in the intricacies of traditional diplomacy.

Napoleon certainly considered an Austrian alliance, but rejected it for a number of reasons. In the first place the unhappy alliance of 1756 was still green in the memory; secondly, Austria's position in

Central Europe was already weakened, and would be weakened
further in any division of the continent with France. Thirdly, Austria
would not contemplate becoming merely a power of Eastern Europe
unless she were crushingly defeated first; she would never give up her
traditional rôle in Europe as Talleyrand's scheme required. Consequently, he rejected Talleyrand's advice and sought an alliance with
Russia. It was an alliance he had lost when Tsar Paul had been
murdered (see page 87). Rostopchin, who had been in charge of the
negotiations on the Russian side in 1800, had sown some fertile seeds:
he had argued that the Ottoman Empire would not long survive,

> all measures taken by it now are nothing more than medicine given
> to a hopelessly sick man whose real condition his doctors do not
> wish to tell him.

Rostopchin had outlined a partition of the Empire; Russia to have
the Balkans, France to have Egypt and Austria and Prussia to have
compensation. There was even the hint of a joint expedition to India,
Russia crossing from Persia, France from Egypt. If the scheme was not
entirely to his taste, it now became the basis of Napoleon's approaches
to Russia: it would give him a free hand in Europe, turn Russia
towards the East and isolate Britain.

Talleyrand persisted in his advice – indeed, that Napoleon rejected
it may have provoked the wily politician to seek ways of freeing himself from Napoleon. On 17 October 1805, at the moment when the
Austrian army was surrendering, he wrote a memorandum from
Strasbourg putting his points clearly. France, he argued, was at odds
with the other great powers of Europe. She was the natural rival of
Britain in the colonial and commercial field, of Austria in Europe, and
of Russia so long as she contemplated absorbing the Ottoman
Empire. So far as Europe was concerned, Britain could easily co-
operate with Austria and Russia against France, and therefore
France should aim to ally with Austria in order to oppose Russia over
the Ottoman Empire. This would turn Russia towards expansion in
Persia and central Asia, away from the Balkans, and thus divide
Russia from Britain because of the latter's fears for her position in
India. It was a shrewd assessment of the situation that might well
have secured a French hegemony – he even appended a draft treaty
with Austria, turning her to the Balkans away from Central Europe.
The scheme was similar to one already suggested by Herzburg in
1787 and it presented the issues that were to dominate diplomacy

until the First World War. But Napoleon had made up his mind: if it was necessary to fight Russia to secure her alliance, it would be cheap at the price.

Russian policy, by the nature of things, was dominated by the Tsar himself. A nervous instability made Alexander I a victim of extremes of passion and peculiarly susceptible to his advisors, who changed rather frequently. He had never freed himself from feelings of guilt over the murder of his father, and the difficulties of conducting policy often led to his violently changing course. At times he was much influenced by liberal ideas – the trauma of 1812 led him even to talk of freeing the serfs – and the wave of religiosity that afflicted aristocratic circles swept him along. But he was never able for long to free himself from reactionary court circles, who insisted upon his maintaining traditional tsardom and called to their aid the prevailing mysticism that the Romantic Revival had made so popular. It was not long before he was thinking of himself as a new Messiah and identifying Napoleon by numerology as Antichrist. Anna Pavlona knew she would strike a responsive chord when she wrote in 1805,

> Russia must save Europe ... The Tsar will fulfil his vocation and crush the hydra of revolution which has become more terrible than ever in the person of this murderer and villain [Napoleon]! We alone must avenge the blood of the just one. [Enghien]

The Enghien affair had affected Alexander badly, for Napoleon had not been slow to remind him of his own connexion with his father's death and to argue that Alexander would have done the same as he. But the prospect of expansion into the Ottoman Empire appealed greatly to him, and Czartoryski had produced a partition scheme of his own when he became Russian foreign minister in 1804. Such ideas, involving penetration into the Balkans and round the Black Sea into the Levant, were in opposition to the schemes of both Talleyrand and Napoleon. As yet he would not serve as Napoleon's willing vassal: rather, he saw himself as the arbiter of Europe.

It was this desire to play the major part on the European stage, quite as much as fear of Napoleon's intentions in the Mediterranean and the Levant, that led Alexander to favour an English alliance in 1804. He proposed a general revision of European frontiers. Pitt was more interested in securing an ally to turn Napoleon's attention away from invasion and to deprive France of Belgium and the Rhineland. Negotiations at last led to a formal treaty in April 1805, providing that Britain should pay one and a half million pounds for every 100,000 troops put in the field against Napoleon, and for an Anglo–Russian force to go to Corfu to attack Naples. After the defeat of France, Holland should have Belgium and Prussia the Rhineland, while some attempt should be made to restore Louis 'XVIII'.

Pitt's horizons, clearly, were limited by self interest. It was the common failing of all the coalitions hitherto; the Third was no exception. As yet, the appeals of Gustavus IV for a European crusade against Napoleon 'the beast' were regarded as the prattlings of a fool dreaming of the days of Charles XII. Under Frederick William III Prussia might have altered the course of history had she taken any firm line of policy: both Britain and France sought her alliance. But the fear of isolation caused Prussia to break off negotiations with France in April 1804, when Hardenberg became foreign minister, and after the Enghien affair a defensive alliance was signed with Russia (May 1804). This was as far as Hardenberg could go in terms of commitment.

Austria was the obvious focal point for a European coalition, for she had lost her hegemony in central Europe. But her recovery after the peace of Lunéville had been slow, hindered both by rapid inflation and a bad harvest in 1804. The powerful Count Colloredo argued for peace, while Cobenzl, the foreign minister, fearing that Napoleon's lack of progress against Britain might lead him to attack in Europe, hoped for an accommodation with France (though not on Talleyrand's terms). But there was a strong war party in Vienna, fostered by the British and supported by the pro-Russian Stadion and the ambassador to Saxony, Metternich (who feared that an agreement between France and Russia would leave Austria helpless). The growth of French influence in Italy was a further point of conflict, and feelers had been put out in 1803 for an alliance with Britain and Russia. The declaration of the Empire in France, with its implication of French influence over Europe coming so soon after the Imperial Recess of 1803, presaged the formal ending of the Holy Roman Empire and thus necessitated action on Austria's part. When he recognised Napoleon's new title Francis demanded a reciprocal recognition as Emperor of Austria. Cobenzl, fearful now of French ambitions and having failed to obtain anything from Prussia, signed a defensive pact with Russia on 6 November 1804.

Aware that the Imperial title would offend Austria, Napoleon had taken the precaution of writing to Francis before he declared northern

Italy an hereditary kingdom, assuring him that 'Italy' would never be united with France. Although Napoleon had declared himself President of the Italian Republic (January 1802), he seems to have intended making his brother, Joseph, king there. Joseph, however, hoping to succeed him in France, refused, and so, by a senatus-consultum of 18 March 1805, Napoleon became King of Italy, nominating Eugène de Beauharnais as Viceroy. He was crowned at Milan in May. On 6 June, on the advice of Salicetti, the Ligurian Republic was absorbed into France. Expansion was continuing. On 17 June Austria agreed to join the Anglo–Russian alliance, with no declared aims beyond depriving France of her recent gains and re-adjusting the balance between the powers.

Both sides redoubled their efforts to draw Prussia out of her neutrality. At Berlin, the war party, strengthened by the romantic attachment between Queen Louisa and Alexander, could not yet get Frederick William to allow the passing of Swedish and Russian troops over Prussian territory. In August Napoleon offered him Hanover, allowing him to occupy it after Bernadotte's troops had moved south: Prussia had declined to join the coalition. The South German States, fearful of Austria, joined Napoleon in September, forming the Fürstenbund against both Austria and Prussia. But in Italy, on 10 September, Maria Caroline of Naples concluded an alliance with Russia, and Napoleon, needing all available troops, withdrew to occupy Etruria and Ancona, ignoring the protests of the Pope. An Anglo–Russian invasion was daily expected. When it came, however, on 19 November, the situation had changed, for the coalition faced defeat, and Trafalgar could not save it.

Austria was unready for war and the principal Russian forces under Kutuzov did not arrive until November. Although she invaded Bavaria on 11 September, Austria's principal attention was directed towards Italy, where Masséna warily faced the Archduke Charles with a disorderly Lombardy at his back. The campaign, however, was decided in Germany, where Napoleon moved with incredible speed and precision, desperate to prevent the Russians joining the Austrian forces. Crossing the Rhine on 25 September, his army corps were on the Danube by 7 October and Mack, out-manoeuvred, surrendered at Ulm on 20 October. Talleyrand offered Austria compensation in the Balkans, but she refused to leave the coalition. Napoleon hastened on to engage the remains of the Austrian forces and the Russians, fearful lest Prussia be drawn into the struggle – for Alexander was at Berlin on 25 October. Frederick William signed a convention with Russia at Potsdam on 3 November and presented Napoleon with an ultimatum in the form of peace proposals on the basis of Lunéville, or Prussian intervention in the war.

Napoleon simulated a retreat. Kutuzov was not to be drawn, but Alexander, hoping to snatch the crown of saviour of Europe, moved with superior forces against Napoleon at Austerlitz on 2 December 1805. The result was Napoleon's most complete victory. Austria signed a truce on 6 December, and the humiliated Alexander withdrew towards Russia.

The coalition had been destroyed before Prussia's entry. Austria was at Napoleon's mercy, and he strengthened his alliance with South Germany by compelling Prussia to cede Neuchâtel–Ansbach to Bavaria in exchange for Berg and to annex Hanover, thus offending Britain. Prussia had been punished for dabbling. Francis, for his part, dismissed Cobenzl and Colloredo and signed the Treaty of Pressburg (26 December) yielding up Venetia, Dalmatia and the Tyrol to the Kingdom of Italy. Here was French expansionism, and yet, by a curious survival of eighteenth-century 'compensation', Austria exchanged her South German lands for Salzburg which Ferdinand of Tuscany exchanged for Würzburg, taken from Bavaria. Already Napoleon was playing the Grand Monarch. Bavaria and Württemberg were elevated to kingdoms and (with Baden) released from all feudal ties with the Holy Roman Empire. Once more Austria had borne the brunt of the French attack and suffered for it. She was now excluded from Italy and in Germany she retained a discredited empty title of Holy Roman Emperor, which itself was abolished without ceremony on 6 August 1806. Napoleon had clearly made his choice: he would pursue a Russian alliance and exchange a European balance for French hegemony.

The 1805 campaign opened a new era in the Napoleonic saga. The speed of the manoeuvres, the huge size of the armies, and particularly the completeness of the victory justified a policy of seeking a major battle in order to hinge the whole future upon its outcome. But the stakes were becoming greater, and in the celebration of victory the tremendous risks were forgotten. Austerlitz gave Napoleon a totally new idea of his powers. It produced a wave of expansion that swept him on to Moscow, and then to St Helena. Hitherto Napoleon might have claimed to be fulfilling the expansionist policy of Louis XIV and traditional France: from now on the expansionism was Napoleonic.

And France, bemused, followed the Caesarist path in the footsteps of the man who was to become what Talleyrand was to call the enemy of Europe. A new era had begun, and it was symbolised by the formal re-adoption of the Gregorian calendar as from 1 January 1806, and by the appearance of 'Napoléon' in place of 'Bonaparte' upon diplomatic dispatches.

[34] THE GRAND EMPIRE

It was now possible to strengthen a new division of Germany. The princes, who had been sequestering the lands of the Imperial Knights since the Recess of 1803, began to adopt French methods and to introduce the Code (although Napoleon had often to insist upon this himself). On 12 July 1806 sixteen princes somewhat unwillingly renounced the Holy Roman Empire and formed the Confederation of the Rhine, agreeing to supply 63,000 troops and to form a diet and accept a constitution (which never appeared). Baden, Hesse-Darmstadt and Berg (with Murat as Grand Duke) became Grand Duchies, and Dalberg became Prince Primate of the Confederation. It merely remained formally to abolish the title of Holy Roman Emperor, and Francis accepted a new title as simply Emperor of Austria on 6 August. As yet Prussia was not included in the new arrangements for Germany, so that a final settlement had still to be made.

The cost and inconvenience of maintaining the French army in Germany soon caused resentment and there began to appear, especially among the bourgeoisie, some degree of national sentiment transcending the local patriotism that had characterised German feeling hitherto. Palm, the Bavarian bookseller, was executed in the summer of 1806 for distributing an anti-French pamphlet, and it was becoming clear that the French were not now welcomed as the Liberators of the 1790s. They were conquerors. The Dutch, for example, received Louis Bonaparte as king on 5 June, aware that a refusal would mean annexation to France.

Italy presented a clearer picture. The Kingdom of Italy stretched from the Alps around the Adriatic, and Napoleon's sisters were made Italian princesses. But Naples admitted an Anglo–Russian force on 27 December 1805. Masséna defeated them, the Russians retiring to Corfu, the British to Sicily, and Joseph Bonaparte was installed as King of Naples on 30 March 1806. Guerrilla warfare broke out in Calabria, aided by the priests, although the prime grievance of the guerrillas was that the French were intent on ending the state of incipient brigandage in Calabria. The English were encouraged to make a second landing, and their easy victory at Maida (4 July) caused a large scale rising and tied down 40,000 troops until 1808, Masséna suppressing the rebellion as mercilessly as the guerrillas fought. It was a foretaste, on a smaller scale, of what was to be encountered in Spain – but it was not a national rising, the guerrillas had more in common with the *mafia* than with the *carbonari*. Only Parma, Tuscany and the Papal States remained outside French direct control – and that merely until 1808. Napoleon was not the midwife of Italian unity – for him Italy was no more than a vassal state.

The Grand Empire that now emerged beyond the confines of the immediate French territories was a product of aggrandisement. It was too extended to admit of a homogeneous administration – indeed the common bond that came to link the non-French members of the Empire was to become resistance to French aggression. In a Europe of 167 million people, the Grand Empire contained 44 million. Its organisation was original. At the outset it was intended to be on federal lines, but the requirements of the Continental System (see page 153) made it increasingly unitary. The kings and princes were hereditary and sovereign, but had to acknowledge the granting of fiefs to deserving Frenchmen (Talleyrand as Prince of Benevento, Bernadotte as Prince of Neuchâtel, for example). From March 1806 all kings and princes became personal vassals of Napoleon. His own family enjoyed a special civil status; Eugène Beauharnais and Jerome (now divorced) were married to German princesses and there was increasing talk of a second marriage for Napoleon – Joséphine had dreaded this consequence of her inability to produce an heir, and the successor of Charlemagne, 'our illustrious predecessor', could not long remain without a legal son.

[35] RUSSIAN ALLIANCE SECURED

Russia, Prussia and Britain still remained outside of his 'system', and his diplomacy remained for a year after Austerlitz full of improvisation, negotiating with anyone until the next great victory gave him the trump cards – indeed, the great victory was beginning to take the place of diplomacy in his eyes.

Since Prussia had seized Hanover at French command, Britain

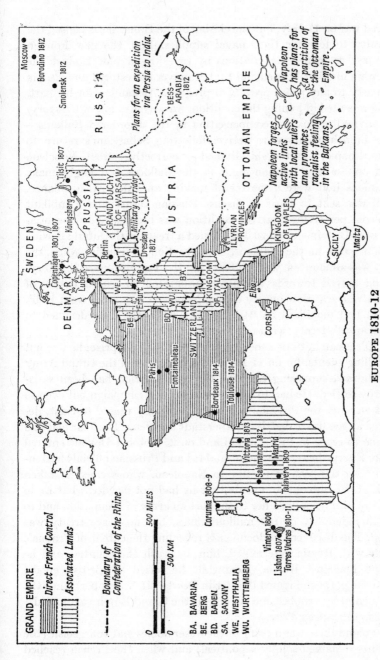

EUROPE 1810-12

Note the extension of France to control the North Sea and Adriatic coastlines because of the Continental System

GRAND EMPIRE

  Direct French Control

  Associated Lands

  — · — Boundary of Confederation of the Rhine

0   500 MILES

0   500 KM

BA. BAVARIA
BE. BERG
BD. BADEN
SA. SAXONY
WE. WESTPHALIA
WU. WURTTEMBERG

Moscow
Borodino 1812
Smolensk 1812

RUSSIA

Plans for an expedition via Persia to India.

BESS-ARABIA 1812

Napoleon has plans for a partition of the Ottoman Empire.

SWEDEN

Copenhagen 1801, 1807

DENMARK

Lübeck

Tilsit 1807

Königsberg

PRUSSIA

GRAND DUCHY OF WARSAW

Military corridor

Berlin

Dresden 1812

SA.

WE.

BE.

Erfurt 1808

AUSTRIA

Paris

Fontainebleau

SWITZERLAND

BD. WU.

BA.

KINGDOM OF ITALY

Elba

CORSICA

Bordeaux 1814

Toulouse 1814

Vittoria 1813

Salamanca 1812

Madrid

Talavera 1809

Corunna 1808–9

Vimeiro 1808

Lisbon 1807
Torres Vedras 1810–11

ILLYRIAN PROVINCES

KINGDOM OF NAPLES

OTTOMAN EMPIRE

Napoleon forges active links with local rulers and promotes racialist feeling in the Balkans.

SICILY

Malta

declared war on 11 May, but the closing of the Hansa ports caused the admiralty to fear for their naval supplies. Fox, the new Foreign Secretary, re-opened negotiations by revealing a plot against the Emperor's life, but his demand that Hanover be restored and Russia be a party to any peace prevented progress. Alexander, for his part, having repented of joining the coalition, was eager to follow Czartory-ski's advice to look for compensation in the disordered Balkans – where French agents were active, following Sebastiani's return to Constantinople. Czartoryski divined – correctly – that Napoleon would oppose any Russian gains in the Balkans, but might make concessions if it were a matter of making an anti-British alliance. Oubril was sent to Paris to discuss Russian terms, and a jubilant Napoleon, perceiving that the coalition was broken, ended negotiations with Britain and on 20 July signed a treaty with Oubril allowing Russian gains in the Balkans. The reaction in Russia, when the treaty was announced, was so great that the Tsar dismissed Czartory-ski and moved towards war again, prompted by Queen Louisa of Prussia who was now openly calling Napoleon 'the scum from Hell'. Prussia had mobilised on 24 July, and when the Tsar declined to ratify Oubril's treaty, went to war in September.

The Prussian initiative took Napoleon quite by surprise: he was not controlling events, for on 17 August he had ordered the Grand Army to withdraw, supposing that the German question had been satis-factorily settled. He had to improvise a hurried campaign but even so by 14 October the Prussian army had virtually ceased to exist, de-stroyed at the linked battles of Auerstädt and Jena. The Tsar had had no time to come to Prussia's aid and on 25 October Davout entered Berlin. Everywhere resistance crumbled and Prussian officials hasten-ed to take the oath of loyalty to Napoleon, who seemed so taken aback at the outcome of events that he had not decided what to do with Prussia: he obliged her to support an army of occupation and to pay an indemnity of 160 million francs, but no peace treaty was signed. The discovery of documents revealing the extent of Prussia's *entente* with Russia determined him to crush the country, and he advanced against Russia. Meanwhile he seized all British goods, closed the ports and issued the Berlin Decree (21 November); thus the Continental System became possible as the Grand Empire expanded – it was not its *raison d'être*.

In Poland there was a rising of the lesser nobles and bourgeoisie (the peasants remained solidly a-political) and when the French reached

Warsaw (27 November) many anticipated a revival of the old kingdom
of Poland. Napoleon had no such intention, for to revive the Poland
of 1773 would bring Austria and Russia against him. He was happy to
have a small vassal state, which, incredibly enough, seemed to
satisfy many Poles. In Russia a flood of patriotic feeling was released
as the Polish question was reopened and as the French drew near the
Russian frontier. The Holy Synod proclaimed a holy war against
Napoleon and there was appearing a type of popular reaction that he
had not before encountered. Furthermore, despite Austerlitz, he
realised he had to press the campaign against Russia in order to
control Austria where stirrings of resistance were already disturbing
the surface.

The terrain proved difficult and the weather was very bad – deep
mud made the poor roads impassable and the Russian army cautiously
declined to give battle. On 8 February 1807 Benningsen felt strong
enough to engage an outnumbered French army at Eylau. The result,
despite Murat's famous charge across the ice, was indecisive, but
rumours began to filter through that the Grand Army had been
defeated. Napoleon was well aware of his exposed position, the more
so as intercepted couriers revealed that Stadion was preparing a war
of revenge for Austria. Gigantic efforts were made to bring up men
and supplies to reinforce the French army. The levies of 1807 and
1808 marched untrained into Germany, where the Grand Army
numbered 410,000 – but it was divided into three, so complex was
Napoleon's scheme of things, one section to watch Austria in Italy,
one for the defence of the northern coast and one for the summer
campaign. Napoleon even made overtures to Colonel Kleist suggesting
a peace treaty with Prussia, so great was his desire to keep Russia
isolated. He was even prepared to listen to Stadion's proposal for a
general European congress to determine the basis of a general peace.
Clearly, Napoleon was hard-pressed, and his negotiations indicated
that he was calculating, not simply pursuing, a paranoic ambition.

Alexander had his own embarrassments, a minor war on his Persian
frontier and another in the Balkans helping a Serb revolt. Napoleon
sought to increase these Balkan troubles by inducing Ali Pasha of
Jamina to attack the Ionian Islands and having Marmont send
artillery and instructors to the Pasha of Bosnia. Sebastiani pressed the
case for an alliance with the Porte, and Britain, thoroughly alarmed,
sent Admiral Duckworth to force the Straits (19 February 1807) –
unsuccessfully because of the excellence of Sebastiani's defences. In

May a treaty with the Shah of Persia provided for French guns and instructors and the provisioning of a future French army across Persia to India. Clearly, Alexander was finding a net closing round him, and Britain declined either to send a diversionary raid on the French coast, or even to pay subsidies for a march by Gustavus IV across Napoleon's lines of communication.

However, only a complete Russian defeat could save Napoleon. Benningsen made this possible by trying to relieve Königsberg, and the Russian army was shattered at Friedland on 14 June 1807. A truce was signed and Alexander once more determined on peace. But on 22 June, Hardenberg produced a daring plan for an alliance of Prussia, Russia and France against Britain for the purpose of achieving general peace and a new European settlement. Russia and Austria should partition the Balkans, Prussia should gain Saxony, whose newly-made King should be compensated by ruling a reconstituted Poland. Alexander accepted the plan in principle, but next day he received an offer of alliance with Napoleon. Flattered, and imagining he could seduce Napoleon, he proposed a personal meeting on a raft moored in the middle of the Niemen river on 25 June. This meeting of the two Emperors, the one representing legitimacy, the other Revolution, was a climactic moment, with each seeking to dazzle the other with dreams of world domination. From it came the Treaty of Tilsit, 7 July 1807.

Prussia provided a difficulty for Napoleon now refused to consider her and the Tsar desired to negotiate on her behalf. But Napoleon held the kingdom by right of conquest, and the Tsar was seduced into accepting a general peace and a French alliance. Prussia lost all her possessions west of the Elbe where the new Kingdom of Westphalia was formed for Jerome Bonaparte. Prussian Polish lands were constituted the Grand Duchy of Warsaw (no new kingdom of Poland was made) and Danzig remained a free port. The remainder of Prussia was left to Frederick William but it had to maintain an army of occupation until a heavy war idemnity was paid. ('False as friends, futile as foes', was Napoleon's comment on the Prussians – but it was fully six years before he had need to revise his opinion.)

Alexander renounced his Mediterranean gains, ceding Cattaro and the Ionian Islands to France. He withdrew from the Danubian Principalities on condition that Napoleon would oblige the Sultan to make peace under threat of joint action against Turkey. In compensation Alexander gained Bialystock in Poland, but had to recognise all

Napoleon's reorganisation in Italy and Germany. Also he accepted the Continental System and agreed to approach Britain to restore her colonial gains and recognise the freedom of the seas; if she refused then Portugal, Sweden and Denmark were to be obliged to join the Continental System, thus theoretically closing the Continent to British goods. The Polish question remained unsettled (even though Napoleon granted a Polish constitution, insultingly enough at Dresden on his way back to Paris). The Grand Duchy of Warsaw was linked to the Confederation of the Rhine (of which it became a member) by a military cordon across the neck of Prussia, and had to contribute to and maintain the 30,000 French troops that remained on Polish soil. Poland remained a pawn in Franco–Russian relations.

Tilsit was a brilliant success for Napoleon. He had gained the ally he sought and isolated Britain and closed the continent against her. Europe was divided between Russia and France and both emperors spoke glibly of gains at the expense of Turkey – concrete proposals for partition were sent by Napoleon to Alexander in February 1808. There was some truth in Canning's remark that Austria distrusted Russia far more than she did France. But Napoleon would not allow Russia extensive gains in the Balkans nor hand her Constantinople, 'the centre of world empire' as he enigmatically called it. It was enough that he had duped Alexander into entering his 'system': it was not to be a partnership. He had gained the peace he so badly needed to control Austria, consolidate his position in central Europe and restore his battered army. There was even the possibility of England succumbing to economic warfare. As for Alexander, he had extricated himself from the defeat of Friedland and might dream of world domination, but he soon discovered that the Russian nobility regarded the peace as a betrayal. Brilliant triumph it may have seemed in the summer of 1807, but it soon became apparent that it was not to be a permanent peace.

PRINCIPAL EVENTS, 1802–8

Napoleon and France	*Events beyond France*
1802	**1802**
Peace of Amiens	Leclerc's expedition to San Domingo
	20 May. Slavery revived for French colonies – slave revolts
	August. Sebastiani to Egypt and Syria
1803	**1803**
30 January. Sebastiani's report on Egypt	
	25 February. Imperial Recess
	Decaen to India, Cavaignac to Muscat
	3 May. Louisiana sold to America
11 May. Whitworth leaves Paris, war renewed	May. Hanover and mouths of Elbe seized by French
2 December. Army of England officially nominated, gathered at Boulogne	
1804	**1804**
	Czartoryski produces partition scheme for Ottoman Empire
21 March. Execution of Duc d'Enghien	April. Prussia breaks off negotiations with France
18 May. Napoleon declared Emperor	May. Prussia signs defensive alliance with Russia
	6 November. Austria signs defensive alliance with Russia
1805	**1805**
18 March. Napoleon declared King of Italy	
	11 April. Anglo–Russian treaty of alliance
26 May. Napoleon crowned in Milan	
6 June. Ligurian Republic annexed to France	
	17 June. Austria joins Anglo–Russian alliance. Third Coalition
	10 September. Naples signs alliance with Russia
25 September. French troops cross Rhine	
20 October. Austrians surrender at Ulm	
21 October. Trafalgar	

Napoleon and France
1805

2 December, Austerlitz
26 December. Peace of Pressburg,
Austria makes peace

1806
1 January. Revolutionary Calendar
ended

20 July. Napoleon signs in Paris a
treaty with Oubril, but Tsar refuses to
ratify it

21 November. Berlin Decree –
Continental System launched

1807

1808

Events beyond France
1805
3 November. Prussia signs convention
with Russia

27 December. Anglo–Russian force
lands in Naples

1806

30 March. Joseph Bonaparte King of
Naples
5 June. Louis Bonaparte King of
Holland
4 July. British victory at Maida
12 July. Confederation of Rhine

6 August. Francis assumes title of
Emperor of Austria
September. Prussia enters the war
14 October. Jena and Auerstädt

27 November. French reach Warsaw

1807
8 February. Indecisive battle at Eylau
French activity in Balkans
19 February. Admiral Duckworth fails
to force the Straits
May. French treaty with Shah of
Persia
14 June. Friedland
7 July. Treaty of Tilsit

1808
February. Napoleon proposes a
partition of Ottoman
Empire with Russia

PART VI
Economic Policy

The Consulate and the first years of the Empire coincided with a burst of prosperity. No doubt the products of a successful war and Napoleon's professed policy of 'France first' played their part in this prosperity, and historians have often credited it to the general glory of the régime – oddly enough, in almost the same breath, denigrating Napoleon for supposed ignorance of economic forces in launching the Continental System. The contrast with the decade of the 1790s and with the years from 1811 to 1816 is sharp, but until much more work is done on the intervening decade, it would be dangerous to lay the credit upon Napoleon's shoulders, or even to talk in terms of a decade of expansion between two cyclical troughs (France was still too agricultural for a cyclical economic pattern to emerge).

Despite the wastage of war, France's population rose by 10 per cent in the Revolutionary and Napoleonic period, providing an abundance of manpower for war and an expanding market at home. In 1801, with some 28 million people, she had some 15 per cent of Europe's population. But fertility was diminishing. Despite the incentive to early marriage provided by the possible evasion of conscription for married men, fertility dropped from 476 per 100 marriages (1780) to 318 in 1810. The dynamic eighteenth-century growth was checked. The decline continued after 1815, suggesting contraception within marriage was the likely cause – the illegitimacy rate rose from 4·6 per cent (1802) to 6·5 per cent (1812). No doubt the loss of young men had its impact, but this can be exaggerated – losses were not excessive up to 1806, but thereafter very severe (the campaigns of 1812–15 probably account for more than half the total). Perhaps there were a million deaths in battle and 2½ million died of wounds. The decline in death rate (especially infant mortality) from 31·5 per cent in 1792 to

26·3 per cent in 1806–10 compensated a little for the losses (and the censuses of 1801 and 1806 may have understated the numbers of males partly in hopes of evading conscription, partly to evade extra taxes).

[36] FINANCIAL REORGANISATION

It is difficult to assess Napoleon's contribution to the prosperity of the Consulate and Empire. Certainly he built upon the reforms begun by the Revolution and not only added to the tax burden, but made the tax system so efficient that his successors maintained it until the present century. But much of the credit rightly belongs to the maligned Directory, especially Ramel's 'bankruptcy of the two-thirds' (see Jones, *French Revolution*, p. 189), a technique Napoleon emulated in the deflationary liquidation of 21 March 1801, and the return to metallic currency (government salaries were paid in cash from the Year VIII), aided, of course, by the inflow of precious metal by conquest. The metric system had also been promoted by the Revolution: its adoption was slow, but the French Empire ensured that it spread throughout much of Europe and helped the flow of goods. Even Chaptal's *Bureau de Statistiques* (22 November 1800) grew out of François de Neufchâteau's work as Minister of the Interior in 1798.

But the Consulate remained, like the Directory, dependent upon loans from bankers. Gaudin, as Minister of Finance, strove to raise the revenue by tax reforms: within days of the Brumaire coup he had placed the assessment and collection of taxes in the hands of central government agents responsible to a Director General in Paris and the skilled staff assembled by the Directory was enlarged, often using senior men whose training had been under Calonne in the 1780s. In 1802 the budget was balanced with a small surplus – until 1804. Revenue agents (*receveurs généraux*) were appointed in each Department in March 1800, empowered to issue bills in anticipation of revenue – a primitive form of Treasury Bill. The discounting of government bills presented problems and Gaudin established a *Caisse de Garantie* under Mollien to back the bills by assuming control of revenue and bonded warehouses. It hoped to hold up the price of government bonds, a task in which it was assisted by the *Caisse des comptes courants* (1796) under established bankers such as Perregaux, Recamier and Desplay with funds made available by its rival, the *Caisse d'escompte du commerce* (1798). It was the former that was transformed into the Bank of France (13 February 1800) with a capital of 30 million francs, in return for half the security bonds of the *Caisse de Garantie* as bank stock and half for commercial practice. The Bank was to manage government pensions and annuities, too; but it was not a central bank, nor really a 'Bank of France': it was a bank for big Paris financiers.

Two economic crises disturbed the first decade of the century. The first in 1802 was short-lived and a familiar agricultural crisis from which recovery was rapid due to peace and business confidence. The second in 1805–6 was superficially more serious, but it was a bankers' crisis, more concerned with arrangements to finance the war than with the working of the economy. The first years of the decade saw some fall in prices – sugar in Paris fell from 4.40 francs in 1799 to 2.60 francs in 1802, coffee from 6.10 francs to 3.26 francs, and cocoa from 4.85 francs to 3.38 francs. But it ended with a severe industrial crisis (1810–12) aggravated by the Continental System and complicated by a food shortage, a crisis showing signs of a nineteenth-century financial crisis.

The short crisis of 1802 was soon over, and special measures were taken to organise food supplies in Paris. As early as November 1801 Chaptal was purchasing grain abroad and Napoleon brought the veteran financial wizard, Ouvrard, out of retirement. Paris was quiet, but the riots elsewhere, severely suppressed, helped to unite the propertied classes and peasant proprietors around Napoleon as a bulwark against social disorder. A further offshoot was the reorganising of the Banks' discounting operations in order to curtail speculation. On 14 April 1803, the Bank's capital was raised to 45 million francs and it was granted a monopoly of note issue in Paris, absorbing its rival, the *Caisse d'escompte du commerce*, in return for discounting all *reçeveurs'* bonds.

Gaudin's tax reforms extended beyond improving the system of collection to new taxes; like the revived indirect taxes through the Excise Bureau, February 1804 (see page 128). At first these were modest and confined to liquor, but later they were extended to salt, tobacco, playing cards and public vehicles. By 1810 these taxes brought in more than direct taxes, and the collectors ('cellar rats') were as unpopular as they had ever been under the *ancien régime*. There was some attempt to shift the burden of expenditure from central to local government, and some Prefects even re-introduced a modified *corvée* system (requisitioning labour). Even so the Treasury under Barbé-Marbois had still to have recourse to bankers and contractors to obtain ready cash.

The 1805 crisis revealed the perils of depending on bankers. Business confidence had been momentarily shattered by the renewal of the war, and royalists were hopeful of the régime collapsing. Like its predecessors, the Grand Army of 1805 marched with few supplies and suffered deprivations on the extended campaign – Barbé-Marbois, the Minister of the Treasury, simply lacked the necessary money. In desperation, he turned once more to the pro-royalist banker, Gabriel Ouvrard, whose financial connexions were wide enough to attract sufficient funds. Ouvrard wove an intricate web of speculation, revealing at once his own brilliance as a financial wizard and the dangers of a government depending on him – for the scheme failed and the subsequent financial crisis of 1805 was so severe that the very future of the Empire was imperilled. The great victory at Austerlitz saved the régime.

The centre of Ouvrard's web was Spanish finance. Spain's annual subsidy to Napoleon was in arrears and Ouvrard secured the product of Spanish taxes to himself by advancing the money from his own resources. His intention was to get a treasure of some seventy million piastres from Mexico to Spain, and partly on the strength of this he provisioned the French and Spanish fleets for the war with Britain. To do this he raised a large sum in Amsterdam. His scheme for transporting the Mexican treasure across the Atlantic involved international bankers taking stupendous risks. Through his Amsterdam banker (who was the son-in-law of Baring, a leading British banker and a close friend of Pitt) he appears to have gained Pitt's consent for the safe conduct of the treasure in United States ships, in return for a cargo of silver. The scheme went awry and creditors demanded payment for outstanding accounts – in particular the merchants who had provisioned the fleets and were in the red to scores of millions of francs. By September 1805, the reserves of the Bank of France had fallen to less than 2 million francs and its note-issue had risen to the fabulous total of 92 millions. Ouvrard defaulted and his Spanish credits were frozen. Panic seized the money market in Paris. The news of the victory at Ulm steadied things a little, but panic revived when the destruction of the fleets at Trafalgar was reported. Several banks failed. Army contractors could not be paid – the biggest of them had to terminate his contract because he was 147 million francs in the red. Austerlitz saved the Empire in a very real sense.

The speculators appeared before Napoleon on his return to Paris in January 1806, and surrendered their assets to the new Minister of the Treasury. There still remained some 60 million francs owing and this debt was given to Spain to pay. The Spanish king, Charles IV, had to expropriate clerical land to raise the money, and this hastened the political crisis that was to culminate in his abdication in 1808 (see page 167).

Mollien replaced Barbé-Marbois and introduced a new accounting system. The Bank was brought more closely under state control by the appointment of a Governor (22 April 1806) and on 14 July a *Caisse de service* regulated the bills issued by the *reçeveurs* and reduced speculation by agents. In 1807 a Public Audit Department was created, but it was not allowed to examine the legality of expenditure – the financial reforms of the Younger Pitt were as far removed from Napoleonic France as was parliamentary democracy.

Napoleon, even as Emperor, was never able to free himself from speculators and dependence on bankers. He had his own civil list, crown lands and private estates – he hoped to have a fund of 100 million francs at his personal disposal, as well as the financial machinery of the Empire. Indeed, in January 1810, a *Domaine Extraordinaire* was established under Defermon to manage the Emperor's estates and revenues in vassal states; it was used to control the flow of money and to make advances to industry and cover pensions. But Napoleon was never able to build up adequate financial reserves because his wars were too frequent and too costly – this double problem of lack of time and the continual strain of war is too easily forgotten.

Receipts from vassal and defeated states helped, but were not enough. The Italian Republic annually supplied 30 million francs from 1802. Austria was charged an indemnity of 118 million at Pressburg in 1805 (some 75 million was actually paid), and a further 250 million (of which 164 million was paid) in 1809. Portugal was charged 100 million in 1807 (she paid only six million because of the British presence), but Prussia, between 1806 and 1812, may have paid as much as 500 million – no wonder the Prussians hated France!

As in the days of the Directory, warfare remained the key to finance. The Army Fund (October 1805) for levying contributions from Austria and central Europe was said to have exacted 743 million francs between 1805 and 1810. Spain is said to have contributed some 350 million, and still the campaign there proved a heavy drain on France. Despite Napoleon's celebrated motto in his letter to Eugène (1810), 'My principle is *France first*', victory and the huge contributions of the defeated and vassal states did not mean a reduction of taxation in France. There was never enough money available, and if the war did not prove swiftly over, the tax payer soon felt the pinch.

Napoleon did not create a customs union for the Grand Empire. This was partly because the vassal states feared they would be totally absorbed if they lost their customs revenue – which they needed to pay for Napoleon's exactions. (The Grand Duchy of Berg persistently petitioned to be allowed within the French tariff, but was crushed between the Empire and her larger German neighbours for her industries competed with France.) It was also because Napoleon failed to see the European market as a whole and thus maintained trade barriers that were essentially irrelevant to him. Instead, pursuing the best mercantilist principles, he closed his frontiers against allies, vassals and enemies alike.

[37] ENCOURAGEMENT OF INDUSTRY

French commerce and industry received direct privileges in the best mercantilist traditions that had served so well in the past. State monopolies in weapons, powder, minting, tobacco continued and private ones were allowed by the reintroduction of trade marks (1802), and the restored corporations and Chambers of Commerce (1802) strengthened the tendency. Industrial exhibitions, emulating the famous 1798 exhibition on the Champ de Mars patronised by François de Neufchâteau, were officially encouraged by Chaptal's Society for Encouraging National Industries (1801). Special prizes, honours and orders for machines were awarded to inventors, like Douglas for his woollen machines; for the light steam engine (1807); Philippe de Gerard's flax spinning machine (1810); and Nicholas Appart's factory for tinned food (1804). But there was little organised direct investment in industry. The Continental System encouraged particular industries like refining sugar from sugar beet (using the process developed in Silesia in 1757) at the factories in Auby and Lille (1811) – by 1813 some $3\frac{1}{2}$ million kilogrammes were being produced in 334 factories – or extracting sugar from grapes, or woad for dyes in Alsace, or coffee from chicory. But there was no deliberate policy of autarky.

Another form of industrial protection was the provision of low interest loans at 2 per cent in the winter of 1806–7. Again, the foreign tariff protected French industries from British and other competition, so that industries in Paris, Alsace, Upper Normandy, Belgium and French-occupied Rhineland made progress (whilst those of the Grand Duchy of Berg declined). There were signs that France was beginning to follow Britain's lead in mechanising the textile industry.

Crouzet estimates French industrial production in 1800 at only 60 per cent of that of the 1780s because of the effects of war and the loss of colonial and continental markets. But the first decade of the century saw a big increase to over 50 per cent above the peak of the 1780s – an increase assisted by extensive building and public works. But the crisis of 1810–11 checked expansion and the recession was prolonged after the fall of Napoleon. The big advances in textiles (there were 11,000 Jacquard looms by 1812, spun yarn had more than doubled during the decade, and there were perhaps a million spindles for cotton by 1812) and in the chemical industries did not represent an 'industrial revolution', although it was not far away, for cylinder printing of calicoes had been introduced in 1805, and in 1810 the first reverberatory furnace was opened at Le Cruesot. Napoleon, for his part, was not above industrial espionage and sabotage – in 1804 he closely examined the means necessary for putting the Newcastle area coal mines out of action and for seizing Swansea to put out of action the nearby coal mines and iron works.

Agriculture, by contrast, was not advanced. Chaptal was anxious to publicise the value of organic manures, but the Revolution, in guaranteeing the peasant proprietor his small-holding, had effectively stopped the major agricultural changes that were at this time transforming British agriculture (see Jones, *French Revolution* p. 32). Sheep rearing was improved, however, the Rambouillet herd of merinos were by 1815 reputedly better than the Spanish.

Transport, the key to economic advance, was neglected by Napoleon, except in so far as it served military purposes. The canals of the Paris Basin, national routeways, the famous Simplon road to Italy (completed 1805), were predominantly military, although, like the Mont Cenis roadway (1806), they might also help trade. Strasburg and Lyons gained a monopoly of German and Italian trade respectively, but vassal states paid for this. The maritime ports, and even Marseilles wilted: a commercial treaty with Britain might well have served him better than the Tilsit settlement!

Napoleon's direction of the economy of France has been exaggerated: he did not so much maintain the mercantilist tradition of the Enlightened Despots, as use economic policy as a branch of warfare. In this he was well within his generation: the age of Free Trade had yet to be born in Europe. In Britain, what was to become nineteenth-century capitalism was helping to create the wealth necessary to continue the struggle against France: but the British government was no more aware of the significance of this than was Napoleon. He can be forgiven for supposing that Britain would collapse because her credit was too strained – did not the Empire pride itself on its metal coinage while Britain was forced to use a depreciating paper currency? But the Empire depended too much on war, and its merchants on government contracts and contraband trading rather than on competitive prices and seeking new markets. Its banking methods lagged behind those of Britain, and the continental blockade saved its industrialists from facing the cold blast of competition with British machinery.

[38] THE CONTINENTAL SYSTEM

The Continental System was the name given to Napoleon's policy of extending a blockade of British commerce across as much as possible of the continent. It began officially with the Berlin Decree (1806). It failed in its object of forcing a British surrender and it raised resentment and hostility among Europe's merchants who had hitherto been well disposed to the French. To this double failure historians, schooled in a Free Trade century, have added the judgment that it was doomed on theoretical grounds, since it was conceived in terms of mercantilism which the century was about to reject. The Continental System has frequently been condemned as among Napoleon's grosser errors: but the judgment is too facile, for whenever it was properly applied the system came perilously near success in defeating Britain.

There is nothing novel about economic warfare, as the experience of the eighteenth century had clearly demonstrated. In 1793 the Convention naturally adopted a blockade of British goods and hoped to cause a collapse of the pound sterling by imposing intolerable strain upon the British balance of payments (the crucial factor in mercantilist trading). Their desire to defeat the 'vampire of the seas' resulted in restrictive measures of mounting intensity, culminating in the draconian law of 29 Nivôse VI (18 January 1798) authorising the seizure of all British goods and of any neutral vessel that had submitted to a search by a British ship, or was carrying on board anything of British origin, whether a chronometer or a seaman's knife. This measure raised so much protest from neutrals, including America, that Napoleon repealed it in December 1799.

Napoleon was not intent on peace, and even during the truce of Amiens he raised French tariffs against British goods and British colonial goods. He was convinced that France alone could induce bankruptcy in Britain through damaging her balance of payments and thus undermining confidence in her paper currency. This would not only take Britain out of any war, but end the payment of subsidies to her allies. (Britain was fortunate that her finances were strong enough to sustain herself.) He had good advice from Hauterive, Talleyrand's principal assistant, who advocated this very policy in *The State of France in Year III*; from the Chevalier de Guer in 1801 and from Lassalles in 1803. But, for all this support from economic experts, the policy was nevertheless an error.

Between 1803 and 1805 the blockade was more a policy of trade and industrial protection than anything more – the tariff against foreign cotton and silk was in response to the demands of the Lyons merchants who feared competition from Italy, rather than a blow against Lancashire. But, if a blockade could be extended across Europe and also include America, an extended economic crisis could be induced in Britain which, with attendant distress, unemployment and wretchedness to cool the ardour of the British workingman's patriotism, might provoke a revolution. More realistically, Napoleon recognised that British merchants feared for their profits and Whitehall feared a financial collapse.

When the Third Coalition had been destroyed and then Prussia defeated it became possible for the first time to extend what had been a mercantile policy of draining gold from Britain into a blockade of economic warfare in the strictest sense. 'I intend to conquer the seas with my land armies,' Napoleon declared, and the Berlin Decree (November 1806) gave effect to this. In this sense only was the Continental System a turning point. It grew stronger as the means became available. The First Milan Decree (November 1807) strengthened the blockade by requiring a certificate of origin to be produced for all goods carried in ships touching in at French ports. When Britain replied with the Orders in Council, regulating the trade of neutrals, Napoleon replied with the Second Milan Decree (December 1807) denationalising any ship submitting to a British examination – returning effectively to the situation at Nivôse VI, but now upon a European scale, for the rest of Europe was brought within the French system. Russia enforced the Continental System as part of the Tilsit Agreement (June 1807); Denmark joined in October, after the second battle of Copenhagen; Spain and hence her Empire was secured in 1807; and, in November 1807, Junot occupied Lisbon (but failed to capture the Portuguese fleet). The Porte was friendly, and Austria agreed to close the Adriatic, whilst by April 1808 Italy, including Rome, was directly under French control. Across the Atlantic, America was taking counter-measures. The System was formidable.

The British counter-blockade, 'to subordinate the trade of the whole world to the development of the navy and the shipping of Great Britain', as the Orders in Council put it, was plainly mercantile in theory and practice. Its purpose was less to defeat France than to enrich Britain. As we have seen, this was Napoleon's original position, but by 1807 he had returned to the policy of the Directory, actually seeking now to seal off the whole continent from British trade. It would involve immense suffering – but Napoleon calculated that the suffering in Britain would be the greater, which would encourage her to make peace or at least inhibit her from paying subsidies on the same scale as before. On the Paris Exchange the pound sterling had depreciated by 25 per cent at the end of 1808 from its peak in 1805. It was to drop a further 10 per cent by 1811. The System seemed to be working.

Within the French Empire opposition came first from shipowners, great merchants and bankers. But industrialists benefited from the absence of British competition – Saxony textiles did well between 1805 and 1812, and Silesian and Westphalian mines, Thuringian iron, sugar beet in Frankfurt, Magdeburg, Holland and Prussia, and the chemical industry at large, all benefited. France, of course, did best. But where there was less industry and a surplus of agricultural produce there was less benefit – as in eastern and southern Europe. The great maritime cities suffered: Venice, Trieste, Genoa, the Dutch and the Hansa ports all felt the pinch. Marseilles had 330 ocean-going ships in 1807 and only 9 in 1811, her population dropping from 120,000 in 1789 to 90,000. At Bordeaux the population fell from 120,000 to 70,000. No wonder these ports were royalist citadels by 1811.

Britain, commanding the seas, had no great difficulty finding substitute markets. But the French Empire had a more difficult task. European trade concentrated on the great Frankfurt and Leipzig Fairs and an organised packhorse trade route developed from Vienna to Salonica to bring in goods from the Levant. Had the System lasted longer new east–west trade routes might have been forged with incalculable results for political history – Napoleon lacked railways, for the transport problem was the greatest obstacle! But the System crumbled too soon. Britain, concerned as much for her position in the Mediterranean as for Russian activity in Persia, so increased her influence at Constantinople that Napoleon recalled Sebastiani in April 1808 and the Porte eventually made peace with Britain in January 1809. The Spanish revolt (see page 167) not only began the 'Spanish ulcer', but opened Latin America and the Philippines to British trade and curbed the activities of Decaen in the East. Napoleon had gone into Spain partly to end the contraband trade with Britain: this trade was relatively insignificant, whereas the consequences of the Spanish revolt were grave – as Crouzet puts it, the game was not worth the candle.

In Europe contraband became big business, with Heligoland serving as an English depôt known as 'Little London', and 120 ships calling there between August and November 1808. British firms quickly adopted French methods of packaging to help evade detection of smuggled goods. The islands off the French coast, and even marked buoys in the Quiberon roads served as rendezvous for smugglers who often discovered that the French commissioners of customs and even local army commanders were corruptible. In the Mediterranean, Malta and Sicily and by 1809 the Ionian Islands (except Corfu) played their part. Even the Barbary pirates came to terms with Britain and the carefully constructed chain of pacts with local pashas that Napoleon had forged from Morocco to Persia was broken. That control of the Levant had slipped from his hands may have contributed to the need for the 1812 campaign in Russia. France herself had lost her old colonial trade before 1806: by 1808 she had lost her Spanish trade, the next most profitable. She was forced to look solely to Europe – yet she did not suffer badly.

In order to overcome shortages, release excess stocks (especially of corn and brandy) and in particular to drain Britain of bullion, Napoleon was prepared to issue licences to trade with the enemy. Britain readily reciprocated, even allowing French ships into the British ports, and issuing some 44,300 licences between 1807 and

1812 (26,000 in 1809–10) – a profitable source of income at £14 a licence! Neutral shipping frequently carried two sets of papers – one for British and one for French authorities. A Liverpool firm openly advertised the documents for sale.

When the system was rigorously applied, Britain suffered – but it could never destroy her because of her extra-European markets. If the American market were denied her, then perhaps half her trade was at peril and the situation became very serious indeed when President Jefferson imposed an Embargo on trade with the European belligerents (22 December 1807) in retaliation against the blockade and against interference with American shipping. Hostility was increased by Napoleon's Bayonne Decree (17 April 1808) and the Rambouillet Decree (23 March 1810) directed especially against American smuggling. In 1809 America had passed a Non-Intercourse Act that hit Britain more than France.

Britain, for her part, sought new markets desperately in the Levant and especially Latin America, and these were opened chiefly in 1808. Without them she would have been very sorely pressed. But this was the year of Napoleon's attack on Spain – it was this that had opened the Latin American markets: thus the Spanish campaign was more than an ulcer – it was the key to Britain's survival, for Britain remained in the war quite as much because of the activities of her merchants in Latin America, as because of Wellington's success in Spain.

However, in 1809, with Austria once more defeated (see page 175) and the possibility of Napoleon regaining Spain and also of Russia allowing a Franco–Russian expedition through Persia, there was no reason to suppose that the Continental System would fail of its purpose. In Latin America the endemic civil wars severely restricted the markets, and the hostility of the U.S.A., eventually resulting in the war in America of 1812–14, caused serious embarrassments to the British Admiralty over naval stores – their ships had even to be constructed in India as well as at Halifax in Nova Scotia. The System was biting hard, and the economic crisis in Britain 1810–12, aggravated by poor harvests, high prices and demands for parliamentary reform and the repeal of the Orders in Council, as well as the Luddite Riots (which required a larger army than Wellington had in the Peninsula to suppress them), was threatening to bring Britain out of the war. By July 1810, Holland had been occupied by Napoleon and Louis expelled for failing to enforce the System, and the North Sea coast through to Lübeck on the Baltic was occupied to make the System effective. Napoleon, with his hands for once fairly free in 1810, could have made the System work, however corrupt his marshals proved to be in enforcing it.

Chaptal, Crétet and Montalivet, Minister of the Interior, concerned for the effects of the System on France, were anxious to return to the purely protectionist position of pre-1806, but Napoleon refused, arguing that the System brought gold into France by means of which, in due course, the peasants could pay their taxes and so help pay for the costly Austrian war of 1809. By 1810 the sale of surplus corn to Britain had drained her of a million pounds in gold, and by the Saint-Cloud Decree (3 July 1810) French licences were made official policy, at 1,000 francs a time: they were to be signed personally by Napoleon and to be available only to French citizens (494 had been issued between October 1810 and November 1811). Important concessions were made for U.S.A. traders in the hope of bringing her to war against Britain. But in 1810 came two further Decrees, that of the Trianon (1 August) increasing sharply the tax on colonial goods, and the extremely severe 'burning' Fontainebleau Decree (18 October), creating a new special *cours douanières* to seek out smugglers and to destroy all contraband goods (in actual fact the goods burnt were frequently worthless substitutes for the captured smuggled goods). The Confederation of the Rhine and Prussia had to accept very close surveillance and Frankfurt was invested and made an example of. Movement of goods almost came to a standstill because of the many bankruptcies of firms caught in the smuggling net, and this aggravated the 1811 crisis.

The Trianon and Fontainebleau Decrees were bitterly resented and resisted – Alexander opened his ports to neutral shipping on 31 December 1810 partly as a delayed protest. By 1811 Napoleon had to admit the gravity of the resistance, but the effect of the economic crisis on England was his justification. He continued to issue licences, hoping to draw off more British gold – indeed, he chose this course deliberately rather than the alternative one of depriving Britain of the much needed corn imports. Holland Rose has argued that Napoleon allowed the 'most favourable moment' to pass in authorising this continued export of grain, since famine and probably capitulation or revolution might well have followed the stopping of the exports. Crouzet, however, destroys this view by demonstrating that the principal exports were sent in the winter of 1809–10. Because the

Non-Intercourse Act rendered supplies from U.S.A. precarious, Britain had issued 1,741 licences for grain imports from Holland or France between September and November 1809. The licences were renewed to the number of 1,125 between May and August 1810, although not all of them could have been used because of the slow movement of corn out of the French ports and because, on Napoleon's specific order, no corn was allowed out of France during the harvest period. In 1810 2,321,000 quarters of grain (a total exceeded only in 1801) came into London – at a cost of £2,701,000. Of this only 396,000 qts. came from France and 267,000 from Holland. Had Napoleon stopped all grain exports it would have affected only 28 per cent of the total, a significant amount, but not enough to provoke famine or revolution, or even capitulation. What the imports did do was to help 'peg' the price of corn, and also to increase the strain on Britain's balance of payments, which was an important factor in the 1811 crisis.

Britain was already in a serious financial situation before 1811: inflation was rampant and the government was unable to help Austria in the war of 1809; also lack of money was one of the factors in the failure of the Walcheren Expedition (see page 170). The Bullion Committee under Ricardo was demanding severe deflation by returning to the gold standard, while production at home declined and Wellington imagined he might have to withdraw from the Peninsula. Napoleon was near to his goal. But Percival rejected Ricardo's advice:

> I am bound to regard the proposed measure as a declaration by Parliament that we must submit to no matter what conditions of peace rather than continue the war.

The war continued, but the Orders in Council were repealed (23 June 1812).

The effect of the System on Britain if not catastrophic was very perilous. The effect in Europe was equally serious. Bankruptcies in the Hanseatic ports, in Holland and Paris caused panic, lost production and rising unemployment. Corn prices soared because the harvest was short and the granaries had been cleared the previous spring. There were no disturbances to compare with those in Britain, but Napoleon had cause to worry and he offered local aid to the tune of 12 million francs; he even allowed Fouché to permit Ouvrard to arrange a reciprocal licensed trade with Britain on the basis of corn for brandy.

The Board of Trade co-operated (1812) allowing French ships into British ports and City insurers to quote for cargoes intended for France. But by the summer of 1812 the crisis was beginning to lift, and the coming invasion of Russia not only opened Eastern Europe to British trade but gave greater opportunities to smugglers as the Grand Army moved across Europe, from North Germany. If Napoleon had returned victorious from Moscow the Continental System would be an acknowledged success now. Historians have too easily condemned it.

Britain and France had used trade blockades during the eighteenth century for mercantile reasons. Today economic warfare is unashamedly directed towards the destruction of the enemy. Napoleon's System was both a combination of these and a half-way point between them, forward-looking in its attempt to break British resistance, backward-looking in its concentration on mercantile concern for gold. Its effects could not be rapid and so Napoleon was denied success as in so many fields, because of lack of time. Also Britain had too many alternative markets which Napoleon could not close. The System, nevertheless, had come close to success – it collapsed once the vigilance of the Grand Army was removed. As Lefebvre says, Britain was saved not by the arguments of Adam Smith but by the loss of the Moscow campaign. On 25 December 1812 the British cabinet refused further licences to trade, for news of the disaster had reached London: a year before it had in desperation accepted licences on a basis of reciprocity. Even so, it is worth recalling that Davout's efforts in 1813 once more closed the Elbe and Hamburg to smugglers – only the allied victory in 1814 finally lifted the blockade.

The Continental System proper lasted from 1806 to 1812. For most of this time it was not fully enforced, but when it was (July 1807 to July 1808 and Spring 1810 to November 1812) Napoleonic Europe was closed to almost all but licensed British trade, and Britain suffered accordingly. The 1811 crisis was the more serious for Britain because of the coincidence of a cyclical downswing in production, beginning in 1808, a bad harvest and the Non-Importation policy of U.S.A. However, Britain was not prepared to make peace – experience during the Amiens truce had shown that she had nothing to gain from peace in terms of trade with Napoleonic France. The Continental System failed for a variety of reasons apart from Britain's own access to the markets of the world. It was never fully applied for long enough: when it was, war in Spain and then in Russia ruined it (both wars begun partly to enforce the System). Secondly, Napoleon failed to get the U.S.A. to support him, for had he done so in 1808, or 1811 he would very seriously have embarrassed Britain: instead he antagonised the U.S.A. by proceeding against her merchants as smugglers. The American war of 1812 against Britain came too late for his System. Thirdly, the System depended on military force and local commanders were often corrupt, whilst outright defiance by Louis in Holland or Murat in Naples made wide gaps in the System in addition to those in Spain and Turkey and the work of the smugglers. Finally, the merchants of central Europe (and even those of France) were not prepared to adopt measures that would ruin them in the hope of an eventual Napoleonic victory; they were therefore too willing to turn to smuggling and they were supported in their efforts by the masses as much as by the army command. In the circumstances, it is less the ultimate collapse of the System, than its periodic success that is the remarkable thing.

Further Reading

Napoleon's foreign policy is too often absorbed into the general story of his campaigns: this is a pity, for it is worthy of separate study. See particularly the classic work by E. Driault, *Napoléon et l'Europe* (Paris, 1910–27), and a fascinating study by H. C. Deutsch, *The Genesis of Napoleonic Imperialism* (Yale University Press, Cambridge, Mass., 1938). Godechot, *L'Europe et l'Amérique* (Paris, 1967) helps to relieve the myopia of looking only at Europe, while V. J. Puryear, *Napoleon and the Dardanelles* (Berkeley, California, 1951) looks at the Near East question. For Central Europe, E. V. Gulick, *Europe's Classical Balance of Power* (New York, 1955), O. Connelly, *Napoleon's Satellite Kingdoms* (Free Press, New York, 1965), J. Droz, *L'Allemagne et la Révolution française* (Paris, 1949), N. Brunschwig, *La crise de l'état Prussien* (Paris, 1947) and H. Kohn, *The Mind of Germany* (Macmillan, London, 1961) are all useful. Napoleon's relations with Fouché are considered in H. Cole's biography (Eyre and Spottiswoode, London, 1971) and with Talleyrand in significant biographies by Madelin (London, 1948), H. Kurtz (1958) and J. Orieux (Paris, 1970).

The classical work on *The Continental System* is by E. F. Heckscher (1922) but this has been seriously revised by F. Crouzet's *L'Economie Britannique et le Blocus continental* (Paris, 1958, 2 vols). Other works dealing with the economic development of France and Europe are

PRINCIPAL EVENTS, 1798–1813

1798.   18 January. Law of 29 Nivôse (draconian economic measure)

1799.   December. Napoleon repeals Nivôse Law

1800.   13 February. Bank of France established

1801.   21 March. Deflationary liquidation of public debt

1803.   14 April. Bank of France gains monopoly of note issue

1804.   25 February. Excise Bureau established

1805.   Ouvrard's complex financial dealings induce a serious bankers' crisis.
        Confidence restored by victories at Ulm and Austerlitz

1806.   22 April. Bank of France under State control
        11 November. Berlin Decree begins Continental System.

1807.   Britain retaliates with Orders in Council
        June. Tilsit Agreement. Russia agrees to enforce Continental System
        September. Second Battle of Copenhagen
        November. First Milan Decree
        Junot occupies Lisbon
        December. Second Milan Decree (return to Nivôse Law policy)
        Jefferson in America imposes Embargo policy

1808.   February. Rome occupied
        April. Sebastiani recalled from Constantinople
        17 April. Bayonne Decree

1809.   January. Turkey makes peace with Britain
        Spanish revolt keeps Iberian ports open to trade and opens Spanish
        empire trade to Britain
        Jefferson's Non-Intercourse Act

1810.   23 March. Rambouillet Decree
        3 July. Saint-Cloud Decree (licences made official policy)
        Louis expelled from Holland
        Holland and North Sea coast occupied
        1 August. Trianon Decree (tax on colonial goods)
        18 October. Fontainebleau Decree (burning of confiscated goods)
        13 December. Alexander opens Russian ports to British trade

1811.   Growing resistance in Europe to Continental System
        Deepening economic crisis in Britain
        Britain accepts licences as a basis for reciprocity

1812.   French ships allowed into British ports for licensed trade
           23 June. Britain repeals Orders in Council in response to public pressure
           Moscow campaign
           25 December. British cabinet refuses to issue any more licences

1812–14.   British war with America

1813.   Davout once more closes Elbe and Hamburg to smuggled trade

PART VII
Nemesis

[39] EUROPE, 1807–12

The Tilsit settlement, extending the Continental System, appeared to deliver Europe to a French domination. But the far-flung Empire, in which the revolutionary pattern of satellite republics was giving way to a complex of dynastic states, was not easy to control, and for the first time, Napoleon found he could not effectively deal with each foreign threat. It is illusory to point to the Tilsit settlement and say that in 1807 he reached a peak of achievement, after which mistaken policies and the pressure of events crowd upon a collapsing régime: his achievement is to be measured not only in the triumph of Tilsit, but also in his capacity to control the growing problems his policies produced. After 1812 he had little chance of maintaining his empire, but that campaign had been deliberately planned and launched after five years of uncertainty had demonstrated the unsettled nature of the empire: this was an achievement greater than the gambler's throw of Tilsit.

These years reveal a new European situation that was to give Napoleon's enemies that bond of unity they had formerly so conspicuously lacked, namely the growing resistance to the increasing oppression of French imperialism. This oppression took two obvious forms. The burden of taxation and requisitions for war indemnities and the garrisoning of troops, together with the pressures of the Continental System, raised powerful economic interests against the French; while the demand for recruits to maintain and expand the existing armies continued to grow. Both these points of resentment raised a ground-swell of resistance from the bourgeoisie and common folk who formerly had welcomed the French, while administrative changes and the expansion of a French imperial nobility directly threatened the interests of the aristocracy. At the same time, the Romantic Revival was inspiring among intellectuals a new cultural nationalism that fed on economic and political discontent and gave moral strength to resistance. Napoleon was no longer faced by a disorganised ancien régime but by a rapid coalescing of opposed interests whose force was only dimly recognised.

Another feature of these years was that Napoleon, again for the first time, was unable satisfactorily to deal with each area of revolt before having to face another elsewhere. Thus the revolt in the Peninsula was not contained whilst that in Austria in 1809 proved peculiarly difficult to suppress, and both were played out against a background of deteriorating relations with Russia which meant constant anxiety over the situation in Eastern and Central Europe. Each of these areas must be dealt with separately for convenience of understanding, but one must remember that the events were contemporaneous. There were other problems, too: when all are taken together, the magnitude of Napoleon's achievement in these years can be the better appreciated.

Russia

Russia featured large among Napoleon's difficulties. In 1807, Alexander stood by the Tilsit settlement and spoke openly of a liberal reform programme with Speranski. But he was well aware of the hostility of the nobles and soon appreciated the economic consequences of the Continental System. By the spring of 1808 pressure at court began to tell on the Tsar, and as the prospect of reform receded, a disappointed Speranski commented, 'Alexander is too weak to rule, and too strong to be ruled'. Speranski was dismissed, sacrificed to the reactionaries at court, in 1811.

Alexander had surrendered the Adriatic but he was unwilling to withdraw from the Danubian Principalities until Napoleon had withdrawn from Prussia. He suggested being compensated by the Principalities for the losses incurred through the breach with Britain. Napoleon recognised his resentment and wrote on 2 February 1808, reviving the dreams of Tilsit by suggesting a partitioning of the Ottoman Empire and an expedition via Persia and Afghanistan to India. The offer was taken up, but differences over the control of the Dardanelles led to a meeting of the two Emperors at Erfurt. The meeting was the more necessary since Napoleon had omitted to help

Alexander to gain Finland from Sweden, and the Tsar had realised, by the summer of 1808, that France had reaped the advantages of Tilsit.

But in July 1808 Napoleon was in need of Alexander because of the Spanish revolt (see page 167) and of the disturbed state of Central Europe (see page 170). He had determined to withdraw the Grand Army from Germany in order to deal with Spain and needed Alexander to defend French interests in Central Europe. He was, therefore, now prepared to withdraw from Prussia and allow Russia to occupy the Principalities (Napoleon's diplomacy was always something of a poker game). Hopefully, Napoleon assembled his vassal kings at Erfurt (27 September 1808) and received Alexander with great pomp. But the Tsar was not overawed. His ambassador in Paris, Count Tolstoi, was in contact with discontented politicians and engaged in a web of espionage that revealed the low morale of Napoleon's leading administrators.

Talleyrand, closely followed by Fouché, was fast preparing for his reception into the bosom of France's enemies, should Napoleon be overthrown. Metternich, the Austrian ambassador, had already grasped the significance of Talleyrand's opinion that Napoleon was showing megalomaniac tendencies that would end in destruction. At Erfurt, Talleyrand took his self-interest to the limits of perfidy by secretly counselling the Tsar to resist the madman now threatening the security of Europe:

> It is up to you to save Europe, and you will not succeed by giving Napoleon his head. The French people are civilised; their sovereign is not. The sovereign of Russia is civilised; his people are not. Therefore, it is up to the sovereign of Russia to be the ally of the French people. The Rhine, the Alps, the Pyrenees are the conquests of France. The rest is the conquest of the Emperor; they do not belong to France.

New visions of dominion rose before the Tsar's eyes, and it is scarcely surprising that Napoleon achieved nothing at Erfurt. The Tsar refused to be drawn into a discussion of a possible marriage of Napoleon to his sister, nor would he agree to do more than offer 'good advice' to Austria over the problem of Austrian rearmament. In private, he now referred to Napoleon only as Bonaparte.

The Erfurt agreement (October 1808) provided for Russia to have Finland and the Principalities, but not Constantinople or the Straits.

Napoleon was to evacuate Prussia (which he was already doing for the army was needed in Spain) and Alexander agreed to offer good advice to Austria and to recognise Joseph Bonaparte as King of Spain. But Napoleon was not duped: he was merely gaining time, for once the Spanish rebels were destroyed, the Grand Army would be back in Germany. Meanwhile, Davout could retain a French presence for a year: if the Erfurt agreement gave him so much time, it would be enough. Events in both Spain and Austria were to ruin his calculations.

[40] REVOLT IN SPAIN

For the British, the Peninsular War occupies a special place in the Napoleonic saga. Napoleon himself admitted that the 'Spanish ulcer' did much to undermine his position. But it was not until the defeat in Russia that the 'ulcer' became a logistic disaster, and, despite the encouragement Europe derived from Spanish resistance, Spain was only the centre of Napoleon's attention in the winter of 1808–9 when he was there with the Grand Army. Otherwise, Central and Eastern Europe were his prime concern. It is easy to exaggerate the significance of the Peninsular War among the causes of Napoleon's overthrow, although some have argued that it was the decision to invade Portugal and occupy Spain that led him to reject the possibility of consolidating the Tilsit agreement as a basis for European stability.

The government of Spain was in chaos for the weak Charles IV was at odds with Godoy, the queen's lover and effective ruler, and with the heir, Ferdinand, Prince of the Asturias, whom the king arrested in October 1807 for plotting. Spain's alliance with France had brought her the destruction of her fleet and the probable loss of her empire, yet the rival rulers were unlikely to turn upon Napoleon. For his part, Napoleon realised how unreliable Godoy was, and desired to see a regeneration in the country, as much for greater efficiency as to obtain greater monetary contributions. At least Spain enforced the Continental System. But Portugal did not, and her trade with Britain was an obvious breach to be closed. On 27 October 1807 he signed the Treaty of Fontainebleau partitioning Portugal to Spain's advantage and Marshal Junot set off to occupy the country. But he made slow progress and found little to provision his troops in his march across Spain. He occupied Lisbon on 30 November, too late to capture the Portuguese royal family (who left for Brazil) or the fleet, which joined the British. He imposed an indemnity of 100 million francs.

Meanwhile, on the excuse of securing Junot's exposed position, Napoleon began to occupy Spain, culminating in Murat's entry into Madrid on 23 March 1808. The Spanish nobles rebelled at Aranjuez, the King abdicated in favour of Ferdinand and Godoy was imprisoned. Napoleon offered the crown to his brother Louis and invited Charles to meet him at Bayonne. A rising in Madrid on 2 May was viciously suppressed by Murat and both Charles and Ferdinand surrendered the crown to Napoleon on 5 May. Since both Louis and Jerome refused it, he imposed it on Joseph, sending Murat to be King of Naples. At the same time he granted Spain a constitution on lines similar to his other vassal states, save that this one guaranteed the position of the Roman Catholic Church. Urquijo might present Joseph with a detailed plan of reform, but when he entered Madrid, his kingdom was in revolt.

Legend clouds the story of the revolt and it is not easy to isolate the motives of the differing rebel groups. Ferdinand had been preparing an insurrection against Godoy since October 1807, and these preparations were feverishly hastened after the Bayonne meeting. In part the revolt was by nobles opposing Godoy as much as the French – Dumouriez, the former Revolutionary general (see Jones, *French Revolution*, p. 119), actually prepared a plan of campaign and Canning in England promised on 12 June to send supplies and offer diplomatic support. Yet there was also a spontaneous peasant revolt, independent of the power struggle of the nobles, provoked by discontent with the economic, social and political system, but also by resentment at the indignity heaped on the Spanish dynasty at Bayonne, and fanned by the priests who feared French anti-clerical measures. (French troops had entered Rome in February 1808 and the dispute between Napoleon and the Pope was common knowledge.) The local influence of the clergy was great and Napoleon called the revolt 'an insurrection of monks'. There was a fierce patriotism, too, and perhaps something of a national awareness, although this manifested itself more as hatred of the foreigner because of exactions and executions (Goya catches the spirit well). However, the revolt began in |Asturias, Galicia and Andalusia, areas as yet free of the French. Spread by clergy and nobles, fearful of their privileges being reduced by social reforms, and desiring to seize power from Godoy, the revolt was joined by peasants who tended to associate Godoy with Napoleon, by brigands and by those seeking vengeance for French atrocities.

The revolt was ostensibly directed by local juntas whose jealousies were enough to prevent a national movement emerging. Napoleon at this stage had no reason to regard the situation as potentially danger-rous: in any case his attention was more concentrated on Austrian rearmament and Russia's Balkan ambitions. By October he had sent 160,000 troops into the Peninsula, too few to control the country and of inferior quality in view of the rigours they had to face. Logistically there were few preparations, and from the outset this was a vital error, for the country was known to be short of fodder and food. The French forces were divided into small armies which often won against grouped Spanish forces, but were as often unable to press home an engagement. The war was conducted throughout with a brutality unknown elsewhere, the Spaniards torturing prisoners and the French retaliating with burning, pillage and massacre.

On 22 July 1808, Dupont was outmanoeuvred at Baylen and signed terms to repatriate his army. It was not worthy of the great notoriety the occasion has been given (nor was Napoleon's treatment of Dupont justified – he imprisoned him until 1814, when he under-standably joined the allies), especially as the Junta disregarded the agreement and left the prisoners to starve at Cabrera. Meanwhile, Sir Arthur Wellesley landed in Portugal and defeated at Vimiero (21 August) the outnumbered Junot whose army was repatriated under the Convention of Cintra. It returned for the winter campaign.

The loss of Portugal was a grievous blow, but it was Baylen that caused a sensation in Europe. Misrepresented as the victory of a popular army, it was held as proof that the French were not invincible, and the good news echoed throughout Germany. It was this that determined Napoleon to end the revolt by transferring the Grand Army to the Peninsula, where both Spanish and Portuguese were demonstrating their ineptitude by taking not the slightest advantage of their favourable position. The only sizeable force of consequence there was the British in Lisbon under Sir John Moore.

Quitting Erfurt in October, Napoleon was at Vittoria in November and in Madrid on 4 December. There he issued decrees, without consulting Joseph, reorganising Spanish administration, abolishing the Inquisition, reducing the number of convents and seizing clerical property. Sir John Moore advanced towards Burgos to threaten Napoleon's communications and save the South from being crushed. He beat a hasty, ill-organised retreat across the snowy mountains of Galicia to Corunna, where, on 16 January 1809, Soult just failed to prevent the main part of the force embarking on the British fleet. The

Spanish campaign seemed over, and the British expelled. But news that Austrian military preparations were well advanced caused Napoleon to leave Spain (17 January) for Central Europe, dealing with a threatened conspiracy in Paris on the way. The Grand Army was withdrawn and he was never again able to concentrate his forces to clear the Peninsula. The British re-established themselves in Lisbon and Spanish resistance entered a new phase of guerrilla warfare that the French found as impossible to crush as their descendants in Algeria, or the Americans in Vietnam in our own day. Thus Spain became an ulcer, draining off resources and men who were badly needed elsewhere: it was not a fatal disease, but it required a second army at a time when Napoleon dared not call on France for further levies. Consequently, he drew increasingly on the vassal states, and if this was impressive in terms of manpower, the quality of the army was not improved and there grew up a fierce resentment among the vassal states.

[41] WEAKENING FRENCH MORALE

An atmosphere of disillusionment and uncertainty seemed to be growing in France, and the lack of response to the challenge of fresh troubles in Spain and Central Europe was symptomatic of this disillusionment. The police continued to harass known Jacobins and royalist activity in Normandy and the West remained troublesome, but these were not serious and Fouché was easily able to silence a republican plot of 1808 that implicated General Malet. The malaise arose from continual war. Fontanes complained to Napoleon, 'France is sick with anxiety'. Decrès went further: 'The Emperor is mad, completely mad: he'll bring ruin upon himself and upon us all'. Already leading administrators and politicians contemplated treason to save their skins, and some were looking for a successor who would guarantee them their power. In December 1808, Talleyrand and Fouché contemplated proclaiming Murat, but Napoleon learned of their plans from an intercepted letter, and returning from Spain, he dismissed Talleyrand from the office of Grand Chamberlain after a violent scene. Fouché was spared for his police work and because he would be useful in securing the divorce he had broached shortly after Tilsit. There were signs of plottings among army officers, for public confidence was waning, reverses in Spain had damaged morale and Napoleon was playing for very high stakes in Central Europe.

N.—6*

In 1809 the old cry of 'one last victory' was wearing very thin. Yet Napoleon pushed forward with his plans, calling up the 1810 class of conscripts and combing through the previous classes. By March he had an army of 300,000 (a third for Italy), but he was under no illusions as to its fighting quality, since about half were foreigners unreliable in action, and the French contingents had too many untrained recruits. Already the fighting quality of the army was being seriously affected by problems of manpower – problems that were to lie heavily upon the 1812 campaign and the armies raised in Napoleon's last three years of power. Had the Archduke Charles of Austria struck quickly (as Talleyrand secretly urged) he might well have won in the early spring. As it was the campaign began badly for Napoleon with indecisive battles at Aspern and Essling (21 May) – checks of greater significance than that of Baylen, for here Napoleon himself was concerned.

In France, 1809 proved a difficult year, for the news from Spain was not encouraging and the Austrian campaign did not end in another Austerlitz. Meanwhile, the British had landed at Walcheren (July). Fouché, left in charge during Crétet's indisposition, took vigorous action worthy of a former Jacobin, and placed Antwerp's defence in the hands of Bernadotte. At home he organised a mass levy of the National Guard lest there be further landings on the Channel coast or in Provence. The public was alarmed at moves so reminiscent of 'the country in danger' and the army command was restless. Fouché may have been in communication with British agents, and his energetic measures could have served as the basis for a coup should the occasion have arisen. Napoleon was suspicious: he replaced Bernadotte and countermanded the preparations, although he made Fouché Duke of Otranto (15 August), perhaps for his support of the divorce proposal.

[42] GERMANY, 1807–12

The Austrian rising of 1809 followed naturally on that of Spain and the withdrawal of the Grand Army. But it was of greater significance than a reaction to troop movements. The Romantic Revival meant little to German peasants, but it promoted a new cultural nationalism among some German intellectuals, most clearly among the Heidelberg Romantics like Tieck, Brentano and Armin who were appealing to distant traditions of German medievalism. Görres, the former Jacobin, whose *Rheinische Merkur* Napoleon called the 'fifth great power', was publishing popular legends and his *Volksbücher* (1807). The *Nibelungenlied* was translated and Adam Muller was cleverly contrasting a free medieval Germany with present-day Napoleonic slavery. Stein later commented, 'It was Heidelberg that chiefly kindled the German flame which later swept the French out of our country'. Already German intellectuals were rejecting France as the measure of political liberty and Arndt's *Geist der Zeit* (1805), undisguisedly anti-French, boldly called for natural frontiers for the German people.

The end of the Holy Roman Empire caused little stir, but the collapse of Prussia in 1806, followed by the requisitions and exactions of French occupation, the forced disbandment of regiments and unemployment arising from economies in the civil service, had a telling effect. There was a rising in Hesse in December 1806, and sporadic attacks on French troops in Pomerania and Prussia continued. The customary apathy of town-dwellers was changing and Schleiermacker's sermons and Fichte's *Reden an die Deutsches Nation* (1807) awoke a national pride not felt since Luther. Liberal nobles, impoverished bourgeoisie and office-holders dismissed without compensation provided an anti-French leadership among circles that had once welcomed the Revolution, and in Königsberg in 1808 the Tugendbund was founded and spread rapidly among intellectuals as a potential nucleus for organising anti-French opinion. The Spanish revolt added fuel to the flames and Arndt proclaimed,

> Further and further rolls the Wheel of Destruction . . . Bonaparte will be vanquished if we attack him with his own devices.

But the cultural nationalism was no simple resistance to the foreigner, for the Tugendbund argued that the People should rise against Napoleon and secure their political rights and abolish social privilege in return. Such ideals inspired Turnvater John's *Deutsches Volkstum* (1810) despite its showing 'some of the most ludicrous traits which marred the new Germanism' (Treitsche). But the danger of social revolution was too patent in this idealism, and the aristocracy still feared to appeal to the people as they had feared to do in the 1790s.

Prussia
These years saw a positive regeneration of Prussia, a regeneration that was in effect an extreme form of the intellectual movement current in

Germany. It was hastened by the collapse of 1806, and among the soldiers and administrators who directed it, the leaders were Stein, the dispossessed Imperial Knight, and Hardenberg. Both were keen reformers and much impressed by the achievements of the French Revolution and Napoleon, which they intended to emulate without disturbing the existing social structure. 'We must do from above what the French have done from below', Hardenberg advised the king in 1807. Neither of them was a liberal, and both knew the king and the Junkers (noble landowners) would resist an appeal to the people. Thus the regeneration of Prussia was not comparable with the French Revolution and it produced a Prussia much nearer the old order than later propaganda would have us believe.

Both Stein and Hardenberg were responsible for the Emancipation Edict (9 October 1807) which abolished serfdom. This was less concerned with the political and social implications of ending feudalism than with a desire to release land for agricultural reform. It allowed for the gradual replacement of caste status by a more modern class structure based on property and wealth, so that nobles could enter professions and trade, and bourgeois and peasant could own land directly. By 1810 the Edict had created a widespread peasant land-ownership but the settlement terms were at considerable profit to the State and the Junkers and involved the destruction of many common law rights hitherto enjoyed by the peasantry. Feudal dues and magisterial authority – even forced labour – were retained. Clearly, the Edict did not herald a social revolution: its impact has been exaggerated. Stein arrived at Königsberg (where the King now held court) on 30 September 1807, and directed his efforts to reorganising the bureaucracy on authoritarian lines. His proposed Prussian Landtag was not proceeded with, and his actual reforms were few apart from the local government reform (19 November 1808) allowing extensive authority to new municipal bodies elected by householders. Stein's brief ministry of just over a year was more remarkable for its promise than for its achievement. It did, however, serve as an inspiration to others – notably to Humbolt whose educational reforms resulted in the foundation of Gymnasia (1809) and the University of Berlin (1810) with Fichte, Savigny and Niebuhr as professors.

The military reformers, led by Scharnhorst, Gneisenau, Grollman and Clausewitz, were not ashamed to adopt French methods for the army and to encourage a purge of the high command. Their reforms took time and therefore they resisted moves for a rising in 1808, although, encouraged by Dupont's capitulation at Baylen, secret negotiations had been opened with Austria. With the Grand Army withdrawn, Napoleon imposed a limit of 42,000 men in the regular Prussian army and forbade a national guard. It was at this time that the Krümper system was introduced, calling up recruits for a short period of basic training to be followed by reserve training. Later, the legend appeared that the system was devised in order to produce a large army, basically trained, without the French realising it. Recent research suggests that the system was introduced as an economy measure only, and in any case did not produce the massive army of 1813, which depended for its large numbers on ordinary volunteers.

The reformers were determined to drive out the French. Stein was concerned with an organised conspiracy to achieve this end that owed its inspiration to French experience in 1793. There was to be a *levée en masse* with the evacuation of women and children and the formation of guerrilla bands: nobles refusing to lead a national uprising were to be deprived of their privileges and the appeal to the people was to be completed with a constitution granted by the King, perhaps extending to all Germany excluding Austria. The plan upset the aristocracy because of its threat of social revolution and a fundamental change in the structure of Central European politics. Frederick William was prudent enough not to commit himself without first consulting the Tsar and then rejected Stein's plan in August 1808. Stein produced a simpler version designed to produce a popular uprising in November, before the Grand Army could return, but his efforts were not appreciated by the more conservative reformers, like Hardenberg, and the chorus of protest, led by the Queen, resulted in Stein's dismissal on 24 November, and York was able to write

> There's one of those madcap's heads broken, at any rate; the rest of the viper's breed will succumb to its poison . . . Germany will never lend itself to any Sicilian Vespers or Vendéan uprising. The Prussian peasant will do nothing unless he is ordered by his king . . . . Our situation begins to look distinctly better, both at home and abroad.

Belatedly, having intercepted plans for the conspiracy, Napoleon declared Stein an outlaw of the Empire (15 December 1808) and he fled to Prague.

The Prussian reform movement lost momentum and Prussia lost the opportunity to lead a new Germany. In April 1809, Major Schill led some troops to help Dörnberg's rebellion in Westphalia, but he marched as an individual, not as a German, nor even as a Prussian. The rebellion was easily suppressed and men turned to Austria for a lead. The war of 1809 might have been the War of Liberation, but then that war had not been preceded by the Moscow campaign and by Castlereagh's formation of the final coalition of the allies against Napoleon.

Austria

Austria had no self-conscious regeneration as had Prussia, but then her showing in the wars had been better, and the complexity of the Austrian empire with its many races and languages, made the path of the reformer fraught with difficulty – as Joseph II had discovered. Philip de Stadion, Chancellor since February 1806, was not prepared to tamper with the traditional social structures. He looked to another war to make his reputation. This was not immediately possible because of lack of money and the unwillingness of Hungary to assist, while from Paris, Metternich urged restraint. The Tilsit agreement provided another reason for caution, and reluctantly Stadion agreed to enforce the Continental System.

But Stadion's successful use of propaganda, aided by the news of Dupont's capitulation and by Stein's renewed efforts from Prague, as well as those of romantic writers like the Schlegels, and of diplomats like Pozzo di Borzo, made an Austrian rising more likely and encouraged Hungary to assist. An additional reason was provided by the seething discontent in the Tyrol against the French and the Bavarians. The withdrawal of the Grand Army and Talleyrand's efforts at Erfurt brought Stadion to a decision. But for him the struggle was in the name of legitimacy (even when helping Tyrolean rebels): the patriots who looked to Austria were under no illusions.

By the spring of 1808, the Archduke Charles's army reforms had produced a new army based on French organisation and with artillery regiments and regrouped cavalry, a pioneer corps and a corps of Tyrolean *chasseurs* (September 1808) who proved very useful as skirmishers. A Landwehr of volunteers began in June 1806 and by 1809 numbered 150,000: there was even a hope that a *levée en masse* would follow the departure of the Grand Army. Even if Stadion was disappointed in this particular, the Austrian showing in the Wagram campaign was very effective – a warning Napoleon could not afford to ignore, especially in view of the declining quality of his own forces.

Stadion was right to seize the opportunities provided by the situation in 1808–9; he was unlucky in having to fight without allies, for Russia would not commit herself and Britain was not prepared for direct intervention because of her commitments in the Peninsula. In London a dispute between Canning and Castlereagh over the use of Britain's army delayed the Walcheren expedition until it was too late (and certainly too inadequate) to help Austria. Stadion had to act quickly before Napoleon returned from Spain and whilst the Tsar was prepared not to intervene.

As Napoleon hastily gathered a new Grand Army in the early months of 1809, the Tyrol rose in revolt, prompted by Bavarian maladministration, the burden of conscription and new taxes, and encouraged by the clergy. On 29 May Andreas Hofer captured Innsbruck. This revolt of local patriots was no more than a nuisance, but it imperilled Napoleon's communications and absorbed valuable troops until it was suppressed (Hofer was executed on 20 February 1810). Meanwhile Austria was active in Galicia and in Saxony and for a moment there was the possibility of a German insurrection with Prussia joining the war. But disarray among the allies saved Napoleon.

Calmly, Napoleon risked Europe's displeasure by annexing Rome (17 May) and, despite the indecisive battles of Aspern and Essling, imprisoning the Pope on 6 July, the very day of the victory at Wagram. That battle ended the war: its tactics showed that Napoleon had lost none of his brilliance, yet it was not the crushing victory of earlier years. Nor did the agitation in Germany subside: a new atmosphere, strengthened by a common bond of resistance to French imperialism, inspired the patriots. Stapps, a young student, failed to assassinate the Emperor and in a personal interview refused a pardon, insisting on being executed.

This is the result of the secret societies which infest Germany, Napoleon complained. This is the effect of fine principles and the light of reason. They make young men assassins. But what can be done against Illuminism? A sect cannot be destroyed by cannon balls.

Napoleon was now anxious about the Tsar who had secured Finland and was fighting Turkey in the Principalities. The Tsar was not yet prepared to break with France and so Austria had to make peace at Schönbrunn (14 October). By this peace Bavaria gained Inn and Salzburg, Napoleon took the Illyrian provinces and Istria, the Grand

Duchy of Warsaw gained Lublin and Cracow with much of Western Galicia, and Russia gained Tarnopol. Austria lost some $3\frac{1}{2}$ million subjects and all direct access to the sea, and had to pay an indemnity, confirm her acceptance of the Continental System and recognise Joseph as King of Spain.

If it was a savage blow to Austria, it was also a disappointment for the Tsar who had hoped for gains in Galicia – a disappointment worsened by the introduction of the Code Napoléon into the Grand Duchy of Warsaw in 1810, a move that terrified the Russian nobility with fears of the abolition of serfdom. But Napoleon was in need of a bride and sought the Tsar's sister. Since the birth of an illegitimate son, Napoleon had been anxious to provide for his succession. The Tsar temporised, Joséphine accepted the divorce on 15 December, and it was legalised (without Papal consent) on 12 January 1810. Joséphine retained a high place in Napoleon's affections, and still retained the title of Empress, a substantial dowry and the house at Malmaison. But when the Tsar rejected the proposed marriage, the half-anticipated mortification mattered less, for Austria provided an alternative bride.

Metternich replaced Stadion in 1809 (see Milne, *Metternich*, University of London Press. Like Talleyrand (though not so nobly born) he was a brilliant diplomat and a libertine. As becoming the son-in-law of Kaunitz he sought a re-establishment of a European balance of power, which involved the defeat (but not necessarily the removal) of Napoleon. Metternich was no blind reactionary; he was prepared for reform to increase efficiency and relieve distress – but not to threaten the social order. The experiences of 1809 convinced him that Austria's best interests lay in a rapprochement with France in order to avoid dominance by Russia. Marie-Louise, the simpering eighteen-year-old daughter of the Emperor would serve this policy admirably – provide a wife and divide Russia from France. Negotiations were opened even before Alexander's refusal. Fouché, Joséphine and the Beauharnais favoured the match: Murat and the Bonapartes preferred a Russian princess. An engagement was announced on 7 February 1810, before Alexander had returned his answer. Napoleon had already decided that the Russian alliance no longer served his purposes well enough.

He married Marie-Louise on 2 April and the heir, King of Rome, was born on 20 March 1811. Napoleon had now cut himself free of the Revolution. The former governess to Louis XVI's children, Mme de

Montesquieu, was made personal attendant to Marie-Louise and the old aristocracy took the upper hand at court. There was even a rumour that surviving regicides would be punished and a solemn rehabilitation of Louis XVI staged. As if to strengthen the impression of a return to the *ancien régime*, arbitrary arrest (in effect by *lettre de cachet*) and full censorship were restored. A new chapter was opened in the Empire's story: Napoleon, recognising that his son would survive only if he were a genius, began to confine the influence of his family, whose predatoriness and wranglings had already brought disrespect on the Empire. The régime was becoming increasingly centred on Napoleon. The Kingdom of Italy was assigned in advance to Napoleon's second legitimate son and even the faithful Eugène de Beauharnais lost his title of heir presumptive – he was compensated with the Grand Duchy of Frankfurt.

But the Austrian détente was not another Tilsit: Napoleon would stand alone. Surprisingly, he did not take the opportunity to return himself to the Peninsula and once again underestimated the nature of that war by sending insufficient reinforcements. It may have been because of the marriage, or suspicion of the Tsar's next move, for he expected a breach in the Continental System and a Russian approach to Britain. In June 1810 disputes over the succession to Charles XIII of Sweden led a pro-French group to approach Bernadotte. A French Marshal as Crown Prince of Sweden would secure the Baltic against the British and prove a useful ally in any war with Russia – particularly to regain Finland. Despite Bernadotte's unreliability, Napoleon consented to his becoming Crown Prince (21 August) and Sweden declared war on Britain on 17 November.

Alexander affected to be furious – but in secret Bernadotte assured him he had no reason to fear an attack on Finland. Russian preparations for war were well advanced. In the spring of 1810 Czartoryski had been sounded out about Russian troops crossing the Grand Duchy of Warsaw as far as to the Oder, and Pozzo di Borgo had gone as ambassador to Constantinople, but had travelled by way of Vienna where he had discussed with Metternich an Austro–Russian partition of the Balkans. At the end of 1810 the Russian army moved up to the western frontiers. By that time the impact of the Continental System upon Russia's agricultural economy had been so pronounced that Alexander had refused to enforce the Trianon and Fontainebleau Decrees. On 31 December 1810 he allowed trade with Britain. The Continental System was breached in the east as it was in the west. In

January Napoleon annexed the Duchy of Oldenburg, belonging to the Tsar's brother-in-law, in order to stop smuggling. It was in defiance of the Erfurt agreement and was interpreted by the Tsar as a calculated insult. War would follow.

[43] BREACH WITH RUSSIA

By 1810 Napoleon was finally convinced that the Tsar was prepared to defy him. The Tsar must be humbled – and Russia defeated if France were to gain Constantinople and control of the Levant. The breach in the Continental System provided a good excuse. He was well aware of the risks of a Russian campaign: the lesson of Charles XII was but a century old, and his own experiences in 1807 had revealed many difficulties to be overcome. French preparations during 1811 were so enormous that Nesselrode nervously suggested the Tsar should strike whilst he yet had time – but Alexander's finances would not stand the strain. However, troops were massed on the frontier and a suggestion of reconstituting Poland made to Czartoryski, in return for free passage to the Oder where Prussian forces might be recruited. Feelers were put out to Stockholm and to Vienna where Metternich was even offered the Principalities (February 1811). But the negotiations failed for Prussia was growing suspicious of the Tsar's ambitions and Metternich preferred to wait on events. Bernadotte offered Napoleon 30,000 troops in return for Norway.

At the moment that Masséna (see page 181) was retreating from the Torres Vedras, Napoleon was completing his preparations for the coming war. The administration at Dresden was put on the alert and defensive treaties with Austria, Prussia, Sweden and Turkey were signed. By September 1811 he had decided the war would begin in the June of the following year, allowing the summer months for a short campaign and the destruction of the Russian army by an overwhelming force. By March 1812 Prussia was reoccupied and Victor entered Berlin, obliging Frederick William to supply 20,000 men and provision the Grand Army (setting off the cost against the still unpaid indemnity). The war party at Königsberg disintegrated and Stein felt it best to leave Prague – he was given asylum in St Petersburg in May 1812.

Metternich's position was not enviable: whoever won the war would have Austria at his mercy. He chose France, signing a treaty on 14 March 1812 to supply 30,000 men in return for the Illyrian provinces,

Galicia and a guarantee of Turkish integrity (which secured him against a Franco–Russian partition of the Balkans). On the surface, Napoleon's diplomatic position was strong, but the treaties were mere documents, and Metternich made it clear to the Tsar on 2 June that Austrian mobilisation would be a façade only. Sweden was feeling the ill effects of the Continental System and when Davout occupied Swedish Pomerania (January 1812) Bernadotte relaxed the System and on 5 April made a treaty with Alexander allowing for Russian aid in taking Norway in return for Swedish harassment of Napoleon's lines of communication in North Germany. On 18 July Bernadotte made peace with Britain. On 28 May Alexander had made peace at Bucharest with Turkey. His diplomatic situation was far stronger than Napoleon's.

French troops were moving towards the Niemen early in 1812, using Danzig as a base. Between February and May troops from Italy, France and Germany moved up and the plains of Poland grazed herds of cattle to provide food for the campaign. On 8 April the Tsar demanded evacuation of Prussia and Swedish Pomerania, compensation for the Duke of Oldenburg and a new commercial treaty. Napoleon did not reply but sought desperately to settle things in Spain by even suggesting to Canning that he would allow a restoration of the Portuguese monarchy. On 9 May he left Saint-Cloud and on 25 May at Dresden he received in great pomp the Emperor of Austria, the King of Prussia and his other vassals. It was a grandiose anti-Russian demonstration and the peak of his career. There was no similar gathering of monarchs until the Vienna Congress in 1814–15.

On 28 May, leaving Marie-Louise and his court at Dresden, he set out for the Niemen which he intended to cross with an army of 380,000 men with Macdonald and Schwarzenberg, each with a further army of 30,000 men, on either wing. But the invasion was that of a conqueror, not of a liberator: Napoleon had no intention of abolishing serfdom in Russia, only of using Russian troops in his next campaign, perhaps in Persia or the Himalayas. War had once more become the sport of kings, but now the stakes were immeasurably greater than anything coming within the eighteenth-century scheme of things.

[44] THE PENINSULAR WAR

The significance for Napoleon of the continued struggle in the Peninsula was that it consumed resources and men badly needed elsewhere and prevented a settlement in Central Europe. But the continuance of the British presence was not certain. After the evacuation of Moore's army in January 1809, there was active support for opening another front in the Netherlands to help the coming Austrian rebellion. The failure of the Walcheren expedition once more concentrated attention on the Peninsula, but as Napoleon restored his power across Europe in 1809–10 and the economic crisis of 1811 deepened, pressure increased for a complete withdrawal of the British troops.

Wellesley (created Viscount Wellington in July) returned to Portugal on 22 April 1809. His position was weak, both militarily and politically. Hence his caution. His tactical skill stood him in excellent stead, however, and it was not until Waterloo that Napoleon realised how good a general the British had produced. Wellington had every advantage of easy and secure sea communications and a friendly Portugal as a base: the Spaniards, however, were as unco-operative as their successive administrations were corrupt and weak. They resented Britain's open trade with Latin America, and despite hatred of the French, conscription was unpopular. Guerrilla warfare was more popular, for the guerrillas were a law unto themselves. By constant attacks on forage parties, convoys and isolated posts, they wore down French morale and obliged the French to occupy the country, thus absorbing more troops. But their effectiveness is difficult to gauge and it may have been exaggerated by popular legend. They could not stand against a strong force, and sometimes they were mere brigands who mulcted all alike for profit.

Had Napoleon returned after Wagram with his full army the war would probably have ended quickly. In the event, King Joseph proved unequal to his difficult task and the local French commanders, lacking overall direction and jealous of each other, failed to cooperate – Ney even refused to obey Masséna. Wellington was usually able to meet individual commanders and rarely had to face a combined army. The French, with a high proportion of 'foreign' troops, their morale sapped by guerrilla activity, poor leadership, lack of success, irregular pay, insufficient food and bad communications, proved no match for the British. The Peninsular War was different from the other campaigns: the supply problem dominated the movement of troops – and partly accounts for Wellington's continual counter-marching into and out of Spain from his Portuguese base.

It was lack of co-operation between Soult and Ney that gave Wellington the opportunity to defeat Victor at Talavera on 27 July

1809. But he retired to Portugal and the French thought it wise to secure southern Spain before pursuing him. When Masséna in September 1810 at last invaded Portugal, he found his progress checked first by a 'scorched earth' policy, and then by the defensive lines of the Torres Vedras which he could not penetrate without a siege train. He retired in April 1811. Wellington, for his part, was unable to make any progress before the spring of 1812 – the war was far from one-sided. On 22 July he defeated Marmont at Salamanca and occupied Madrid. But even with French forces depleted for the Moscow campaign, he felt constrained to retreat to Portugal. It was in 1812 that the Spanish liberals secured a liberal constitution – it was to be discarded without protest in 1814. Fugier suggests that there was little nationalism in the Spanish resistance to Napoleon.

Napoleon failed in Russia and more troops were withdrawn from Spain to fight in Central Europe, so that Wellington was able to rout Jourdan at Vittoria (21 June 1813) – a victory that echoed throughout Europe and determined Austria to join the Fourth Coalition. Thereafter, it proved surprisingly difficult to cross the Pyrenees and enter France. Toulouse fell on 10 April 1814, four days after Napoleon had abdicated.

PART VIII
Napoleon's Fall

[45] THE MOSCOW CAMPAIGN

The risks implicit in the War of 1812 were well understood by Napoleon. He had made massive preparations and anticipated a short campaign, so that his absence from the Empire would be at a minimum and he could return triumphant having imposed on Russia a defeat as humiliating as that on Prussia in 1806. This was unlike the War in the Peninsula, for the troops were well supplied and the Russian army may well have quaked at the thought of what faced them. It is necessary to stress this, because, since the campaign proved a total failure, it has been too readily dismissed as the effort of a madman who could never succeed. The invasion was not ill-conceived, the preparations could scarcely have been better: it was not the invasion itself that ruined his career, it was the loss of the army after taking Moscow. It is also worth recalling that from December 1812 to March 1814 is fifteen months – a long time for the defeated Napoleon to continue to hold out against Europe.

The war was launched to settle Napoleon's command of Europe, but his proclamation to the Army (22 June) declared he fought in defence of Poland, and he crossed the Niemen on 24 June without a formal declaration of war. The principal army marched with Napoleon. Macdonald, assisted at first by a Prussian contingent under Yorck, commanded the small army in the North; Jerome (later sent back for incompetence) that in the South. These were to act as pincers to trap the Russian forces and so bring on the main battle. Had this happened in the early weeks of the hot summer Russia might well have been destroyed.

Safe in St Petersburg Alexander was under pressure to make peace.

The Russian commander, Barclay de Tolly, knew he could not face the French: despite army reforms, especially Arakcheyev's work with the artillery, the Grand Army would overwhelm him. He had no alternative but to fall back – although he was accused of treasonous connivance with the French for doing so by Rostopchin, Mayor of Moscow. Bagration, commanding the second army, was all for a fight; but he, too, had to fall back. As the armies retreated, peasants escaped with what remained of their property and burnt their villages: this was no planned strategy, Barclay simply withdrew; it was Napoleon who first spoke of a 'Scythian plan' to lure the French into the interior.

Time and again the Russians escaped the clumsy French man-oeuvres. The Grand Army was a motley one, its movements slow and its discipline bad, while the poor roads and the |lack of cover made surprise moves impossible. The country yielded nothing, but despite the slowness of the advance, the supply trains were left behind so that food was short and draught horses died quickly from heat, exhaustion, and lack of fodder. Meanwhile the persistent failure to catch the Russians damaged morale and desertion was soon a massive problem. The supply problem got out of hand, and large contingents of troops were sent back to Poland in August to relieve the pressure on food and fodder supplies.

The Russians made a stand at Smolensk but retired before a major engagement could be brought on and the city was surrendered. This was a new type of warfare for Napoleon and he contemplated going into winter quarters at Smolensk, but he decided to press on to catch the Russians whom he knew to be suffering as badly as he was. Kutuzov succeeded Barclay but was no more inclined to offer battle until Bagration joined him at Borodino on 7 September. Fearful of losing contact, Napoleon pinned the Russian army by successive waves of men, eventually carrying the day by sheer weight of num-bers. It was a clumsy, bloody battle that caused Ney to say the Emperor had forgotten his trade.

By 14 September he was in Moscow and Rostopchin caused fires to be lit to destroy much of the city. Still there was no response to Napoleon's repeated messages to Alexander calling for surrender. Russia seemed defeated, yet already the gigantic scheme seemed to have misfired and Napoleon's position was precarious. Supplies were not getting through, partly because of the distance, partly because the Cossacks attacked the columns. If he were to winter in Moscow, some

1500 miles from Paris, he might lose control of Central Europe to
Austria. The Poles already were disaffected because he had refused to
annex Lithuania to the Grand Duchy of Warsaw or to re-create the
Kingdom of Poland. Ill-discipline and shortage of supplies added to
his difficulties and he ordered a retreat on 19 October, moving first
southwards towards Kaluga where Kutuzov kept his distance. On
25 October, he was almost captured by a Cossack patrol: he ordered a
phial of poison which he kept by him – he would not be taken alive.

Alexander, meanwhile, had found new strength and courage in the
suffering of his people. The court now called for a fight to the finish
and Mme de Staël arrived to add her voice. The Tsar had fallen under
the spell of mystical writings and already imagined himself God's
chosen instrument to destroy Anti-Christ and to lead the crusade the
reactionaries had been preaching for a decade – it served also as a
happy cloak for naked self-interest. His confidence was the greater
because he now knew the Russian people would resist Napoleon to the
end. There had been a fear that Napoleon might win the war immediately by granting emancipation to the serfs – a fear already reported
in the 1807 campaign by Rostopchin. It is amazing the serfs did not
welcome the French as deliverers, for the Russian army was as
savage in its marauding as the French. The Pugachev rebellion (1775)
was still green in the memory and the invasion gave them another
opportunity: rumours of emancipation spread rapidly and the landowners of White Russia appealed to Napoleon in person for protection.
He responded and French troops crushed the serf riots. Here was
Napoleon the conqueror and monarchist.

This sealed his fate and the Russian peasant responded with a
fierce patriotism and a vicious and destructive guerrilla activity. Such
deliberate self-sacrifice was an inspiration to the coming century;
there were rumours that the Tsar would grant them their freedom,
there were even mutinies by peasants who determined to kill the
officers who ordered them to retreat and instead to destroy the
French and then go to the Tsar to be rewarded with freedom. Thus the
defeat of the French in the peasant mind became synonymous with the
end of serfdom. Napoleon had forgotten the Revolution. The Russian
bourgeoisie were few and antagonised by the Continental System; the
nobility rejected the French as Napoleon had rejected his natural
allies the Russian peasant.

The retreat was not a rout until Smolensk was reached. By then
the French forces were starving: it was this logistical problem that

was the reason for the destruction of the army. Cannibalism had begun. It was not the snow – Dr Angervo, the Finnish meteorologist, has demonstrated that the 1812 winter was not severe by Russian standards. The rivers were not properly frozen, and the frosts and snow did not begin until the army left Smolensk, by which time it was already a rabble. Only at the Berezina river did Kutuzov attempt to check the French and in forcing the crossing, 'Napoleon not only completely saved his honour, but acquired new glory' (Clausewitz). The Russian army was suffering as badly as the French: barely a third of it reached Vilna and it was in no more fit state to fight than the retreating French, who left their artillery and struggled on without pretence of discipline. On 13 December, Ney and the rear-guard crossed the Niemen. The most serious loss was not the massive loss of life, but the loss of artillery and cavalry – the lack of which was seriously to reduce Napoleon's effectiveness in the next fifteen months.

Kutuzov allowed the French to leave. Russia had suffered enough and he saw no need to fight battles for Europe: he stopped at the frontier. But in North Germany there was a call for a national rising which was to welcome the Russians as liberators. The opportunity to extend Russian power whilst being welcomed as the champion freeing Europe of the scourge of Napoleon was too much for Alexander: he launched the 1813 campaign. After the bloody defeats of Lutzen, Bautzen and Dresden, the ideas of Kutuzov did not seem so strange. But the victory of 1812 was not won by the army; it belonged to the peasant, and vague talk of reform, soon forgotten, was a poor re-compense.

Napoleon had left his army on 6 December. He needed to resume the reins of the administration before news of the disaster reached Paris. He needed also to rebuild a new army – amazingly, he even expected to get levies from Prussia and Austria. What finally decided him to leave for Paris was the news that had just reached him that on 23 October General Malet, a royalist priest and a mixed bag of conspira-tors, including some former Jacobins, had forged a document announc-ing Napoleon's death in Russia, declared a new constitution and formed a provisional government under the banished General Moreau. The conspiracy was quickly checked and Malet shot on 29 October. The régime was never imperilled, but what disturbed Napo-leon was that no one thought to proclaim the King of Rome as heir.

[46] THE WAR OF 1813 AND THE FIRST ABDICATION

Stein reverted to his plan of 1808, encouraging the Tsar to appeal to the people and dispossess those princes who would not follow. But there was too much support for a patriotic war among aristocracy and upper bourgeoisie to make an appeal to the people necessary. Patriotic enthusiasm had the effect of allowing rulers to lose their inhibitions: they could safely rely upon the support of their subjects for the first time.

On 30 December 1812, in defiance of Frederick William, Yorck signed the Convention of Tauroggen allowing Russian troops to approach the Oder, while the Polish nobles, hopeful of a restored Poland, followed Czartoryski in supporting the Russians. The French continued to withdraw. Frederick William was slow to realise that this restored his freedom of action: perhaps wisely he feared Napoleon's return and suspected that the Tsar desired to annex Poland and even East Prussia. His reticence may not have been utterly inappropriate: but he was forced into action by the patriots. Stein appeared at Königsberg demanding the summoning of the estates, but patriotism was kept in check by restricting the choice of officers in the Landwehr, which was now raised, to nobles. The social order was not to be imperilled. But the King had to issue an Appeal to the People (10 February). The Landwehr took time to organise and was only a sizeable force at the end of the war, while the Landsturm of older men (founded 12 April) was little used. There was no *levée en masse*. Much has been made of the War of Liberation: one must distinguish between myth and reality. There was no trouble from guerrillas in Prussia as there was in Spain. Napoleon's principal worry was for the loyalty of the German princes.

> The myth of the national uprising against Napoleon was later fostered by German intellectuals who had been present at Leipzig in the same sense as George IV was present at Waterloo ... In fact, Germany turned against Napoleon only in the sense that the German Princes sensed the coming storm and changed sides. (Taylor)

The Princes took good care to watch over their territorial interests, for all their enthusiasm for a patriotic War of Liberation. Under pressure from Stein and Yorck (the leading reactionary general) a treaty between Prussia and Russia was signed at Kalisch only on 28 February. Napoleon was being given time to recover. The Prussian declaration of war came only on 17 March, and the Appeal to Germans on 19 March, calling on the Princes to lead their people on pain of forfeiture and declaring the Confederation of the Rhine at an end, was issued jointly by the Tsar and Frederick William. The Princes were nervous of Napoleon and feared Russian and Prussian ambitions. They looked to Austria to save them from a possible threat from below and the threat from the two Powers.

Metternich viewed Europe from the Austrian position. The 1812 campaign restored his freedom of action, but he saw three dangers. First, a possible fresh outbreak of French power; secondly, the threat to the social order and to Austria's position in Germany implicit in the views of the German patriots, especially those who talked vaguely of national unity. The third danger was the emergence of Russia as the predominant power in Europe, for Russia's interests in Central Europe, in Poland and in the Balkans conflicted with Austria's: there was no point in exchanging French imperialism for Russian dominance.

Metternich was in no hurry to commit Austria to the allies and would do so only on his terms. He refused to help Napoleon, despite Marie-Louise, for a French victory would leave him at Napoleon's mercy. By 30 January 1813 Schwarzenberg, who had scarcely taken part in the 1812 campaign, had withdrawn, leaving Poland to the Russians and Metternich, while keeping negotiations with Napoleon open, awaited the right moment to join the allies. In Italy he was rapidly gaining influence, for Murat, back in Naples from the Grand Army, was negotiating for the retention of his kingdom. If the British (having links with the Bourbons and with the *carbonari*) had not favoured a restoration of the former royal house, Murat would have deserted Napoleon at this juncture.

Castlereagh, meanwhile, was anxious to consolidate the allies both to avoid the risk of defeat through disunity and to prevent Britain becoming isolated. The Treaty of Kalisch had persuaded him to intervene and on 3 March he gained Bernadotte for the coalition by promising him Norway. In April he offered subsidies on condition that Hanover was enlarged and the allies did not make a separate peace. The war would go on with France facing an increasingly united coalition.

Napoleon had acted with his accustomed vigour. He had called up

the 1813 levies from Moscow on 22 September, and in January he
called those of 1814. They responded without enthusiasm. Troops
were recalled from Spain and the Paris municipal guard were sent to
Germany. Sufficient cannon was collected, but the lack of horses
reduced his efficiency, and finance was a major problem – he had to
draw heavily upon his own personal reserves. By May he had a
crushing superiority over the Russians and Prussians in North
Germany and took the initiative in a manner that showed he had not
lost his genius. But there were many failures among the field commanders, so that Napoleon did not always achieve the full success he
anticipated. He won at Lützen (2 May) but Eugène failed to cut off
the allied retreat. Then the Russians and Prussians were trapped at
Bautzen (21 May), but the possibility of a brilliant victory was
thrown away by Ney's bungling and once again the allies escaped,
there being no cavalry to force a pursuit. He feared Metternich might
march on his flank: he could deal with two powers well enough, but
three stretched his resources. Furthermore, he needed time to call up
reserves. He therefore negotiated an armistice at Pleiswitz (4 June).
Perhaps this was a mistake, for had he followed up his victories with a
third, his position might have been restored. But he knew Austria to
be unreliable and he had lost too many men to risk an extended
campaign.

The armistice gave time to both sides, and on 14 June Castlereagh
bound the allies together with a guarantee of £2 million in subsidies
and the assurance that none should make a separate peace. At
Reichenbach, on 27 June, Austria agreed to join if Napoleon's response to Austrian mediation was inadequate. Metternich met Napoleon
at Dresden, but it was too much to expect him to make concessions:
he had, after all, just won the campaign. Metternich reported him as
saying,

> Your sovereigns, born on the throne, may be beaten twenty times
> and still go back to their capitals. I, an upstart soldier, cannot do this.
> My reign will not survive the day when I cease to be strong and
> therefore feared.

News of Wellington's victory at Vittoria caused the allies to raise
their terms and Austria declared war (11 August) confirming her
alliance with the allies at the Treaty of Teplitz (9 September). By this
time the allies outnumbered Napoleon. They were joined by Bernadotte who brought with him Moreau, the Revolutionary general who,

like Bernadotte, had once conspired for Napoleon's place. They persuaded the allies to adopt a new approach, using Napoleon's tactics to divide the French and to engage only the local commanders, never Napoleon himself. Eventually their plan worked, but not before the allies had been terrified by Napoleon routing Schwarzenberg at Dresden (27 August). Moreau was killed in the battle, but the final victory was denied Napoleon by his own gastric illness and the exhaustion of his troops who could not pursue the defeated Austrians. On 18 October he was cornered at Leipzig, outnumbered two-to-one. Bernadotte's arrival and the desertion of the Saxons hastened his defeat in what has romantically been called the 'Battle of the Nations'. The South German States joined the allies, Murat returned to Naples and resumed his contacts with Metternich, and the Grand Army was forced back to the Rhine, leaving some 120,000 men blocked in German fortresses. In Italy, Eugène was routed at Valsarno (26 October). The Grand Empire was about to fall.

But Metternich was anxious lest hasty action deprive the allies of the advantage of their position, and it was agreed to offer from Frankfurt (9 November) a negotiated peace on the basis of a general settlement of Central Europe and France retiring to her natural frontiers. Metternich was no doubt sincere in putting forward the terms, for it would consolidate his position in Italy (where he was still negotiating with Murat) and Germany, reduce the danger of Russian dominance and prevent the Tsar replacing Napoleon with Bernadotte, a scheme to which he was utterly opposed. Napoleon was happy to negotiate to gain time to raise another army and to endeavour to divide the allies. To accept the natural frontiers would be more than difficult for Napoleon, but he was aware that France would not rise to defend him. A draft treaty was produced by 2 December. But events overtook the Frankfurt proposals, for on 17 December Holland revolted and declared for the Prince of Orange: this breached the natural frontiers and Britain refused to consider a France that continued to be in control of Belgium.

Castlereagh was now emerging as the moulder of allied policy – he was their paymaster, after all – and already was negotiating for a union of Holland and Belgium to serve as a buffer state, and to compensate Holland for the loss of her colonies. Castlereagh arrived at Basle on 18 January 1814 and presented his conditions to the allies: none should negotiate a separate peace with Napoleon; Belgium should be joined to Holland and Prussia have gains on the Rhine; the

Bourbons should be restored (not for any principle of legitimacy, but to avoid Bernadotte ruling in Paris as a Russian puppet); and the freedom of the seas and British colonial gains were to be matters for Britain to decide. A new era had dawned: the Revolution was long past and the allies were concerned for the problems of the next fifty years. The Age of Metternich had arrived.

Napoleon might have divided the allies by supporting Austria against Russian ambitions, had he responded to the Frankfurt proposals more quickly. As it was, the invasion of France was begun with Schwarzenberg moving from Switzerland towards Lyons and Blücher penetrating Lorraine. Napoleon was in desperate straits over manpower. There would be no *levée en masse:*

> Rouse the nation when the Revolution has destroyed the nobles and priests and I myself have destroyed the Revolution?

Lack of money was another problem, for France was having now to pay for war (for the past decade her defeated enemies had paid). The politicians already had made their position clear: in December the Legislative Body had dared to demand to be informed of the allied proposals. It agreed to fight to defend the integrity of France in return for a guarantee of civil liberty, but blamed the present situation on

> a vexatious administration, excessive taxes ... a barbarous and endless war swallows up periodically the youth torn from education, agriculture and the arts.

Napoleon prorogued the Legislative Body.

War weariness characterised France's reaction to invasion. There was passive resistance to conscription, requisitioning and taxes, but no great enthusiasm for a restored Bourbon. Only where the allied armies were indisciplined was there any popular resistance. In the South, where the British paid for their requisitioning, the invasion was even popular. Officials anxious to provide for their future paralysed the administration, and the royalists were active in aiding 'our good friends, the enemy', raising rebellion once more in the West, and on 12 March the Mayor of Bordeaux, a member of the Chevaliers de la Foi, surrendered the town to the British and welcomed the Duc d'Angoulême.

Napoleon remained full of vigour. Handing over the administration to Joseph and Marie-Louise, he left Paris on 25 January intent on preventing the allied armies uniting. He defeated Blücher at Brienne

(29 January) only to be overwhelmed by weight of numbers at La
Rothière (1 February). Caulincourt was sent to a futile conference at
Châtillon. He was offered the 1792 frontiers and temporised (7
February). Talleyrand would have used his initiative. Perceiving an
opportunity to divide the allies, Napoleon rejected the terms,
defeated Blücher again and checked Schwarzenberg. But fresh troops
were on the march from Germany, and Bernadotte was joining them,
having obliged Denmark to surrender Norway to him. The allies still
continued negotiations, but on 9 March Castlereagh secured the Treaty
of Chaumont, binding the four powers against France for twenty
years, each to supply 150,000 men and to guarantee a settlement of a
new European order. Only then did he release the £5 million he now
promised in subsidies.

Napoleon contemplated a drive into Lorraine to cut the enemy
communications, but his plans were revealed by a captured letter and
after Schwarzenberg had overwhelmed him at Arcis, the allied armies
made a dash for Paris where Marmont, hoping perhaps to play the rôle
of Monk, surrendered the city on 30 March, and joined the Austrian
forces by invitation on 4 April. On 31 March, the Tsar entered Paris
and a proclamation invited the Senate to form a provisional government with Talleyrand at its head. On 3 April the Senate deposed
Napoleon and on 6 April called Louis XVIII to the throne. Meanwhile
the Marshals gathered at Fontainebleau and refused to fight further:
they urged Napoleon to abdicate in favour of his son, but when the
Tsar demanded unconditional surrender, he gave way on 6 April. Five
days later he signed the Treaty of Fontainebleau, retaining the title
Emperor and agreeing to be sovereign of Elba with a pension of 2
million francs, annually paid by the French government. The terms
were the Tsar's, and Castlereagh and Metternich, coming up from
Dijon, were enraged. By the same treaty, Marie-Louise and his son
(whom he was not to see again) were to go to Parma. On the night of
11 April Napoleon attempted to commit suicide with the phial that
had been prepared after Moscow. He survived, and took a tragic
farewell of his soldiers who alone remained faithful to him. On his
journey through Provence to Elba, he was subjected to such hostile
demonstrations that he felt obliged to disguise himself.

[47] THE HUNDRED DAYS

Louis XVIII's restoration was not an occasion of general rejoicing either among the allies or in France. In his twenty years' exile Louis had learnt political wisdom, and he was now guided by Talleyrand whose skilful advocacy saved several towns on the Saar frontier that might otherwise have been lost to France when the First Treaty of Paris (30 May) restored the frontiers of 1792. French colonies were not restored, but the incredible leniency of the terms – no indemnity or army of occupation – was not a measure of the allies' compassion, but of their disagreement.

The four great powers were sensitive of their strained relations. A preliminary meeting in London had revealed the extent of their division, and when the brilliant gathering assembled at Vienna in September, agreement was no nearer. Britain rejected all discussion on freedom of the seas and decided problems of restoring colonial conquests unilaterally. On the continent, Poland was the principal problem. The Tsar wanted it all, with Prussia getting compensation in Saxony. Prussia wanted Alsace and Lorraine. The discussions became so acrimonious that on 3 January 1815 Castlereagh and Metternich signed a secret treaty of alliance with Talleyrand directed against Russia, and the prospect of war was real. However the Tsar was deeply under the influence of Mme de Krüdener, whose evangelical appeals concentrated the Tsar's earlier ideas of a league of sovereigns to maintain peace into a formal proposal for a Holy Alliance, which was established in September. Napoleon's return from Elba had the effect of holding the allies together – committees sat throughout the Hundred Days.

The final treaty was signed on 9 June and the Vienna Settlement proved a triumph of the statesmanship of Castlereagh and Metternich. A ring of buffer states confined France: Holland united with Belgium, Prussian gains on the Rhine, Piedmont enlarged. Austria was saved from Russian dominance by becoming herself predominant in Central Europe: in Italy she gained Lombardy and Venetia, Istria and Dalmatia, while she dominated the Central Duchies and was happy to have the Papal States restored. In Naples the Bourbons returned and Murat, routed at Ferrara and Tolentino in May 1815, lost his opportunity of remaining king. Russia gained Finland and 'Congress Poland' as a separate kingdom (Austria regaining Tarnopol and Galicia and Prussia retaining Thorn and Posen). Prussia gained a third

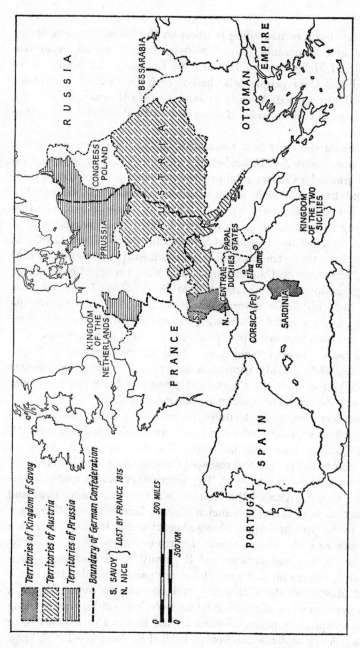

EUROPE IN 1815

Compare with the maps of Europe in 1799 (page 24) and 1810-12 (page 137).

of Saxony and a commanding position on the Rhine. Sweden, losing Finland and Pomerania, gained Norway from Denmark (who also surrendered Heligoland to Britain). In Germany the princes were restored and their people, who had fought the War of Liberation, remained unrewarded. As early as January 1814 Görres had made the columns of the *Rheinische Merkur* ring with denunciations of the Princes.

In France the brief first restoration of the Bourbons was not a happy one. Louis XVIII landed at Calais on 24 April 1814 and on 4 June granted a Charter retaining the principal gains of the Revolution and the Napoleonic administration. There would be equality before the law, the career open to talent, no conscription, taxation according to wealth, no arbitrary arrest, freedom of worship and of opinion, inviolability of property, including the National Lands. It was, as Artz says, 'the most liberal instrument of government that existed anywhere on the Continent'. The King exercised government through responsible ministers. A Chamber of Peers (chosen by the King, but containing several marshals, many of the Napoleonic nobility, and Cadoudal as a reward for his faithful services) voted on taxes and laws presented by the King. A second chamber was to be elected on a narrow franchise, and until this had been done, Napoleon's Legislative Body continued to serve. The upper bourgeoisie were delighted with the Charter. It preserved their power against democrats, liberals, and counter-revolutionaries alike.

Louis, however, was not vitally interested in politics: his ministers were in effect superior clerks and he allowed Wellington and Pozzo di Borgo quite considerable influence. The French people remained indifferent to the régime and resented the substitution of the Bourbon white cockade for the tricolor. The reactionary nobles under Artois and the clergy, regarded the Charter as a temporary expedient and were set upon restoring the ancien régime. Louis did not discourage them, for he gave prominent places at court and in the administration to former *émigrés*, while Dupont, imprisoned since Baylen, became Minister of War and demoralised the army by discharging a large number of officers on half pay. The clergy gained the abolition of the Grand Master of the University and concessions over education. Anger grew as signs of reaction became obvious, and it was not long before conspiracies began. Fouché looked to the Duc d'Orléans, or even a regency under Marie-Louise, backed by Austria – for he knew Europe would not consent to Napoleon's return. Maret unashamedly worked for his master's return, keeping him informed, while Drouet tried to provoke a rebellion in the North.

Napoleon himself had grievances. The allies refused him his son (it mattered less that Marie-Louise had taken Neipperg into her bed), and Louis XVIII declared he would not pay the pension. On 1 March 1815 he returned amid general acclamation and on 14 March Ney, sent to arrest him, joined him at Auxerre. Louis XVIII left Paris for Lille, where he found the garrison hostile and moved on to Ghent.

There was no serious resistance to Napoleon – Angoulême's attempt to raise Languedoc failed. But there was a new atmosphere in the France of the Hundred Days. Political life was active and the spirit of the Revolution walked abroad. Napoleon himself invoked it by his violent attacks on priests and nobles. Jacobin bourgeois revived the old federations in Brittany (April) and Paris (May) and in the East, the 'Marseillaise' was sung again and dim memories of 1793 revived. Napoleon was alarmed – indeed, he complained that he would have stayed in Elba had he realised the concessions he was to be forced to make. Arrived in Paris, he played a clever card by issuing the *Acte Additionnel* allowing a liberal constitution very similar to the Charter. It paved the way for the Napoleonic Legend with its sham constitutionalism, that was to forge the link between the Bonapartes and the Liberals of the Second Empire (1852–70) and added fuel to what Guizot called

> the old quarrel which the [First] Empire had smothered and the Charter was designed to extinguish, the quarrel of the old France and the new, of the 'emigration' and the 'revolution'.

Napoleon issued the *Acte* in conjunction with Benjamin Constant, Mme de Staël's protégé and leader of the liberals: but this was too curious an alliance and the *Acte* was soon contemptuously referred to as 'Benjamine'. Universal male suffrage was restored, but with the former electoral colleges to control it, and life peerages for the restored Senate. A plebiscite brought a disappointing response and only half the electorate voted for the deputies. The liberals were already becoming suspicious and Fouché, in charge of the police, was lenient to them, and was himself in secret contact with Metternich and Talleyrand in Vienna. Carnot, recalled to be Minister of the Interior, did not prove as effective as in 1793 and the royalists took advantage of the abolition of censorship to exploit discontent with the economic crisis, and fears of a return of conscription. La Vendée was in revolt once more in May. Lamarque defeated the rebels on 20 June at Légé but his 30,000 troops might have made all the difference at Waterloo.

Napoleon's offers of peace remained unanswered by the allies and he prepared rapidly for the coming campaign. The shortage of men, horses, arms, ammunition and money proved serious and the indifference of the populace was worrying. Had he appealed to old Jacobin traditions he might have rekindled the old enthusiasm, but this he dared not do. Nor dared he amalgamate regular troops with National Guardsmen and volunteers (as Carnot had done in 1793): his last army was his final breach with the Revolution. It was hastily assembled and suffered from inadequate staff work (Berthier had died mysteriously on 1 June), a lack of cavalry and draught horses, a shortage of seasoned officers and an uncertainty of command among field officers. On the eve of the battle of Ligny, Bourmont went over to the enemy.

The conception of the Waterloo campaign was brilliant and the speed of its execution in the early days showed Napoleon at his best. He aimed to destroy the two forces of Britain and Prussia separately, then, perhaps to seek Austrian aid against Russia. But his early advantages were wasted by poor staff work and field officers failing to press home their tasks. Napoleon's own illness as well as the heavy rain stopped the pace on the last day and the advantages of Quatre-Bras and Ligny were dissipated on the field of Waterloo (18 June).

Napoleon was back in Paris on 21 June, but the Chambers were not prepared to continue the war and he abdicated next day. Fouché made himself effective head of the government and the Chambers declared against a second restoration of the Bourbons. Talleyrand urged the cause of Orleans, while the Tsar also was opposed to the Bourbons. But Davout surrendered Paris on 2 July and Wellington secured the return of Louis XVIII on 8 July, 'in the baggage train of the allies'. He accepted Talleyrand and Fouché, a regicide, as ministers – 'Vice leaning on the arm of Crime' was Chateaubriand's shocked comment as he saw them retire from their royal audience.

Meanwhile, Napoleon had reached Rochefort (3 July) and demanded a frigate to take him to America. This was refused and he surrendered to Captain Maitland on the *Bellerophon*. The British government, after refusing him permission to land in England, sent him to St Helena, where he died on 5 May 1821.

The Hundred Days posed problems for the diplomats. Talleyrand's argument that Napoleon, not France, was the enemy could no longer hold, and there was keen pressure for a savage treaty. But Metternich and Castlereagh were anxious to preserve France as a great power in order to maintain a balance in European diplomacy. Once more the allies were bound together by a Quadruple Alliance (20 November 1815), the logical conclusion of Chaumont (1814): but, despite the Holy Alliance (26 September) and the widespread earnest desire for peace, they were still aware of differences. The Second Treaty of Paris (20 November) deprived France of Philippeville, Marienbad, Saarlouis, Landau, Saar, Savoy and Nice; it imposed an indemnity of 700 million francs, the return of art treasures and an army of occupation at French expense under Wellington. The Bonapartes were excluded from the French throne in perpetuity, and ambassadors of the Big Four were to meet in Paris regularly as a control commission. The wars were over, but the Hundred Days forced open chasms left by the Revolution, chasms which Napoleon's régime in its early years had gone far to close, chasms that grew wider during the next two generations until another, very different Bonaparte, Napoleon III, temporarily sealed them. For, if France lay stunned after the Hundred Days, and the Bonaparte cause seemed lost, it was less than a generation before the glories of the Napoleonic era were lovingly recalled by old men who had walked to Moscow and back, and the Napoleonic Legend had become a force in politics.

Further Reading

The fall of Napoleon occupies a special place in each book about him. Some useful observations will be found in the following volumes, M. Raeff, *Michael Speransky, Statesman of Imperial Russia 1772–1839* (The Hague, 1957); Grunwald, *Alexander I* (Paris, 1955), Tarlé, *Napoleon's Invasion of Russia 1812* (Allen and Unwin, London, 1942), R. C. Raack, *The Fall of Stein* (Harvard University Press, Cambridge, Mass., 1965), F. D. Scott, *Bernadotte and the Fall of Napoleon* (Harvard University Press, Cambridge, Mass., 1935) and J. Thiry, *La Chute de Napoléon* (Paris, 1938). The force of European diplomacy is presented in C. J. Bartlett, *Castlereagh* (Macmillan, London, 1966); A. Milne, *Metternich* (University of London Press, 'The London History Studies', London, 1975); H. Nicolson, *The Congress of Vienna* (Constable, London, 1946); and an important book, H. Kissinger, *A World Restored* (Boston, 1957).

PRINCIPAL EVENTS, 1807–15

France and Central Europe	*The Peninsula*
1807	1807
June. Tilsit agreement	
9 October. Emancipation Edict (Prussia)	
	27 October. Treaty of Fontainebleau partitions Portugal
	3 November. Junot occupies Lisbon
1808	1808
2 February. Napoleon's suggested partitioning of the Ottoman Empire Napoleon omits to help Tsar gain Finland	Napoleon occupies Spain
Grand Army withdrawn for service in Spain	
	23 March. Murat enters Madrid
	April. Spanish monarch at Bayonne to see Napoleon
	2 May. Madrid rising suppressed
	10 May. Spanish monarchy replaced by Joseph Bonaparte
	Murat becomes King of Naples
Signs of Austrian resistance	23 July. Dupont capitulates at Baylen
	21 August. Wellesley defeats Junot at Vimiero
September–October. Abortive meeting at Erfurt of Napoleon and Tsar	
	November. Napoleon enters Spain
19 November. Local government reform (Prussia)	
15 December. Stein declared outlaw of Empire	
	December. Moore chased to Corunna
1809	1809
	16 January. Soult fails to stop British evacuation at Corunna
	Some of Grand Army withdrawn to face threat in Central Europe
April. Major Schill's rebellion suppressed	
	22 April. Wellesley returns to Portugal
21 May. Aspern and Essling, indecisive battles	

France and Central Europe

1809

29 May. Andreas Hofer captures Innsbruck

6 July. Wagram, Austria defeated Pope imprisoned

29 July. British expedition to Walcheren

14 October. Peace of Schönbrunn Metternich, Austrian Chancellor

15 December. Joséphine accepts divorce

1810

Code Napoléon introduced into Grand Duchy of Warsaw

20 February. Andreas Hofer shot

2 April. Napoleon marries Marie-Louise

21 August. Bernadotte becomes Crown Prince of Sweden

Russian troops begin to mass on western frontiers

31 December. Tsar opens ports to British trade

1811

January. Napoleon annexes Duchy of Oldenburg (offends Tsar)

February. Russia secretly offers Austria the Danubian Principalities

20 March. King of Rome born

September. Napoleon plans an invasion of Russia for June 1812

1812

14 March. Austrians sign an alliance with France v. Russia

French troops reoccupy Prussia

5 April. Bernadotte signs treaty with Tsar

May. Stein welcomed in St Petersburg

The Peninsula

1809

27 July. Talavera, British victory Wellesley retires to Portugal French troops secure southern Spain

1810

September. Masséna invades Portugal: unable to penetrate Torres Vedras

1811

April. Masséna retires from Portugal

1812

French forces weakened to supply Grand Army for Russian campaign

France and Central Europe	The Peninsula
1812	*1812*

France and Central Europe
1812
25 May. Dresden meeting of Napoleon and his allied Princes
28 May. Napoleon leaves Dresden
Tsar makes Peace of Bucharest with Turkey
2 June. Metternich assures Tsar of Austria's wish not to fight
24 June. Napoleon crosses the Niemen

7 September. Napoleon wins at Bordino
14 September. Napoleon enters Moscow
19 October. Napoleon begins retreat
23 October. Malet conspiracy in Paris
6 December. Napoleon quits army to return to Paris
13 December. Ney and rearguard cross Niemen
30 December. York signs Convention of Tauroggen
1813

10 February. Prussian King issues Appeal to the People
23 February. Prussia and Russia sign Treaty of Kalisch
3 March. Castlereagh gains Swedish support
19 March. Prussian King issues Appeal to Germans
2 May. Napoleon's victory at Lützen
21 May. Napoleon's victory at Bautzen
4 June. Armistice of Pleiswitz
14 June. Castlereagh binds allies into Coalition at Reichenbach

28 June. Abortive meeting of Metternich and Napoleon at Dresden
11 August. Austria declares war
27 August. Austria defeated at Dresden

The Peninsula
1812

22 July. Wellington's victory at Salamanca
Madrid occupied, but Wellington retires to Portugal

Spanish 1812 liberal constitution

1813
More French troops withdrawn for service in Central Europe

21 June. Wellington's victory at Vittoria

Soult defends Pyrenees, Wellington finds progress difficult

France and Central Europe
1813
9 September. Austria formally joins allies at Treaty of Teplitz
18 October. Napoleon defeated at Leipzig
26 October. Eugène routed at Valsarno (Italy)
9 November. Frankfurt proposals
17 December. Holland revolts

1814
18 January. Castlereagh at Basle to consolidate coalition
Austria and Prussia invade France
1 February. Napoleon defeated at La Rothière
7 February. Conference at Chatillon
9 March. Treaty of Chaumont

30 March. Marmont surrenders Paris
6 April. Napoleon abdicates

11 April. Treaty of Fontainebleau, Napoleon given Elba
28 April. Napoleon leaves for Elba
30 May. First Treaty of Paris
4 June. Louis XVIII grants the Charter
September. Allies assemble at Vienna for Congress

1815
3 January. Castlereagh, Metternich and Talleyrand sign secret treaty of alliance against Russia
1 March. Napoleon returns for the Hundred Days
14 March. Ney joins Napoleon
22 April. *Acte additionnel*
May. La Vendée in revolt
Murat routed at Ferrara and Tolentino
1 June. Berthier dies
9 June. Treaty of Vienna
18 June. Waterloo
20 June. Lamarque defeats La Vendée rebels at Légé
22 June. Napoleon abdicates

The Peninsula
1813

1814
Wellington invades France

12 March. Bordeaux declares for the Bourbons

10 April. Wellington's victory at Toulouse

8 July. Louis XVIII restored again
August. Napoleon transported to St Helena (where he dies 5 May 1821)
26 September. Holy Alliance formed
20 November. Quadruple Alliance between Britain, Russia, Austria and Prussia
Second Treaty of Paris

PART IX
The Impact of Napoleon

[48] MAN AND MYTH

Napoleon's greatness, dominating twenty years of war, reaches beyond his age to our own and the fascination of his name is charted in literature from the great novels of Tolstoy and Dostoievsky to a host of lesser men. He has come to personify the desires of very different men, a Renaissance hero for Stendhal, a friend of the people for Heine, the precursor of bourgeois reaction for Marx, the incarnation of the Superman for Nietzsche and, for Spengler, the belated Caesar pointing to the destruction of the West through the excesses of our own century. He has been called a father of modern democracy and of fascism: the very range of the different groups who claim him as their inspiration reflects the quality of the myth that has grown around his name.

Historians have not agreed in their assessment of his personal achievement, for it is impossible to define the extent to which he dominated the historic situation within which he worked. In 1799 the Revolution had favoured him by making possible the career open to talent, upturning the social and political world, launching a great war and creating a great army: he was young, he had proved his military and political talents, he was married to a useful wife. Furthermore, the Directory had done much to restore confidence and to build up the administration. Abroad, France's enemies were divided and self-seeking, led by older men lacking his vigour and abilities, their people prepared to welcome the French as liberators. Victory in the field meant dominance in Europe, and at home his administration was efficient. But at the end of his career he was faced with united enemies and new armies supported by the people who had come to regard the French as aggressors. If Napoleon dominated the situation of 1800, he did not dominate that of 1813. This argues that his dominance relied upon favourable circumstances and that his failure to perceive the change in the circumstances early enough condemns him to be judged as a mortal prone to the usual range of human failings. His extraordinary career can be explained in terms of the age producing the man: but it is not so simple, for not only was he as convinced of his own destiny as any visionary might be, he was also able, in his exile in St Helena, to recast his career in a manner that launched the Legend which reverberated into our own day for he was able to gather the early threads of emergent nationalism and to spin a web of fantasy that was to fascinate a century. This grasping of the future tendency of events could suggest that his fall was due to a temporary loss of control in the changing circumstances after Tilsit.

His career surpasses the normal bounds even of great men, and the explanation of his continuing attraction may lie in his capacity to speak directly to the elemental feelings of the human psyche. For all that his mind was classical in mould, his career leapt beyond the rational bounds of the eighteenth-century world into the romanticism of the succeeding century. Thus, in a sense more profound than in his political measures, he was a Janus figure. Grandeur in terms of conception and execution was a feature of the Romantics – Beethoven, Goethe, Wordsworth, or the canal builders and their successors of the age of iron, all were enlarging the bounds of human experience. Napoleon was the Romantic hero *par excellence*. His career fits well with the rôle: humble (yet still noble) birth, scaling heights of human pre-eminence, Prometheus-like in the abundance, good order and magnitude of his schemes, then a fall into a lonely exile, too easily represented as a martyrdom to the selfish desires of kings. After the battle of Lützen, 1813, Narbonne declared,

> Sire, some say you are a god, others that you are a devil, but everyone allows you are more than a man.

Men praise the dedication of a Carnot, admire the skill of a Fouché, wonder at the ability of a Talleyrand: they worship at the shrine of Napoleon. It matters naught that Talleyrand profited whilst Napoleon died in exile: Talleyrand is no hero.

> The French Revolution and the Emperor Napoleon I have thrown a certain number of minds, including some of the most distinguished into a feverish excitement which becomes a moral and, I would

almost say, a mental disease. They yearn for events, immense, sudden and strange: they busy themselves with making and unmaking governments, nations, religions, society, Europe, the world. ... They are intoxicated with the greatness of their own design, and blind to the chances of success. (Guizot)

Napoleon, as Lefebvre has said, was 'more than anything else a temperament' or, to quote Napoleon himself, 'I live only for posterity: death is nothing, but to live defeated and without glory is to die every day'.

It is an impossible task to judge such a man in purely human terms, for the normal gauge of morality, achievement, personality, have little relevance. His shortness of stature did not oppress him as it did Robespierre: he possessed an unusual control of his senses. He played upon human passions and had developed to a fine art his capacity to fascinate, cajole, even hypnotise with his piercing grey eyes. Mme de Staël, disappointed of becoming his lover and subsequently a hostile critic, commented

Napoleon was neither good, nor violent, nor soft, nor cruel as ordinary people. ... He hated no more than he loved, there was only him for himself.

Rarely did he lose control of himself, and his rages at official levées were often carefully staged. After the abdication in 1814, Masséna told Lady Bessborough,

Napoleon never loved anybody in his life – women, men, children – nobody but himself. He was passionate in his ambition, hard as iron in everything else.

His capacity for work was legendary and he drove his secretaries mercilessly. At times of nervous and emotional strain he could indulge in fits of temper that often resulted in physical violence upon his servants. These intimate storms relieved the tension (he was a mass of nerves, normally kept in rigid control), and some writers have classed them as a form of epileptic fit, the 'conqueror's syndrome' as it is called, which he shared with Alexander the Great, Caesar, the Elder Pitt and perhaps Hitler. Normally, however, his capacity to take quick 'cat-naps' kept him sane and healthy.

I was born and made for work. I have recognised the limits of my eyesight and of my legs, but never the limits of my working power [was his proud boast].

Hours of detailed work each day, often extending into the night, resulted in his maintaining a precise control of a staggering quantity of information upon a whole range of different subjects. At a moment's notice, he could switch from very detailed work on one topic to similarly detailed work on a quite different topic. This control of detail was the secret of his success both as a general and as an administrator.

> Different subjects and different affairs are arranged in my head as in a cupboard. When I wish to interrupt one train of thought, I shut that drawer and open another. Do I wish to sleep? I simply close all the drawers and then I am – asleep.

When illness struck, it could have disastrous effects, as at Borodino or Waterloo. But this was a consequence of dependence upon one man. His control of detail extended to faces, and he delighted in picking out of a parade an old soldier to praise his record. Such personal attention inspired service: it is not to be wondered at that the Old Guard was faithful to the end.

On the battlefield a keen sense of the possible was always with him, but in politics and administration the range of the possible receded into the distance until the mists of unreality began to cloud his judgment. The assumption of the Imperial title was no more than a change of name for him: as his Caesarism grew so did an impression of paranoia. The impression is deepened by his refusal to delegate. In part this arose from his infinite capacity to command the wide canvas of his Empire in terms of policy and of detailed administration: in part it was due to his refusal to acknowledge the need for help, or to brook a possible rival. It is not surprising that he left no General Staff or strong ministry.

Much has been made of Napoleon's Corsican background: it has even been suggested that he failed to grasp the true interests of France because of it. Yet he could not so perfectly have expressed the French spirit, as the testimony of succeeding generations proves, if France were no more than an adopted country. His concern for his family is also credited to his Corsican background: they proved unworthy and inadequate, and he has been accused of colossal vanity in supposing that anyone related to him, even by marriage, must be a genius. But Napoleon would not delegate – why, then, should he set up kings, unless they were to be his personal puppets? Who better than his family for such a post? But he recognised their incapacity and potential disloyalty, and from 1809 he progressively cut them out of the administration, a process all but complete by the time of the Austrian marriage.

Joseph was scorned as a poor commander and merely used in Spain for want of a better substitute. Louis held a special place in Napoleon's affections, but proved too independent as King of Holland and was dismissed. Jerome was a dandy whom he had married (after a matrimonial escapade in America) to a German princess to become King of Westphalia – his presence in the 1812 campaign was an embarrassment. Lucien had proved himself the ablest brother, especially during the Directory, but he proved also the least co-operative and he seems to have had some contact with the *carbonari* before being captured and 'imprisoned' in Worcestershire. Napoleon secured a cardinal's hat for his uncle. His sisters he made princesses, but if Elisa remained a shadow, Pauline gained a libidinous reputation and Caroline, who had married Murat without Napoleon's approval, encouraged her husband's treason. Madame Mère was a withdrawn figure, hoarding her wealth against a future she insisted on regarding as uncertain even in the heyday of the Empire. None of them was overawed by Napoleon: 'From the way they talk,' he complained, 'one would think I had mismanaged our father's inheritance.' All but Caroline, however, returned to the fold in 1815. But Napoleon preferred his Beauharnais relations – 'Eugène was the only one of my family who never caused me any trouble' – but Eugène was transferred from heir presumptive to the Kingdom of Italy, to be merely Grand Duke of Berg.

[49] NAPOLEON, FRANCE AND EUROPE

The reforms of the Consulate so successfully combined those of the previous decade into an administrative system that it remained almost unchallenged until the crisis of May 1968. It is tempting to view the Napoleonic era as the concluding episode of the Revolution, but it is not possible to take so simple a view. Certainly, the land settlement was guaranteed, the social consequence of the abolition of feudalism preserved, and the career open to talent promoted, to some degree, by the educational system. Certainly, the religious question was settled adequately enough, even if the clergy were to remain a powerful disruptive force on the political right until the Dreyfus Case. The Codes, too, bear his name and are often used to characterise the era.

But these achievements were not the whole of the Revolution. The Empire reduced political liberty to a sham, while the upper bourgeoisie, who had done well out of the Thermidorian Reaction and the Directory, raised no objection as Napoleon consolidated a régime that was to anticipate socially the July Monarchy of Louis Philippe, and the Second Empire. Liberals were less happy, for the régime was a dictatorship of the right in which fascist régimes of our own day could find an antecedent. Napoleon did not complete the Revolution: he ossified it according to the character of the Thermidorians. The Hundred Days and the *Acte Additionnel* gave him the opportunity to argue that his had been a period of necessary dictatorship before liberalism could be launched, but Waterloo ended this strange experiment and Louis XVIII was happy enough – as de Maistre observed – to ascend the throne of Bonaparte as it was in 1814.

The urban proletariat, destroyed as a political force by the Thermidorians, confined by the *loi chapelier* and the *livrets*, supervised by the *conseils de prud'hommes* (some of which did useful work), could well contrast the Empire with what might have been hoped of the friend of Augustin Robespierre and the author of *Le Souper de Beaucaire*. The workers were not neglected: except in the 1811 crisis, employment was plentiful for those not conscripted and there was some desultory effort to deal with the problem of poverty (although vagabonds were severely treated). Public health in Paris was not neglected, new quays, markets and slaughter houses were erected, sewers and water supply improved, and Chaptal began the very first full-scale hospital for training nurses and midwives and encouraged vaccination against smallpox. But Napoleon kept the proletariat in leading strings: their political voice was not heard again until the 1830s and 1840s.

The peasant and the bourgeois right winger found that Napoleon 'completed' the Revolution: the Jacobin and proletarian, as Tarlé puts it, found that he 'liquidated' it. And yet he gave to all Frenchmen a sense of unity, stability and prosperity and two million Frenchmen fought in the campaigns of the Empire. To them and the relatives of the 250,000 killed in the battles of the Empire, he brought a glory that burnished the unity he gave to France. Never again during the century was France to feel that same unity. When Louis Napoleon III sought to close the gaps in French society by wooing the disinherited proletarians with *L'Extinction du paupérisme* (1844) they retained a far clearer memory of the great Napoleon than the liberals who so frequently invoked his name: Napoleon had given France glory and in doing so he had exploited the workers – but not only the workers, he had exploited all classes.

In Europe, welcomed as a deliverer, he was, within a decade, to be driven out by the very forces he had fostered, castigated as an ogre, a despoiler, Anti-Christ. The patriotic reaction against French imperialism was a temporary phenomenon, but it disturbed the sands and gave a preview of the nationalism that was to disturb the diplomacy of Europe half a century later. He also recast the frontiers of Germany on much more rational lines which the allies were prepared, more or less, to adopt in 1815. There was no blind return to the *ancien régime*.

French occupation had brought conspicuous advantages to the Grand Empire: feudalism as a social system (and to some degree as an economic one) was destroyed while the Napoleonic Code helped to synchronise administration and provide a unified code of law. Administration was strengthened by a centralised bureaucracy allowing a career open to talent for the petty bourgeoisie. Freedom of worship, concessions for the Jews, as well as the impact of the metric system, common weights and measures, better public works on roads and bridges, the removal of internal customs barriers, the enforcement of equality of taxation and equality before the law – all these helped to provide unity and centralisation so that in Germany and Italy liberals of the next generation were to look back upon the Napoleonic period as the first major step to nationhood. The Napoleonic Code gave expression to imperial unity and Napoleon was anxious that it should be imposed on vassal states in its entirety. He wrote to Joseph, then King of Naples,

> The Code will confirm your power because it does away with everything that is not protected by entails and no great estates will remain except such fiefs as you will found.

But the threat of a universal empire was already appreciated, and if the Code was introduced throughout Italy (and Illyria in 1812), and many states of the Confederation of the Rhine, it did not penetrate Spain, Bavaria or Württemberg.

Where feudal rights were abolished, heavy redemption payments were often imposed, while feudal dues survived in Holland and South Germany. In Poland, society remained much as it had been before Napoleon, and the same was true in Naples (except that the restored Ferdinand did not dare bring back feudalism in 1815). Thus, whilst bringing the Revolution to Central Europe, he did not ensure that its principles were applied equally throughout, nor did the reforms necessarily cut deeply into society. Indeed, the only consistent principle in his Empire and satellite states was that of exploitation. As his Empire became increasingly dynastic, he leant upon local nobles, retaining their privileges in hope of gaining their support. In this way he failed to tie the peasantry to the French System, especially in Poland, and his failure to free the Russian serf was a fatal error.

In his impact on Europe there is a contradiction. He began as the champion of a new era of freedom but he came to characterise a new despotism made the more monstrous by the threat of a universal empire. The reforms he engendered, when taken up in Prussia and even in Russia (under Speranski) were turned against him, and within the Empire itself, by breaking down provincial autonomy and creating a unified internal trading market, he created the conditions necessary for the future expansion of political nationalism. In so far, he helped in the forming of Italy and Germany, but this he had never intended. He assisted the intellectual tide of romantic nationalism by rousing patriotic resistance against the exactions of French imperialism, even though it was the princes, not the people, who benefited in 1815. The Settlement of 1815, though it used frontiers not unlike those he had created, was a rejection of Napoleonic Europe, for it was founded on the principle of a balance of power, underpinned by the Congress System. Russia might dominate in the East and threaten the Balkans, yet in Central Europe, Austria was the residuary legatee of Napoleon's fall. Abroad, Britain had acquired a huge empire and controlled the seas: France was defeated on the seas, in her century-old imperial struggle with Britain.

[50] REASONS FOR HIS DOWNFALL

It is all too romantically easy to suppose Napoleon was doomed to failure. At crucial moments in his career, luck was on his side in situations where the odds were nicely balanced: later, his luck ran out. Alexander was not caught at Drissa in the summer of 1812, nor did his nerve fail after Borodino; the allies were not destroyed at Bautzen or at Dresden; more effective staff work at Waterloo might have brought a different result. At these crucial moments, the odds were pretty even – but the consequences of failure were gigantic. In risking all, France lost all. His régime was based on military victory and glory: as his Caesarism drew him into a vortex of expansionism each battle took on a new significance for Europe: he could not contemplate a defeat, as Louis XIV had been able to do. Thus he was drawn into further campaigns, and the prospect of peace receded.

The glory became increasingly a matter of the inspiration of future generations, whilst war weariness and indifference gripped France. The Grand Army became increasingly a motley collection of various troops, the foreign element increasing at the expense of the French with recruits who were less reliable, less effective, less well trained than the army that conquered Europe in the eighteen months between Ulm and Friedland. The marshals, too, became war weary and preferred to save their personal fortunes. Napoleon's personal ill health was merely a temporary matter, but because so much depended on him, his incapacity for a few hours could make a world change. He left no staff to carry on his methods.

Beyond the frontiers, the growing demands of French imperialism in terms of men, money and lost trade provoked a hostile resistance among populations that once had welcomed the French. In Italy and Germany, and beyond, romanticism inspired this patriotic resistance with a veneer of cultural nationalism, and princes were induced to lose their inhibitions and to place themselves at the head of this patriotism as leaders of the crusade to expel the Anti-Christ. Their armies had grown to massive size; the common soldier was better equipped and led by younger, more professional officers: those very factors that had once favoured Napoleon were turned against him at the end. As the satellites and vassals fell away in 1813, the Empire was deprived of support, of men and of money.

Insatiable ambition seduced Napoleon with dreams of world domination at the very moment that his defeated enemies were once more growing stronger, and he overtaxed his resources in ventures that were too obviously Napoleonic and not French. And England remained his undefeated enemy, ready to snatch any commercial advantage and to offer coalitions both money and arms. As the complexity of events crowded upon him, he could not effectively deal with each problem in turn; and as the Tilsit settlement crumbled, delusions of power clouded his vision. Molé noted,

It is strange that though Napoleon's commonsense amounted to genius, he never could see where the possible left off. . . . He was much less concerned to leave behind him a 'race' or dynasty than a name which should have no equal and glory that could not be surpassed.

He was his own enemy, for the clarity and precision of his mind meant that he had no need to lean on the advice of others: his personality and his obvious success conspired to make him govern by himself. His distrust of underlings at times became a phobia, and his refusal to give a staff or a ministry a free hand deprived able men of the opportunities and influence they had a right to expect. Once Napoleon was away from the centre of affairs, the administration was automatically weakened. This dependence on himself strengthened his determination to free himself from his revolutionary background and to create a new monarchy with all the trappings of the old. But the traditional nobility in France or abroad had no desire to share special primacy with parvenus. He chose badly in seeking the support of Europe's nobility. Comtesse Voss commented in 1807, 'These people are forcing us down to a lower level than dirt'. For all that he had rejected the Revolution, in the eyes of Europe's nobility Napoleon remained its soldier.

All Europe was not France, and patriotic resistance could not be contained. In Spain, the resistance had serious consequences, for it meant the Peninsular War dragged on, consuming men and resources sorely needed elsewhere, while the need to garrison Germany and to contain serious revolts in the Tyrol and riots in Italy, added to the strain and the popular resistance. Austria, defeated again in 1809, was prepared to take up arms once more when the moment came. Prussia also awaited its opportunity for revenge. But it was in Russia that Napoleon's fate was sealed, where the serf, betrayed by nobles, army command and merchant alike, died at his post to repel the invader: after 1812, Napoleon was denied another Austerlitz.

Lack of time and the crowding in of problems was another reason for his collapse. The Continental System, given time and effective enforcement, could well have succeeded: but time was denied Napoleon and the unemployment and distress consequent upon the enforcing of the System deprived Napoleon of the bourgeois support he had formerly enjoyed. It led to the fatal campaigns in Spain and Russia, and to the enlargement of the area under direct French rule. Meanwhile, the deliberate policy of 'France first' increased resentment in Europe. The attempt to form a unitary empire failed, and its failure was confirmed by the experience of the following fifty years.

But it was not yet the nationalism of the later years of the century: the Princes profited from the patriotic resistance of the War of Liberation. Toynbee puts the point well, for the people in 1815 were deprived of –

> the national rights which in 1812–15 they had earned by pouring out their blood and had lost through being made victims of a political swindle. Thus the non-French national states ultimately owe their origin to Napoleonic France's stimulus but have been founded on the ruins of the post-Napoleonic restoration and not on those of the Napoleonic Empire itself.

Yet in France, weary in the last years of the Empire, there was soon to appear a generation that would look back with longing to the Napoleonic era and be seduced by the Napoleonic legend.

[51] THE NAPOLEONIC LEGEND

Napoleon was a master of propaganda, and the Legend that he launched upon the flood tide of romanticism during his six years of exile at St Helena is an object lesson in the reinterpretation of a career to deceive future generations.

He claimed to be the champion of equality, liberty and nationality against the oppressive forces of the *ancien régime*, characterised after 1815 by the Holy Alliance. He was the mediator between the past and the Revolution whose purpose, after a brief temporary dictatorship whilst reaction was destroyed, was to bring peace and stability and a new social order based on the career open to talent and graced by a new imperial nobility of worth. The campaign of 1812 was the turning point of his career, he argued: it was undertaken both to free Poland and to oblige England to make peace. Victory would have resulted in a new era of constitutional rule, succeeding the French imperium, in which each national grouping, French, German, Spanish, Italian, Slovene, Croat, Pole, etc., would be identified, unified and recognised within a federated Europe.

> Europe thus divided into nationalities freely formed and free internally, peace between states would have become easier: the United States of Europe would become a possibility.

To refute the claims is idle: the wonder is that the legend should have had so great a currency. At the outset, this reinterpretation of his career may have had the simple purpose of refuting the so-called 'black legend', that great quantity of propaganda vilifying his memory in which reactionaries indulged in the few years after Waterloo. But it grew beyond any such limited aim to speak across the years to a new generation in Europe. He had perceived one of the principal problems that would trouble the future and had offered a solution before that problem had been properly identified.

The growth of the legend was aided by numerous memoirs published in the 1820s, among the principal ones being O'Meara's *Napoléon en exil, ou une voix de Sainte-Hélène* (1821), and the more famous *Mémorial de Sainte-Hélène* of Las Cases (1823). The conditions of his exile, under the gruff and tactless Sir Hudson Lowe and early rumours of possible poisoning, added romantic colour to the growing legend, and Napoleon's will itself was splendidly calculated to point to a future Bonaparte prince:

> I desire that my ashes should repose on the banks of the Seine in the midst of the French people whom I have loved so much. ... I recommend my son never to forget that he is born a French prince, and never to become an instrument of the triumvirate which oppresses the peoples of Europe. He must never fight against or injure France: he must adopt my motto: 'Everything for the French People'.

The Restoration was not a glorious era for France and the contrast with that of Napoleon also helped to spread the legend among his soldiers and their sons. The return of the Emperor's ashes to the Invalides in 1840 brought no reflected glory to the régime of Louis Philippe, but it quickened the legend. Already in 1823, Count Rostopchin, governor of Moscow in 1812, could write, 'The Napoleon who is popular today is the Napoleon of the Legend rather than that of History'. It would not be too long before a Queen of England (Victoria), was to order her eldest son and heir to kneel before the tomb of Napoleon.

The myth of a romantic hero too easily gathers round Napoleon, and the men of the nineteenth century found that they could respond to it, as much because of its glory as of its fierce assertion of individuality against what some perceived as the growing alienation of life among the complexities of the century – Raskolnikov was to account for his crime on these lines. Prometheus walked abroad.

The boundless yearnings of the poets is but the negative aspect of the Will to Power unappeased. And the Will to Power, which was to find supreme literary expression in Nietzsche, had already found its most complete realisation in Bonaparte. (Guérard)

As Wellington, that supreme example of common sense, put it, 'Napoleon was not a personality, but a principle'. The legend rises through various levels of intensity, past the absurdity of representing Napoleon as the protector of the Roman Catholic Church, to reach a climax in Louis Napoleon's *Les Idées napoléoniennes* (1840),

> Had it not been for the Consulate and Empire, the Revolution would have been but a mighty drama that leaves glorious recollections but few traces. ... Napoleon ... planted in France and disseminated throughout Europe the most important benefits of the great crisis of '99 . . The Emperor may well be deemed the Messiah of modern ideas.

Further Reading

The impact of Napoleon on Europe will be traced in all general textbooks of nineteenth-century Europe. For Napoleon's last years see R. Korngold, *The Last Years of Napoleon* (London, 1960). An interesting light is cast by I. Baelin in *Benjamin Constant et Napoléon* (Paris, 1965) and H. Guillemin, *Mme de Staël, Benjamin Constant et Napoléon* (Paris, 1959). The early parts of Leys, *Between Two Empires* (London, 1955) and Artz, *France under the Bourbon Restoration* (Harvard University Press, Cambridge, Mass., 1931), are useful. So is C. Harold, *The Mind of Napoleon* (Columbia University Press, New York, 1955). For the Napoleonic Legend see A. Guérard, *Reflections on the Napoleonic Legend* (London, 1924), J. Lucas-Dubreton, *La Culte de Napoléon 1815–1848* (Paris, 1960), P. Gournard, *Les Origins de la legende Napoléonienne* (Paris, 1906), F. Healey, *The Literary Culture of Napoleon* (Geneva, 1959). Also useful are A. Castelot, *Napoleon's Son* (London, 1960) and F. A. Simpson, *The Rise of Louis Napoleon* (Cass, London, 1950).

INDEX